GREEN CLASSROOM BOOK

Dear Reader,

I wrote this book because I'm counting on you to help children become good stewards of the Earth, now and for all their lives. I know it is a heavy load to bear, but the Earth needs so much help and, as always, you educators are on the front line teaching and leading by example.

My son, Clinton Hill, knew kids could lead the way to protect the Earth. He started a club called Kids for Saving Earth (KSE) shortly before he died at age eleven from a brain tumor. He understood that educating kids helps them become Earth-savers, but they also become leaders influencing the "big" people of the world. He was right. His organization has inspired millions of kids and adults with the Earth-saving message since 1989.

Skim through the book and find topics that interest you the most. Your interest and enthusiasm will spill over to your students. The book has been written in a style that will make it easy for you to understand and translate the information. As you read through the book, you will find that the action component of environmentalism helps children retain information and makes it all fun.

Tessa Hill

Welcome to the EVERYTHING Series!

These handy, accessible books give you all you need to tackle a difficult project, gain a new hobby, comprehend a fascinating topic, prepare for an exam, or even brush up on something you learned back in school but have since forgotten.

You can choose to read an *Everything*® book from cover to cover or just pick out the information you want from our four useful boxes: e-sources, e-facts, e-alerts, and e-ssentials. We give you everything you need to know on the subject, but throw in a lot of fun stuff along the way, too.

We now have more than 400 *Everything*® books in print, spanning such wide-ranging categories as weddings, pregnancy, cooking, music instruction, foreign language, crafts, pets, New Age, and so much more. When you're done reading them all, you can finally say you know *Everything*®!

SOURCE
Online information

FACTS
Important snippets
of information

ALERTS!
Urgent
warnings

ESSENTIALS
Quick
handy tips

PUBLISHER Karen Cooper

DIRECTOR OF ACQUISITIONS AND INNOVATION Paula Munier

MANAGING EDITOR, EVERYTHING SERIES Lisa Laing

COPY CHIEF Casey Ebert

ACQUISITIONS EDITOR Lisa Laing

DEVELOPMENT EDITOR Elizabeth Kassab

EDITORIAL ASSISTANT Hillary Thompson

Visit the entire Everything® series at *www.everything.com*

THE
EVERYTHING®
GREEN
CLASSROOM
BOOK

From recycling to conservation,
all you need to create
an eco-friendly learning environment

Tessa Hill, president of Kids for Saving Earth

Adamsmedia
Avon, Massachusetts

To my son Clinton Hill,
Defender of the Planet, whose spirit lives on in the actions of over a
million children and teachers working to protect our beautiful Earth.

An Everything® Series Book.
Everything® and everything.com® are registered trademarks of F+W Media, Inc.

Published by Adams Media, a division of F+W Media, Inc.
57 Littlefield Street, Avon, MA 02322 U.S.A.
www.adamsmedia.com

ISBN 10: 1-60550-351-7
ISBN 13: 978-1-60550-351-6

Printed in the United States of America.

J I H G F E D C B A

Library of Congress Cataloging-in-Publication Data
is available from the publisher.

This publication is designed to provide accurate and authoritative information with regard to the subject matter covered. It is sold with the understanding that the publisher is not engaged in rendering legal, accounting, or other professional advice. If legal advice or other expert assistance is required, the services of a competent professional person should be sought.
—From a *Declaration of Principles* jointly adopted by a Committee of the American Bar Association and a Committee of Publishers and Associations

Many of the designations used by manufacturers and sellers to distinguish their products are claimed as trademarks. Where those designations appear in this book and Adams Media was aware of a trademark claim, the designations have been printed with initial capital letters.

The pages of this book are printed on 100% post-consumer recycled paper.

This book is available at quantity discounts for bulk purchases.
For information, please call 1-800-289-0963.

Contents

Endorsements

"The Everything® Green Classroom Book *is filled with an amazing amount of action-oriented environmental activities that are not just useful to the Earth but also strengthen learning skills for other school subjects such as math, English, and music. Of special importance to me is Tessa Hill's handling of human health issues demonstrating how virtually all problems that negatively influence the health of the Earth can also impact our children's health."*

— Philip J. Landrigan, MD, MSc, the Ethel Wise Professor and Chair of the Department of Community and Preventive Medicine, Mount Sinai School of Medicine

"Working on creating a clean, green, and healthy school? Look no further! You can do it with this great (and easy) resource guide! After years of leading Kids for Saving Earth, Tessa Hill knows how to activate students and instructors. This book will help you know what's most important and how to prioritize. It is full of tips and innovative solutions that will make your school green, and you'll have fun doing it!"

— Christopher Gavigan, Executive Director, Healthy Child Healthy World

Acknowledgments

Each day as I worked on this book, I was inspired by the memory of my son, Clinton, and the hope of a healthy future for my daughters, Karina and Genine, and my grandchildren, Drew and Taylor. For the many hours of research and writing support, I'd like to thank Janelle Sorensen, Children's Environmental Health Consultant. Finally I'd like to thank my husband, Dennis Odin Johnson, for his love, for editing help, and for taking up the slack when I needed more time for the book.

Top Ten Ways to
Create a Green Classroom

1. Stop and smell the flowers, and the pine trees, and the moss, and the bark, and everything else. Take time to get outside and appreciate nature

2. Reduce, reduce, and then reduce some more. Since it would take about six planets to support humans if everyone lived like Americans, people must reduce the use of energy, water, paper, and everything else to protect planet Earth.

3. Look at the life cycle of everything. Discovering where things come from and where they go is enlightening.

4. Empower kids to make change. Kids are capable of much more than they are generally given credit for if they understand why it is so important to change. Give them a chance to find solutions and create a better world.

5. Look for simple beauty and appreciate what the Earth gives you.

6. Don't be afraid to "buck the system" and integrate environmental protection into as many other academic areas as possible.

7. Nature is organic, so let learning be organic. Allow for flexibility in your curriculum; you will find fun, interesting ways to strengthen students' interests.

8. Embrace the butterfly effect. Small changes lead to bigger and bigger ones, so nothing should be considered unimportant.

9. With a smiling face, promote hope and use a can-do method of teaching. The environmental problems we face can be very daunting. To surmount these challenges, people need to maintain hope, optimism, and perseverance.

10. Celebrate success. Use a variety of reward systems to encourage helpful Earth-saving projects.

Introduction

▶ *THE EVERYTHING® GREEN CLASSROOM BOOK* is the essential guide for teaching children about environmental protection. Through you, your students will learn how the little decisions people make every day affect the planet and, ultimately, human health. This book is the most comprehensive resource to incorporate the fundamental concepts of ecology with active steps to protect the Earth. Each chapter contains ways to make Earth-saving fun and empowering. The book provides clear ways to teach children how to make planet preservation a part of their daily life in their school, home, church, or any other place.

The first Earth Day in 1970 represented the true organized launch of environmental protection. Government agencies addressing environmental issues were formed, laws were written, and environmental activists spoke out, but the rapid growth of environmental problems far outpaced the success of protection efforts. Now the sustainability of the Earth is at a pivotal point in history. Between climate change, the rapid extinction of species, and the overwhelming amount of pollution, there is much to be done in order to preserve the planet that all life depends upon. United action now is more important than ever before. What you do and how you empower your students to act will make a major difference. Schools are a vital force in raising the next generation of global citizens, who must be equipped to solve the complex environmental problems.

This book stresses the principle of interconnectedness, which has been historically overlooked. Teaching how humans are tied to and responsible for protecting the balance of nature is the essence of sustainability and must be the wave of the future. Humans live in a web of life. If you pull on any one strand, it affects the rest of the web. This theme guides each chapter, examining every issue from an international perspective, to the local outlook, and all the way down to each individual human body.

Meant to be empowering for students, teachers, administrators, and parents, this book very simply and clearly provides overviews of environmental issues, background information, and tested activities. Instructors are provided with steps to turn their students' education into action. Throughout the book, hands-on experiences in the world of nature will help inspire action. In addition, it is widely known that student success is based on parental involvement. With that in mind, each chapter provides activities to bring the learning home. In this way, not only will the children benefit from potential increased academic success, they also get to act as teachers to their parents and help their whole family green their home and protect the planet.

Each activity in this book is meant to be adaptable to most age groups. There are resource options to help you either lower or raise the skill levels. The book relies heavily on the true beauty and fascination of nature. Art, music, and games lighten up what might seem like a frightening topic. The activities are meant to inspire and encourage appreciation, optimism, and smiles. There are definitely some big issues to overcome, but there are a plentitude of existing solutions to embrace in your own classrooms, schools, and communities. By teaching your students the concepts in this book, you will enable their engaged, excited young minds to come up with many more solutions. Working together on important environmental problems will inspire positivism and confidence.

CHAPTER 1

Green Schools 101

Green, sustainable, environmental, eco-friendly, Earth-friendly. What does it all mean? However you say it, it means you are taking action to protect the planet and all of its inhabitants, including people. It sounds like a big job—and it is—but if everyone works together, it'll be a job well done. At a green school, everyone plays a part in protecting the planet. From the youngest student all the way up to the principal and the superintendent, everyone can do something.

Making a Difference

This is a pivotal time in human history. People have pushed the planet to its brink and it's time to change old habits in order to create a brighter, healthier future. To make these important changes, people need to understand what's going on and how their actions impact the planet.

What the World Needs Now

The planet needs help. People created the problems, so it's up to people to solve them. The atmosphere is warming up, leading to serious storms and causing the ice caps to melt. Pollution from factories, cars, and people makes the air and water dirty. Chemicals that are made in laboratories and used in everyday products end up in the bodies of polar bears and humans alike. Species are going extinct faster than at any other time in history.

It's a pretty dire picture when you examine it all at once, but if you look at it piece by piece you can quickly see how many opportunities there are for people to turn things around. It's time to set aside differences and come together for the common goal of a healthy future.

Many people all over the world have already begun making the changes necessary to protect the planet, but there is still much, much more to do. Every day is a new chance to teach another person, spark another solution, and create a better tomorrow.

How can you create a green classroom if your school isn't thinking green yet? Make the transitions easier by making your intentions transparent. Write letters to the school administrators and parents. Let them know you feel it's important to raise responsible global citizens who care for the Earth. Invite them to share ideas for teaching the students or making changes at the school. If they need additional convincing, tell them that going green is not just about protecting the planet: It also protects human health and saves money. The monetary savings are generally a clincher for schools.

Still, you know your principal, and perhaps the best way to get started is just to do it! Let the administration come to you if they have any concerns. A key to communicating your intentions in a less-than-hospitable community is by making sure you are using positive language instead of coming off as judgmental. Remember to pat people on the back for every small act and every little idea. It's much harder to teach adults to change their behavior (that's why it's important to start with children), so take things slow and encourage cooperation by keeping things easy. It's all about patience, persistence, practicality, and positivism. Before you know it, the children will be leading by example and the adults will have no other choice but to follow.

Children Are the Future

As all good teachers know, children are the future. If you're reading the daily headlines about global warming and pollution, the future can look pretty unappealing and downright scary. Yet there are already scores of teenagers and children who have gotten a glimpse of that future and decided it is unacceptable and avoidable. These young people are making significant changes all over the world. They are an inspiration, and they represent just a fraction of the imagination and hope the next generation has to offer. For example, Kids for Saving Earth (KSE) has been in existence since 1989. The first members have now become adults. Over and over again, KSE receives letters from former kid members—now adult teachers who are continuing to spread the spirit of Earth-saving.

Teachers are some of the most influential people in society. You hold the power to transform young minds. You lay the foundations for tomorrow's leaders. What you teach is what will be carried forth. Whether it's math, history, or sustainability, if you don't plant the seeds, the concepts will not grow. Even though living green is not a core pillar of today's curriculum, it is an imperative concept for maintaining a healthy planet for generations to come.

Luckily, a green education can be woven into the general lessons of reading, writing, arithmetic, and all other curricular areas. The most important thing about teaching sustainability is to empower the children through action. There are already countless examples of teachers engaging children in environmental activities that inspire the students to initiate a wide variety of other actions in all arenas of life—at school, at home, and in the community. Children almost instinctually understand the importance of protecting wildlife and the Earth. They have to live in the future we created, so they know they must change that future. All they need is a little direction about how they can help.

FACT

Going green from the get-go saves a school a lot of green. According to a report for the Massachusetts Technology Collaborative, the cost of building a green school can be 1.5 percent to 2.5 percent more expensive than a conventional building, but the financial savings after twenty years are about $70 per square foot. That's more than ten times the initial cost.

Walk the Talk

Having a green classroom does not simply mean that you incorporate environmental concepts into your curriculum. It's not just about teaching sustainability; it's about trying to live it every moment you spend together. It sounds tough at first, but as you venture down the green path, you'll find that it quickly becomes habit. New ways to discuss it, learn it, and live it will continuously emerge. You'll also find that walking the talk strengthens the educational outcomes by making the learning process experiential.

Making a Green Classroom

Your classroom should reflect the concepts of green living and planetary protection that you intend to teach. It's nearly impossible to transition to a totally sustainable building in the blink of an eye, but there are many small ways you can make the classroom embody what you teach.

Sustainable School Supplies

When you're shopping for the basic supplies for your classroom, look for Earth-friendly options. Here are some examples:

- Choose paper that has been processed chlorine free (PCF), to avoid dioxin and mercury pollution from the bleaching process, and choose the highest percentage of recycled post-consumer waste (PCW) available.
- Opt for folders and binders made of recycled cardboard and paper instead of PVC or other plastic products.
- Find recycled pencils, recycled plastic pens, soybean crayons, and nontoxic unscented markers.
- Pick paperclips, scissors, and other incidentals made with recycled materials.
- Use the Electronic Product Environmental Assessment Tool found at *www.epeat.net* to help you select the most environmentally friendly computer for your classroom.

Green office and school supplies are becoming increasingly available through major retailers, but you may still run into difficulty depending on your location. Shop online and you'll find everything you need and products made from materials you never would have imagined, like paper made from bamboo. Make your purchases "speak" to your students by posting signs by each item that explain what they're made of and how that's better for the planet.

Use your green classroom not only as a model for your students, but also as a model for the rest of the school, the parents, and the community. Take every opportunity possible to have people tour your room to look at what you have and do. Invite a local newspaper or television station to do a story on it. Spread the word!

Keeping It Clean and Green

Many conventional cleaning products have ingredients in them that pollute the air inside your classroom. They can also cause headaches, asthma and allergy attacks, and other health problems. Keep your classroom clean by using products that don't hurt the Earth or human health. You can find safer products at *www.healthyschoolscampaign.org* in its Green Clean Schools resources. Green Seal (*www.greenseal.org*) is another national non-profit that certifies products for offices and institutions.

Beware of what the Center for Ecoliteracy calls "hidden curricula" in schools. These subliminal messages can undermine the good lessons you teach in your classroom. For instance, if your cafeteria uses Styrofoam plates and cups, this contradicts what you say about the harm they do to the environment. What are the hidden curricula at your school?

Taking It Outdoors

As much as possible, take your students outside. Getting in touch with nature makes people more apt to want to protect it. Even if you're not specifically teaching an environmental concept at the time, just being outside in the sunshine is important. You can sit in the grass and read a book or work on math equations. It might be difficult at first to keep everyone focused on the task at hand, but the more often you do it, the more the children will become accustomed to it and appreciate their time outdoors.

Another way to get a quick glimpse of the natural world is to take an outdoor route when you're going from one area of the school to another. It might be a longer walk to find the nearest exit to your classroom and then traipse around the building until you find the nearest entrance to the cafeteria, gym, or library, but the time outside is a tiny opportunity to enrich your class. Did anyone see a bird or some other type of animal? Did anyone see a bug? What types of plants are growing? What was the weather like? The first couple of times, you can devote a little class time to discuss what the students experienced. Make a large bulletin board showing your school and grounds. The students can regularly draw pictures of what they saw and add them to the board. Each time you take a quick walk, pick one or two students to add a drawing during their spare time.

Making It Work

You might be thinking, "Sure this all sounds good in theory, but how will it work in reality?" Just because something sounds good or seems like the right thing to do doesn't necessarily mean it can be done. The golden rule for the green school: Don't dwell on what you can't do; focus on what you can do.

The average person can recognize more than 1,000 corporate logos, but fewer than ten native plants. It is more important than ever to take every opportunity possible to teach kids the basics of nature and the language that goes with it.

Curriculum Connections

You likely have a very full plate of concepts you need to teach your students in order to meet grade and testing requirements. How can you squeeze in more? Fortunately, the concepts of nature, ecology, and sustainability lend themselves easily to all of the other issues children need to learn. Math, science, reading, English, history, social sciences, nutrition, art, and other subjects can be explored while you simultaneously teach your students to be responsible planetary citizens. There's a growing body of resources for teachers to tie these curricular concepts together, and the interdisciplinary framework of sustainability strengthens educational objectives by making all subjects more engaging, significant, and action-oriented. Using an interdisciplinary education model also promotes the systemic thinking necessary for addressing the increasingly complex global issues humanity faces. The world needs responsible citizens and leaders capable of interdisciplinary thought, and it begins with understanding the planet you live on and the way you can impact it.

Events to Inspire

If you're having a tough time linking the concepts of sustainability with your established curriculum, get creative and take it beyond school hours by hosting events that the children coordinate. You could start with a junk sculpture art show, a play about water pollution, an Earth Day celebration, or anything else you can dream up. You can also go green at events that your school already hosts. Have your students set up an informational table with fact sheets and a display describing an important environmental action. Work with the school music teacher to put on an environmental musical for the school's spring concert. You can find a "Rock the World" concert kit at *www.kidsforsavingearth.org*. Sell reusable water bottles at the season's biggest sporting events. There are countless ways to inspire your community at these regular gatherings.

Prompting Parents

Every teacher knows that a student's academic success is largely determined by parental involvement. Successfully nurturing a child who cares about the environment and who takes action to protect it requires parental support as well. Again, make parents aware of your intentions by sending home letters regularly updating them on the issues you're teaching the students and the actions you're taking at school. Throughout this book, you'll also find ways to have the children take the issues home and get families to take action together.

Keeping It Real

There is no perfect prescription for going green. Everyone has to do it their own way. Just as every child learns in different ways, some of the activities in this book will be more successful than others at teaching different children. Teaching sustainability is not like teaching math. There are facts to remember, but it's much more about critical thinking. It's a process and an outcome, and you should feel comfortable in letting the children guide the journey. Always keep in mind that it is a learning process for everyone and it can make a big difference to the health and welfare of the Earth and its citizens.

SOURCE

Check out Edutopia's Go Green Database, which includes links to imaginative classroom projects, green curricula, lesson plans, service-learning opportunities, and online tools. Search by grade level, cost, topic, or location. You also can contribute your favorite environmental education resources, as well as rate, browse, and discuss the resources in this growing green directory. Visit *www.edutopia .org/go-green.*

Making It Meaningful

Melting polar ice caps are easily forgotten when your students are bombarded with advertisements for the latest video games, movies, and junk food the instant they leave school. Buying new toys and watching television is so much more fun than worrying about pollution. It takes a certain finesse to make it meaningful without sending the child home frightened. Here are some basic tips.

Find the Personal Connections

People are a part of a web of life. Make global issues important to your students by discussing how they ultimately impact their lives in your community. Industrial pollution or agricultural runoff upriver from you may find its way into your drinking water. Melting polar ice caps and the resulting rising sea levels could leave your favorite vacation spot underwater. One thing always leads to another. Teach your students the global consequences of their actions, but also empower them to solve these problems.

Storytelling

It's innate to human cognition that stories influence thought and behavior. You can lecture all day long and spew facts and statistics until you're blue in the face, but it won't have the same impact as a good short story. Stories are powerful. Look to global fables and folklore for stories about nature and the environment. There's also a growing number of fictional books for kids that discuss environmental issues and values. Many are listed in Appendix A. Even more compelling, though, are true stories about other kids and other schools. For example, the story of eleven-year-old Clinton Hill, the founder of Kids for Saving Earth, is an inspiration to many. Alternatively, you can have your students write and illustrate their own stories and share them with the class.

FACT

Every year since 1971, ten students or student groups from across the country are recognized with a President's Environmental Youth Award. That's more than 300 examples of exceptional efforts to protect the environment, and all of them were imagined, developed, and implemented by kids!

Accentuate the Positive

It is extremely important that you don't scare your students. It sounds obvious, but it can be challenging when you're discussing environmental destruction and global warming. People of all ages quickly become overwhelmed and scared, which can lead to a sense of futility. You want to empower your students and this can only happen through the power of positivism. There are many problems, but there are even more solutions. Focus on the opportunities. Focus on the success stories. Focus on the possibilities.

Earning Money

Schools are used to fundraising. There are many ways to make some green while being green.

Eco-Friendly Fundraising

Say goodbye to candy and plastic trinkets and hello to high-quality, useful products that people want and need. Here are five resources for innovative, green fundraising that can earn money and educate your community.

- **Green School Project** (*www.greenschoolproject.com*) pays schools to recycle inkjet and laser printer cartridges as well as cell phones and PDA devices. It provides prepaid shipping materials and all other marketing materials free of charge.
- **Mother Earth Fundraising** (*www.motherearthfundraising.com*) is an ongoing way to raise money for your school. You simply encourage your community to purchase Earth-friendly products from the website and designate your school to receive a percentage of their purchase. The site has a wide variety of items, from soaps and cleaners to recycled gift wrap and gardening supplies. Get your community shopping online and your school will receive quarterly checks equal to 25 percent of all purchases.
- **Terracycle** (*www.terracycle.net*) pays you money to collect waste it recycles into new products. Collect wrappers, drink pouches, plastic bottles, yogurt cups, corks, and other simple trash that's turned into treasures like reusable bags, pencil pouches, plant food bottles, and more.
- **One Planet Fundraising** (*www.oneplanetfundraising.com*) has a variety of fundraising programs. Your class can choose to sell energy-saving compact fluorescent light (CFL) bulbs, reusable shopping bags, reusable water bottles, or recycled metal magnets. Each one earns you 40 percent of the profits.
- **Kids for Saving Earth** (*www.kidsforsavingearth.org*) has several suggestions for educational programs that combine earning and learning.

With a growing awareness of environmental issues, new green fundraising programs are sprouting up regularly.

Economical Education

Another way to earn money is by saving money. For example, if you have a certain budget allotted for buying paper, cut back on how much paper you use by using both sides and taking advantage of other reduction techniques. Use the money left over for eco-friendly products or for field trips. Likewise, you can ask the principal if you can have a portion of the money saved if you conduct a school energy conservation campaign. Find out your school's average monthly energy use. Conduct an energy conservation campaign and examine energy usage levels after several months. If it's gone down, it's money in your classroom pocket.

Making This Book Work for You

Now you know the nuts and bolts of creating the environment to nurture a green classroom. Here are the final tips for using this book and making your journey successful.

Meet Your Major Headings

Most of the chapters of this book are organized exactly the same to make it easier for you to get into a rhythm of addressing the entire picture about a particular issue. Here's what the areas are called and what they cover.

- "What It's All About" describes the basics of each issue.
- "Global Picture" attempts to address how the issue impacts other regions of the globe, how different populations are responding, or general lifestyle differences.
- "For the Classroom" brings the issue into the physical classroom space.
- "School Projects" are ideas to address the issue as a school community.
- "Field Trips" are—you guessed it—ideas for field trips that highlight the issue.

- "Human Health" discusses how each issue relates to human health.
- "Take It Home" identifies ways to bring the issue home to parents and caregivers.

Essentially, the framework of this book is to incorporate green living in every facet of life because the environment is everywhere and every action impacts the environment.

It's about Learning and Loving, Not Guilt and Grudge

Whatever you do, keep it easy and fun because if something is not fairly easy and fun, it won't get done. You have a limited amount of time with each child and you want your lessons to last a lifetime, so tackle little pieces every day until it becomes a habit for everyone. Laugh a lot. Smile a lot. You're making the world a better place.

CHAPTER 2

Earth-Friendly Farming

With so many people living in cities, children (and adults!) often have no idea where their food comes from or how it is grown or raised. Establishing an intimate connection between you and your food lays the foundation for healthier eating and a healthier life. By understanding exactly how your food gets to your fork, you will understand better how your food choices affect your health, the environment, and the community. The old cliché "you are what you eat" can now be expanded to "the world is what people eat." Every bite and drink you take has an impact on the planet.

What It's All About

Who needs farms when there are grocery stores? The personal disconnect from farming and food has probably never been greater. School curriculum emphasizes the importance of a nutritious diet, but it is also important to understand the bigger story of food.

Big, Big, Big Farms

Farms grow food, but they've also grown in size over time. Have your students draw their own garden from a bird's-eye view. Have you ever grown or seen a vegetable garden? Imagine that everything you eat in a year is grown in that one garden.

Since most people don't grow or raise their own food, farmers have to use more space to grow enough to feed not only themselves but many other people also. Back in 1940, each farmer fed eleven people; by 2002, each farmer fed ninety people. With a growing population, farms have gotten bigger and bigger and bigger. Put all of your students' gardens together on the wall to show how quickly the farm grows.

These big farms, known as industrial farms, are useful because fewer people can grow more food. That means most people don't need to worry about growing the food they eat. They can do other things with their lives like write books or race cars or fly planes. Yet, in order for fewer people to grow more food, they have to find ways to be very efficient, meaning they can't waste any time or money. They have to be fast and do things cheaply.

Think of your garden, and picture going out and picking the weeds that pop up in between the plants. It's important to get rid of the weeds because they compete with the edible garden plants for water, sun, and soil nutrients (plant food). If you had to pick the weeds from everyone's gardens, it would be a lot more difficult and take a lot more time. Industrial farms use pesticides to kill the weeds because it saves time. However, these chemicals end up killing bugs like butterflies and bees in addition to the weeds. They also sink into the soil and soak down into our groundwater (the water underground that most of our drinking water is drawn from). They can also end up in the food that is grown at the farm.

The Natural Recipe for Farming

People can farm without hurting the planet if they keep the planet in mind while they're farming. Organic or sustainable farms try to grow food and raise animals as close to what Mother Nature intended as possible. They don't use any harmful chemicals for killing weeds; they don't use sewage sludge (which is what people flush down their toilets!) to fertilize their fields; they feed their animals natural food; and they do whatever they can to protect the Earth as they farm. Take a virtual organic farm tour at *www.ecokidsonline.com*. Just look for "My Visit to an Organic Farm" and let your students explore without leaving the classroom. When you're done, write your own organic "Farmer in the Dell" song.

One specific part of the Earth sustainable farmers try hard to protect is the soil. Without healthy soil, they can't grow food. There are a lot of ingredients needed for healthy soil, including our friends the earthworms (actually, it's their poop that makes soil healthy). Make your own classroom worm farm by downloading the worm guide from *www.ciwmb.ca.gov/schools/curriculum/worms*.

A second part of this project is to buy two identical plants. Scoop out the worm poop and worm juice every now and then and feed it to one of the potted plants (mark them so you know which one to feed). Watch and see what happens. Is one growing more quickly than the other? Does it look healthier? This is why it's important to protect the soil and the creatures that live in it. The pesticides and other chemicals that industrial farmers use can kill these helpful creatures. Pick up a copy of *Worms Eat Our Garbage: Classroom Activities for a Better Environment* by Mary Appelhof, Mary Frances Fenton, and Barbara Loss Harris to find more ideas to get your students wriggling.

Earthworm Survey

Spring is the ideal time to check for earthworm activity. Wait until the soil temperature is at least 50°F and soil moisture content at the surface is 20 percent or more. Using a shovel or spade, dig a cube of soil measuring roughly a foot on each side, and lay it next to the hole on the ground's surface. Break it apart and look for earthworms. You'll find at least ten earthworms per cubic foot in healthy soil. Repeat the procedure at several locations in your garden or schoolyard. If your soil's average is fewer than ten worms per cubic foot, it's time to add more organic matter like compost to your soil.

Global Picture

The foods we eat come from all over the world. Things like bananas, chocolate, and coffee are common in every American household, but they have to travel thousands of miles to get to the local grocery store. The farther the food has to travel, the more fuel it takes to get it there. The more fuel it takes to get it there, the more pollution and global warming it creates.

Big Planet, Little Land

The planet Earth is very large, but there's really not that much space on it for farming, which means it's important to protect the soil on the farmland. You can demonstrate how very little farmland there is by cutting up an apple for the class. The apple represents the planet Earth.

1. Cut the apple into quarters; three of those are oceans.
2. Slice the remaining quarter in half; one piece is all of the land people cannot live on, such as swamps, mountaintops, polar ice caps, and deserts. What's left now? One-eighth of the apple.
3. Slice this piece into four equal sections. Three of them represent the land that is too rocky, too wet, too cold, or too steep. It also includes land with soil that is too poor to grow food on and all the land that has been built on or paved. What's left now? One-thirty-second of the planet.
4. Carefully peel the tiny slice of Earth. This tiny bit of peel represents the very thin layer of the Earth's crust that grows all the food to feed everyone on the planet. This layer, called the topsoil, is less than five feet deep and it takes 100 years for nature to create one inch of it.

This visual example usually sparks some lively class discussion. Did you have any idea that people had such little space for farming? How can people protect the soil? Can the students practice cutting an apple (or drawing an apple and then drawing lines through it to represent the cuts) and telling the story to someone else?

FACT

The average fruit or vegetable has to travel 1,650 miles from the farm to your table. It's a long journey and causes a lot of pollution. Map it for the class and calculate how many gallons of gas it would take if you took the same road trip.

Play with Your Food

Have fun with food by having your students create food puppets and write a play that can teach younger students. Divide the classroom into pairs or small groups. Assign each of them a simple food like a potato, banana, kiwi, mango, cinnamon, or cocoa bean. Find common foods that may come from far away. Each group will need to make a puppet of their food and answer the following questions:

- Where is this food from?
- How many miles is that from where you live?
- How many gallons of gas would it take to get here by car if your car gets thirty miles per gallon?
- How many pounds of the global-warming gas, carbon dioxide, would be released by this trip if each gallon of gas releases about twenty-five pounds of carbon dioxide?
- What language do they speak where this food came from?
- How is this food grown and farmed?

Once the students have learned all about their food, they should write a script as though their food is talking and introducing itself to an audience. Have fun with it and let the kids write music for the play and design the set. Encourage them to use their imaginations.

For the Classroom

What's the difference between a teacher and a farmer? One grows bright thinkers and the other grows food. Make your crop of thinkers farm-friendly by engaging them in their own miniature farm.

SOURCE

For a wide range of activities and resources for levels K–12, visit the California Foundation for Agriculture in the Classroom website (*www.cfaitc .org*). It has lesson plans, a teacher's resource guide, a kid's corner with games and coloring pages, and lots more.

Flat Farmers

If you were a farmer, what kind of food would you grow or what kind of animals would you raise? Have each child pick one thing and then go around the classroom to discuss how that food grows or how that animal is raised. For example, if a child wants to be an apple farmer, she has to know that apples grow on trees. Likewise, if a child wants to grow carrots, he has to know that they grow underground. If you have access to the Internet, try to find images of what each type of farm looks like (or at least a picture of what the food looks like before it is picked). For animals, talk about what kind of food they eat and what kind of houses they need. Again, find some pictures to show the students. If the children are younger or you don't have access to a computer, get a variety of farming books from the library and look through them with your students. After you've perused them together, the students can each pick which farm they would want to have.

For the second part of the activity, lay out large pieces of paper on the floor and trace an outline of each child. Have them draw in the details of themselves wearing whatever clothing they think a farmer would wear. For the background of the picture, they should draw what their chosen farm would look like. Voilà! Flat Farmers ready for display in your classroom or hallway.

Petite Patch

Herb gardens are easy to grow indoors, and they give children a chance to grow a plant that can be harvested and used in cooking. Create your petite patch by designating some prime "farmland" by sunny windows. You can either grow herbs from seed or, to increase the likelihood of success, buy seedlings (or ask a nursery to donate them). Use fiber pots, so when the plants grow big enough, they can easily be transplanted to a large pot or even outdoors when the children take them home. For whichever herb you choose, when they are big enough to be used, send them home with instructions for how to pick them off the plant without harming it, as well as some simple recipes for using them. Visit *www.planetnatural.com/site /herbgardening.html* for help and more ideas.

School Projects

Getting your whole school engaged in understanding where food comes from and how food grows can be really exciting and surprisingly rewarding. Establishing an intimate connection between you and your food lays the foundation for healthier eating and a healthier life. By understanding exactly how your food gets to you, you understand better how your food choices affect your health, the environment, and the community.

Farm-to-School

Farm-to-school is a growing national effort to connect school lunch programs directly to local farmers. According to the National Farm to School Program, there are almost 9,000 schools across the country making this vital connection. You can start down this exciting path by visiting the National Farm to School Program website (*www.farmtoschool.org*), where you'll find information about the program and its importance, success stories, how to connect with resources in your state, step-by-step guides for implementing a program, curricular resources, funding opportunities, and much more. Whether it's a simple salad bar or a seasonal supply of apples, little efforts go a long way to teach kids and adults alike about the vital connection between healthy farms, healthy communities, and healthy bodies.

School Gardens

School gardens are an amazing multidisciplinary, hands-on learning opportunity. In addition, they provide an unparalleled experience to empower children to grow their own food. You'll see the pride in your students' faces the first time they get to eat or share something fresh from the garden. You can also expect them to eat foods they may shun in the cafeteria because of the excitement of growing it themselves (and because it just tastes better)!

Once again, all you need to do is hop online and visit *www.school gardenwizard.org*. This site has everything from how to make the case to your school administrators to planning the garden. It also includes tips on how to garden, how to learn in the garden, and how to evaluate your success. Of course, the climate you live in will determine what you can feasibly grow during the school year. If you live somewhere with a short growing season, you may want to raise funds to build a small greenhouse for your garden. You can also focus on fast-growing crops like snap peas and leaf lettuce. Another idea is to have families adopt the garden over summer break, so the children have a bountiful harvest to enjoy when they come back in the fall. Put one family in charge each week, fewer if you have a lot of parents who'd like to participate.

ESSENTIAL

It is very common for school food service managers to initially assume farm-to-school programs are too difficult or too expensive. Don't take no for an answer! For your best chances of success, find the nearest school that has a program in place and have their staff contact your school to explain how it works for them.

Field Trips

The farming and food field trip options are almost endless. You'll find a couple of ideas here, but use your imagination. Think of ethnic restaurants, global markets, farmers' markets, processing facilities, Amish or Native American communities, fisheries, or orchards. Just remember to examine how the farm or facility is affecting the environment.

Visit a Local Farm

Most schools already schedule a farm field trip at some point during the primary years. If it's possible, find a local organic farm to visit so the staff can explain what they do to protect the environment. How do they protect the soil and water? How do they conserve energy and water? How do they deal with weeds and pests?

Have the class brainstorm questions to ask prior to your visit. Even if it's not an organic farm, you can ask staff if they consider the environment or do anything about the farm's impact on it. If you successfully start a farm-to-school program, visit the farms you have partnered with. It's especially memorable for students to see exactly where their food is grown. To prepare your students for visiting the farm, visit Earthbound Farm's website at *www.ebfarm.com* to find basic information about organic farms and a coloring book about Earthy and Bounder, two earthworms that teach kids all about organic farming.

SOURCE

The Center for Ecoliteracy published a comprehensive guide for schools called the "Rethinking School Lunch Guide." It contains all the tools and creative solutions for improving school lunches, academic success, environmental awareness, and the well-being of children. Download it at *www.ecoliteracy.org/programs/rsl-guide.html*.

Grocery Store Scavenger Hunt

Call a local grocery store and find out at what times during the day or what day of the week they usually have very little business. Warn them that you'll be bringing in your class. Break up the class into teams of three or four (depending on your class size and how many chaperones you can wrangle). The goal of the scavenger hunt is to find the foods that came the longest distance and those that came the shortest. Chaperones should all be armed with atlases to help the children find the locations on a map. It's impossible to know at a glance how far the ingredients in processed foods have traveled, so you'll just have to go by where it was packaged or manufactured. If the ones that end up coming from the closest locations are multi-ingredient processed foods, write down the product names and bring them back to the classroom for an investigation to see how far the ingredients had to come.

ALERT!

If you are planning a visit to a farm with animals, make sure you are aware of any animal allergies your students may have. Also, be sure to have students wash their hands well after touching any animals at the farm.

Human Health

How many times have you heard "you are what you eat"? What do you think it means? It means that your health depends on how healthfully you eat. More and more, we're finding that the foods that are healthiest for us are also the foods that protect the health of the planet.

Food Label Forensics

Have students bring clean food labels from home. Each student will only use one label, but they should all bring several to ensure that everyone will get to work with a label from a different product. Go around the room and have them read their product's ingredients to the class. Before you begin, reassure them that it's okay if they have a hard time pronouncing some of the ingredients. As they read each one, write it on the board; whenever an ingredient is repeated, tally a mark by it.

In the end, you'll likely have a very long list and you'll see by the tallies which ingredients are most common. Do you know what these ingredients are? Have the students come up to the board and circle ingredients they are familiar with (likely things such as milk, sugar, and wheat). What's left? Now it's time for some food label forensics. Find out what these things are, what they're doing in your food, and what they might do to your health. The Center for Science in the Public Interest has a food additives safety program. At *www.cspinet.org/reports/chemcuisine.htm* you can find a comprehensive list of these unpronounceable ingredients and what sort of health impacts might be associated with them.

Invisible Invaders

To get an idea of how a chemical pesticide or fertilizer ends up in your food, fill a container with water and add a few drops of food coloring. Place a stalk of celery in the water. When plants are growing, they drink water from the soil they are growing in. To speed up the process for our experiment, we've left the soil out and are letting our plant simply drink all the water it wants. A conventional farm uses strong chemicals called pesticides to help keep weeds and bugs away from the plants, but where does the pesticide go after it's been sprayed? It lands on the plant and the soil and eventually ends up in the water the plant is drinking. The food coloring represents the pesticides. Wait twenty-four hours. What happened? Ask your students what would happen if they ate this celery.

Grade schools in Olympia, Washington, went completely organic and still managed to cut lunch costs by two cents per meal. Their program includes working directly with local organic farms, and they cut out desserts, opting instead to offer fruits to satisfy students' sweet cravings.

Take It Home

Most parents know a healthy diet is important for their child's development. What many don't know is that the healthiest diet is also the one that's best for the planet. Help your students' parents get in the know by giving them easy tips for making changes in their diet.

The Dirty Dozen

Conventionally grown food can have chemical pesticide residues. Pesticides have been linked to a variety of health impacts, and kids are most vulnerable. You can easily reduce a child's exposure to these chemicals by avoiding produce that typically has high levels of residue and choosing those with low levels instead. In a 2003 study published in *Environmental Health Perspectives*, schoolchildren were tested for pesticides in their bodies. Those who ate an organic diet had one-sixth the amount compared to those who ate a conventionally grown diet. When you want one of the most frequently contaminated foods, select an organically grown product instead.

Twelve Most Contaminated
- Apples
- Bell peppers
- Celery
- Cherries
- Imported grapes
- Nectarines
- Peaches
- Pears
- Potatoes
- Red raspberries
- Spinach
- Strawberries

Twelve Least Contaminated
- Asparagus
- Avocados
- Bananas
- Broccoli
- Cauliflower
- Corn (sweet)
- Kiwi
- Mangoes
- Onions
- Papaya
- Peas (sweet)
- Pineapples

This list is from a study conducted by the Environmental Working Group based on U.S. government data. Learn more at *www.beyondpesticides.org*.

Organic Gardening at Home

Growing your own food is rewarding, and it saves money, too! Encourage parents to embrace Earth-friendly farming at home. Whether it's a garden in the yard or simply a few plants in pots on a windowsill, it's a great experience for the whole family. Here are a few tips:

1. **Earth-friendly gardening means ditching the chemicals.** Instead of using pesticides or synthetic fertilizers, find natural ways to eliminate pests and build nutrient-rich soil.
2. **Save space by using vertical gardening techniques.** If you have limited space in your yard, grow things up instead of out. For example, produce that grows on a vine can grow up on trellises if you help it along. The same techniques can be used for deck or indoor gardening (although indoor plants may need the help of a grow light).
3. **Save water by collecting rainwater.** Do you have indoor or outdoor plants that you need to water regularly? Instead of using tap or hose water, collect rainwater. If you own a home with gutters, place a barrel at the bottom of a downspout. You can also buy rain barrels that have a spigot you can attach a hose to. If you live in an apartment or condo with a fire escape or deck, you could leave buckets out during a storm. Get creative!

Go to *www.organicgardening.com* for more information and advice on how to incorporate Earth-friendly practices into your life and your students' home lives.

CHAPTER 3

Radical Reductions

People in the United States spend more time and money shopping than anywhere else in the world. All these purchases certainly don't make the planet a happier place. Every single thing you buy has an environmental impact. Some are much bigger than others depending on how they are made, how much they are packaged, how far they are shipped, what it does, and what happens when we're done using it. One of the most important—and least expensive— choices people can make to protect the Earth is to buy and use less stuff.

What It's All About

Have you ever heard someone say "waste not, want not"? What does it mean? It means that if you don't waste something now, you'll still have it in the future. It's an idea that's especially important to keep in mind if you want to be a good steward of the Earth. Take care of the Earth and it will take care of you.

What a Waste

How much garbage do you create every day? How often do you buy new things? If you look at the facts about how much people buy and throw away, it's pretty shocking.

- If everyone lived like an average American, it would take five or six planets to provide all of the necessary resources.
- Each individual creates about 1.5 tons of solid waste per year. That's about 4.5 pounds a day and 90,000 pounds of trash in a lifetime.
- Every product leaves a trail of waste before it even hits the shelves at a store. For example, the amount of trash created to make a laptop computer is close to 4,000 times its weight.
- Each year 352 million pounds of plastic are thrown into the ocean, killing about 1 million sea creatures.
- Eighty percent of what Americans buy ends up in the trash within six months.

There is only one planet Earth. It has a limited amount of resources and a limited amount of space for garbage. People can't continue to live this way, and the planet is starting to make that clear. Forests are disappearing, the atmosphere is warming up, and everything is becoming polluted and dirty. It's time to start to clean things up by stopping our wasteful ways. What can each person do to stop wasting so much? Do you buy things you don't need? What have you thrown away recently?

Trash Examination

What is waste? It's everything we throw away and then some. Most of what ends up in landfills is paper. There's also food, plastic, metal, glass, textiles, wood, and much more. Challenge students to think of other things that end up in the garbage. Have each student keep a journal of what they throw away for a week. For younger students, have them work together to keep track of classroom trash for a week. After a week, examine your list (or lists) to see what items were repeated most often. Is there a way to keep these items out of the trash? Is there a way to reduce how much we use of them, or to reuse or recycle them?

If you'd like to make it more visual, use your classroom bulletin board to illustrate the experience. Create a picture of a trash dumpster to put on the bulletin board. Place a sign over it that says, "Things I should throw away." Next to the dumpster, place a sign that says, "Things I didn't need to use." Examples of these items include plastic plates, paper plates, plastic utensils, paper towels, plastic bags, and paper bags. Assign the students to draw pictures of what was on their lists. As each child draws a picture, have her pin it on the dumpster or under the items she didn't need.

SOURCE

The Story of Stuff with Annie Leonard is a twenty-minute fact-filled journey into the hidden life of products. From how products are made to how they are disposed of, the video is essential for understanding the social and environmental impacts of shopping. It is meant for adults, but it can be broken down into sections and taught to students. You can watch it for free online or order a DVD at *www.storyofstuff.com.*

Global Picture

Garbage is a growing issue everywhere. Some countries are solving their garbage problems by shipping it to other places. Other countries are coming up with inventive ways to reduce how much they are creating.

Out of Sight, Out of Mind?

Many people forget about garbage as soon as it's taken away, but it doesn't simply disappear. A lot of garbage doesn't even make it to the dump. Instead, it blows around in the wind, gets stuck up in trees, or sails off into waterways. One especially sneaky item that seems to end up all over the place is the simple plastic bag.

Around the world, people use about a million plastic bags every single minute. Hundreds of thousands of whales and sea turtles and other sea animals die every year from mistaking plastic bags for food. Plastic bags don't biodegrade; they photodegrade. This means they break down into tinier and tinier pieces of toxic bits that pollute the air, water, and soil. Many countries—including China, India, Taiwan, South Africa, Somalia, Kenya, Uganda, Switzerland, Germany, Holland, Norway, and Spain—have either gotten rid of plastic bags altogether or are making people pay money for them so they use them less. Individual cities such as San Francisco have also banned plastic bags. Is this an issue in your city?

What happens to the billions of bags that are still being used every year? Many are building up in our oceans and adding to huge masses of floating plastic-trash islands. The biggest one is known as the Great Pacific Garbage Patch that is twice the size of Texas. You can show the kids a great cartoon video about the Great Pacific Garbage Patch and a real-life video of kids who are making a difference at *www.greengorilla.com*.

What can you do? Ban the bag! Make your own reusable bags in class. Work with local grocery stores to provide reusable bags for people to buy. Have the students make signs warning others about the perils of the plastic bag. Help them list ways to reuse the plastic bags already lying around your house. What ways did the students come up with?

Fun with Furoshiki

You don't have to worry about what to do with garbage if you don't make any. Generations of people in Japan have used a fabric-folding technique known as *furoshiki* (f'-ROHSH-kee) to wrap gifts and carry groceries, among other things. Furoshiki eliminates waste-like plastic bags and wrapping paper. It is reusable and can be used for many different things. You can do an online search for furoshiki videos and diagrams for folding to give your students an idea of the process. Of course, the real fun is in trying yourself. Start your search for ideas at *www.furoshiki.com/techniques.php.*

Each child needs a large bandana or scarf (thrift stores and Grandma's closet are great places to look). You can have them make a craft that they then wrap in the fabric or have them make their own bag. You can also have them practice wrapping different shapes like books or cans. See how creative they can get with folding and knotting.

Almost everyone is familiar with the mantra "reduce, reuse, recycle," but unfortunately, most people really focus on recycling. Reducing is the most important thing to do, reusing is second best, and recycling is better than throwing something away. It is imperative to refocus attention on reduction. Embed this concept in as many class activities as possible.

For the Classroom

The typical school classroom has little waste outside of paper, but holy smokes a lot of paper gets thrown away! Let's hope your classroom recycles, but even recycling takes energy and resources. The best option for the planet is to reduce, reduce, reduce.

Paper Purge

Find as many ways to reduce paper use as you can. For example, designate a spot in the classroom for pieces of paper that have only been used on one side. Reuse these pieces for scratch paper. For older students, try to shift to e-documents. Make it an option to e-mail assignments so you don't use any paper at all. Focus on activities that are based on action instead of a final product; for instance, choose oral reports instead of written. Another way to reduce paper use in your classroom is to get parents' e-mail addresses so you can e-mail announcements instead of sending home hard copies. Minimize the number of handouts you use. Research online instead of subscribing to magazines and newspapers. How many more ways can you find to purge paper? Have the kids design flyers that list the different ways your classroom has reduced paper use and waste. They can share them with other classrooms or even other schools. Better yet, make it an electronic document that you can e-mail to other staff and schools.

Take a Load Off at Lunch

Students will see immediate differences in waste levels after starting a paper purge, and they can also see drastic changes if they begin planning waste-free lunches. Split the classroom into two sections: those who bring lunch from home and those who eat school lunches. Have each group brainstorm ideas for how to reduce waste. Ideas for students who bring bag lunches include using reusable containers for food and eliminating overly packaged foods like individually wrapped string cheese and single-serving potato chip bags. Ideas for students who eat school lunches are more limited because the school's practices determine what they eat. One behavior they can control is the amount of food they take. They should only put the food they know they will eat on their plates. They can also be more conservative with using disposable items like napkins.

Take it to the next level and have your students organize a waste-free lunch day at your school. They can educate other students and staff about why it's important and how to do it. If your school has separate lunch periods for different age groups, you can have a contest to see who generates the least amount of waste. There are great resources for conducting waste-free lunch days and even creating year-round waste-free lunch programs online through the U.S. Environmental Protection Agency and *www .wastefreelunches.org*.

School Projects

An entire school's garbage adds up fast, but usually it's only the custodial staff that sees it. Getting everyone thinking about reductions will lighten the load for both the school budget and waste haulers, which will also use less gas.

Paperless Office

If your students are trying to reduce paper use in your classroom, it's time they taught the administrative staff a little lesson about going paperless. Of course, it's highly unlikely you'll be able to get them to go completely paperless, but with a few simple tips they can probably cut their use in half—not a small amount at most schools. Have your students conduct an initial survey with the staff asking how much paper they use and what types of things they print. Back in the classroom, have the students brainstorm ways that the staff could reduce their use of paper. Some of the most important steps they can take include printing on both sides of the paper, not printing e-mails, and trying to keep documents digital instead of printing them. Then have the kids make signs that can be posted to remind staff of these quick tips.

FACT

The average office worker uses 10,000 pieces of paper a year. You can cut that amount in half simply by always copying or printing on both sides of the paper. Set your copiers and printers to default to duplexing. When you assign papers, request that students write or print on both sides if their printer has a duplexing unit.

Make a "Paper Police" badge and regularly send students to the office to act as "paper police." If they see that someone has forgotten one of the tips, they can remind that person to do it in the future. Students love to chide adults. Watch how quickly staff adapt to the new paperless office rules. You can find more ideas for how to reduce paper use by doing an online search of "paperless office" and by visiting *www.reduce.org*.

Dumpster Diving

Having older children do a waste audit allows them to understand exactly what goes into their school's garbage, and it also gets them to use a variety of mathematical concepts. You can find directions for a variety of different audits at *www.recycleworks.org*, but the essence of the project is to sort and weigh your school's garbage. The cafeteria and custodial staff will need to be aware of the project, and parental permission slips may need to be mailed home, too. The day of the audit, wet waste will need to be separated from dry waste. The dry waste is sorted, weighed, and identified as recyclable or nonrecyclable. You can combine a recycling effort with a reduction effort if your school doesn't have a recycling program yet. Still, reduction is the most important first step. What items found during the audit could be reduced or eliminated? Here are some tips for schools to reduce waste:

- Buy products in bulk to cut back on packaging.
- Buy durable products like refillable pens and rechargeable batteries instead of disposable ones.
- Remove your school's name (or staff names) from junk mail lists.
- Use reusable cutlery and trays in the cafeteria.
- Have staff bring in reusable mugs for coffee.

What else can your students come up with after looking at the waste?

Field Trips

There's no better way to get the big picture of how much waste people make than by seeing where it all ends up. Garbage doesn't just disappear. Where does it go in your community?

Unlovely Landfill

Many solid waste facilities offer tours for schools. Call your local facility or local government office of solid waste to find out if there are any tours in your area. Generally, the tour consists of a presentation to the students about how a landfill is built and maintained. They also typically discuss how some garbage is diverted to recycling facilities, as well as what happens when a landfill becomes full. The tour ends with a bus ride through the dump. It is truly a field trip your class will never forget. Seeing the size of landfills and the amount of garbage gives people a sense of why it's so important to reduce waste.

Government Garbage Control

You can call your city, county, or state government offices to talk to someone about solid waste and pollution control. Take the children to the selected government office to see where the region's waste issues are addressed. How much is created each year? What's in it and how much? What do they do with it? What kinds of programs do they have to try to reduce waste? Do they have materials the students can take home to their parents? Have staff talk about their individual jobs and projects. You can even have the students break up into small groups and interview different staff people. When you return to the classroom, they can teach one another about what they learned.

Human Health

It wouldn't be healthy to live in a garbage can, but people are treating the Earth like a big waste container. The more waste people create, the more it ends up polluting the air and water. When you breathe and drink polluted air and water, you can become polluted, too.

Wastewater

Landfills are built like big swimming pools. They have special thick walls that are supposed to keep the garbage from leaking into groundwater. Still, oftentimes, over time the walls start cracking and garbage juice leaks out. You can demonstrate how this happens by creating your own miniature leaky landfill. Fill a jar with about an inch of water. Find a small plastic container, like a small yogurt container, that will sit in the mouth of the jar without falling in. Poke a little hole in the bottom of the container. Now start filling the landfill. What kinds of things end up in the garbage? Candy wrappers, old socks, dirty diapers, and much more. Using colored paper and markers, have the children draw tiny pictures of the different garbage items, or put in tiny bits of real trash. Just make sure you don't pack it in too tight.

When the landfill is full, put in a few drops of a dark-colored dye. This represents toxic substances such as paint and old oil that end up in the garbage. Now slowly pour in some water. This is the rain that falls on the garbage and the moisture that ends up in the landfill from old food. Watch what comes out of the hole. What happens to the water below the landfill? Did you know that many people's drinking water comes from groundwater? What could happen if your drinking water had some garbage juice in it?

Don't Make It, Don't Breathe It

Reducing the amount of "stuff" people use will reduce all kinds of pollution, including air pollution. When China wanted to clean up the air for the 2008 Summer Olympics in Beijing, it shut down factories that were creating "stuff." Those factories were creating air pollution that could make it hard for athletes to breathe. Sometimes that stuff is important, but many times it's not so important—like plastic straws or plastic disposable forks. When people don't use these things, no one will make them and the factories that make them won't create pollution.

You and your students can reduce pollution by reducing your use of disposable items. Have each student create a reduce-use box by decorating a small box and filling it with reusable utensils, washable straws, small cups, salt and pepper shakers, and other items you typically get at a fast food restaurant when you're out and about.

Have them bring their boxes home to their parents to keep in their car. They can reduce waste and save money by ordering a large drink and splitting it up into the cups. They can also stuff rags under the seats of their car for cleaning windshields and headlights. Can your students think of other items to keep in the car to reduce waste?

Take It Home

Where there are people, there is almost always garbage. Keeping our planet from becoming one huge landfill means starting to reduce waste every day, everywhere. The lessons your students have learned at school will transfer home with ease, but here are a couple of additional ideas to really get the reduction ball rolling.

Shop-until-You-Drop Waste

Everything people buy creates pollution. You don't need to stop shopping, but everyone can shop smarter. Here are some ideas to reduce how much waste you create. They'll also help you reduce the amount of money you spend. Follow these easy tips to get started:

- Make a shopping list before you go and stick to it.
- Buy things that can be reused or recycled.
- Look for items that are made from or packaged in recycled materials.
- Look for the least-packaged products and buy in bulk.

One of the most important steps you can take to reduce waste is to bring reusable shopping bags when you go to the store. You can use cloth bags you may already have lying around your house, buy reusable bags, or even sew your own.

Junk Mail Madness

No one likes junk mail, so why not get rid of it? It's irritating to consumers and it's incredibly wasteful, so put your foot down.

Write the Direct Marketing Association and register with their Mail Preference Service, which puts you on a list to not be contacted by solicitors. It's a free service that lasts for five years, but only for national mail. All you need to do is write a letter or postcard with the date, your name, address, and signature, and write, "Please register my name with the Mail Preference Service." Send it to: Mail Preference Service c/o Direct Marketing Association, P.O. Box 643, Carmel, NY 10512. You can also register online at *www .the-dma.org/consumers/offmailinglist.html,* but it costs $5.

CHAPTER 4

Choose to Reuse

Just because you're done using something doesn't mean it's garbage. Just like the old saying says, "one man's trash is another man's treasure." In the case of reusing, sometimes your own creativity can turn your trash into a new treasure—for you!

4

What It's All About

If you can't reduce or avoid your use of something, try to think of ways to reuse it. It's the next best option before recycling because it doesn't require the resources needed to recycle something. The old-fashioned habit of sharing isn't in vogue anymore. But just think if it became a badge of honor to share items like crayons, clothes, and toys. We would save money, energy, and landfill space.

In the Beginning, Think of the End

When you are out shopping and trying to decide which products to buy, look at them closely to see if they might be reusable. If it can't be reused, is there a similar product that would suit your needs but could be reused? For example, bottled water is sold in plastic bottles that are meant to be thrown away after one use. As a result, people in the United States throw away 70 million bottles of water every single day. Instead of throwing it away, you could decorate and reuse the bottle as a flower vase or bath toy. Better yet, if you like having bottled water, buy a reusable water bottle made from a stronger material like stainless steel and just fill it with tap water. Look around your classroom. What will happen to different items when you're done using them? Do they have to be thrown away? What else could they be used for?

According to studies done in California and Massachusetts, about 2 to 5 percent of the waste stream is reusable materials. Organizations like Terracycle would put that number much higher; they continuously find second lives for discarded materials like plastic bags, plastic bottles, juice pouches, wrappers, and more. Reuse is limited only by imagination.

Re-imagine, Reinvent, Rediscover

Reusing requires a little creativity. By nature, kids are some of the most creative creatures on the planet, so get those innovative juices flowing and watch what happens. Either provide some of your own items or have the kids bring in things from home. You want a wide variety of things that could easily end up in the garbage, such as empty food containers, dried-up markers, broken toys, torn or stained clothing, packaging, and wrappers. Everything should be thoroughly cleaned, and nothing with sharp or pointy edges should be used.

Divide the students into several groups and give them each a pile of random junk to work with. What can they make? All of the items can be used to make one new item or several different items. The children should work together to reinvent a use for the junk. Set their imaginations free by allowing them to invent things that have never been seen before.

If your school has a display case, ask if your class can exhibit its projects there for a while. Post a sign asking if people can identify what materials went into each piece. Kids for Saving Earth provides many ideas for turning trash into an eco-carnival. You can even earn money through creative thinking with trash. Put your kids to work thinking of games they can make with trash.

Reusing means giving a second life to the products you've purchased new, but it also means buying things used. Are there items that your classroom or school purchases that you could buy used? How about chairs and tables or shelves and organization systems? Look into buying used items by doing a little research online at sites like eBay and Craigslist.

Second Homes for Secondhand Stuff

Just because you don't want to reuse something doesn't mean somebody else wouldn't want to. Some people have yard sales to get rid of things they don't want anymore. Ask your students to tell you about their experiences with family garage sales. If they haven't had one, suggest that they help their parents put one on. They could be making money and saving the Earth! If a yard sale isn't your cup of tea, thrift stores, secondhand stores, and antique stores all sell used items.

There are also organizations that accept donations of used items for people in need. For example, homeless shelters are often looking for people to donate clothing, coats, and blankets. Some organizations help parents who don't have very much money by collecting donations of baby blankets, clothing, toys, cribs, and strollers.

Global Picture

Around the world, people reuse things in interesting ways. With the widespread use of the Internet, people can easily share all of their great ideas for reusing materials and giving them a new life.

Toys from Trash

A group of artists in South Africa collect aluminum cans, bottle caps, plastic bottles, bits of wire, and other refuse to create functional toys like cars and radios as well as souvenirs like decorative flowers and pens. Challenge your students to make a toy out of trash. For the best results, structure it as a take-home assignment that they can work on with a parent. By having the children work independently from one another, you'll end up with a wider variety of projects. At the end, talk about what types of trash your students used and what they made with their trash.

Reusing takes time and patience. You need to make sure that items are clean and safe. You need to put aside your "garbage goggles." It is a long-term commitment, and you should prepare yourself for the little messes that come along with it. It may seem difficult to wash out the jam container and reuse it for leftover soup, but in the end it will save you money and help the planet.

Idea Sharing

How Can I Recycle This? (*www.recyclethis.co.uk*) is a British blog that has readers submit reuse questions for everyone to respond to. People can send in a request for ideas for reusing old gloves, bubble wrap, banana boxes, and just about anything else you can think of. The authors of the site and the other readers submit their ideas and personal pictures of ways that they've either reused something themselves or seen it reused somewhere else. It's fun just going through the site and seeing all of the imaginative ways people are reusing everyday junk.

You can start your own idea-sharing effort either in your classroom or on a hallway bulletin board. Students (and staff) can share pictures and short descriptions of how they are reusing things.

For the Classroom

By now, you are probably starting to understand that reusing is all about creativity. The ability to reuse something is only limited by the imagination. The more reuse projects you promote with your students, the more they'll begin identifying ways to reuse outside of the classroom. They'll begin seeing the second life in everything.

Create-a-Card

Everyone has lovely holiday and birthday cards they hate to throw away. At the beginning of the year, send out an alert for parents to save their old holiday and birthday cards. Create postcards by cutting off the side with the picture (if there's no writing on the back) and using the blank side to create a postcard-like writing area and address area. Sell them at a reuse sale at your school or other community gatherings. When you send postcards, you don't have to use envelopes. This saves paper and energy costs!

Another good reuse project for older kids who can handle scissors and an iron safely is creating a reusable fabric gift bag. Ask parents for scrap material donations for your classroom. Each child should cut out two 12" by 12" pieces. (Preferably, use borrowed pinking sheers from parents.) You can precut the square patterns out of cereal boxes to make it easier for the kids, or challenge their measuring abilities by having them draw it on the fabric themselves. Instead of sewing together the pieces, use glue tape or fusible webbing to iron the seams together (both are available at craft or fabric stores). Iron three sides together. On the open side, punch holes to weave in one long piece of yarn. Pull the two ends of the yarn together around the gift and create a nice bow. This can be reused over and over again.

SOURCE

The School and Community Reuse Action Project *(www.scrapaction .org)* collects reusable materials from businesses and distributes them to local schools. It protects the environment, provides valuable resources to schools, and inspires creative reuse of a wide variety of materials. While it is only a local organization, its website is sure to motivate you to find new opportunities for reuse.

Notebooks out of Cereal Boxes

Have your students bring in empty cereal boxes from home. Collect paper that has only been used on one side from classrooms and staff offices. Pile the paper so that all the sheets are facing the same direction, blank-sides up. Cut the cereal box so that it is about one-half inch longer and one-half inch wider than the paper. Use a three-hole punch on all of the pieces. Lay the cereal box pieces picture-side out in line with the stack of paper. Use metal rings from a craft store or even strong yarn or twine to bind all of the pieces together. You can make alterations to this project by using small cereal boxes and cutting the paper smaller. You can use old album covers or any type of food packaging that is a stiff cardboard or card stock. These notebooks make good sketch pads to take on hikes for drawing pictures of the wonders of nature.

If you have magazines that need organizing in the classroom or library, simply cut off the top of the cereal box with an angle down the side (a la the magazine organizers you buy at the store). Voilà! Organized.

Swap It

Children are natural swappers. Ride a school bus or visit a playground and you'll see them trading candy for bouncy balls or other small treasures. Ask your students if they've ever done this and have them share with the class what they traded. Then, announce that you will be having a Swap Meet in your classroom (send a letter home to parents, too). Have your students bring in items from home that they no longer want, like books and toys. Check all items for cleanliness and appropriateness. Decorate a large box for all of the items.

When students do well on tests and homework assignments, reward them by allowing them to select something from the swap box. Remind parents throughout the year that gently used toys and books are always welcome donations for the classroom swap box.

ALERT!

You may want to make your swap box donations anonymous or trade with another classroom. You don't want children feeling bad if they have nothing to offer. Likewise, you don't want children to feel awkward for wanting a classmate's old toy. You never know how kids will respond, so make sure it's a respectful process.

School Projects

Get your whole school on a reusing kick by sparking everyone's imaginations with a few simple ideas. With everyone working together, you can keep mounds of materials out of the landfill.

Reclamation Station

Find a spot in your school that is easily accessible and visible to everyone. Use medium-sized garbage cans, recycling containers, or large boxes to set up a reclamation station. Make labels for each container so that the materials are organized. You can have a spot for cardboard boxes (flatten them but don't damage them so people can simply fold them back into shape to reuse). You can also collect other materials such as clean yogurt tubs, broken crayons (they can be melted into new ones), gloves and mittens that have lost their partners (sew and stuff into little animals or puppets), other textiles, wrapping and tissue paper, and whatever else you want to reuse. Teachers and students can regularly visit the reclamation station to find materials for crafts and other projects.

One Person's Junk Is Another Person's Treasure

Make one of your annual school fundraisers a schoolyard sale. Ask parents, staff, and neighbors in the community to donate gently used clothes, toys, books, tools, household goods, jewelry, and whatever else they may have lying around. To facilitate the process, you can request that they put a price tag on each item they donate. It saves the sale coordinators an enormous amount of time, and it also ensures that you are asking a fair price for the item. Make it clear that the items that do not sell will not be returned; instead, they will be donated to a local charity or thrift store.

Prepare for the sale by promoting it widely in school announcements and community newsletters or bulletin boards. Don't have it on a holiday weekend. Make plenty of readable, attractive signs for the day of the sale. Make sure you have plenty of volunteers, snacks, and drinks to sell to customers, and extra-extra small bills and coins for change. You'll also need calculators for totaling purchases and piles of plastic and paper grocery bags (reused, of course!)

SOURCE

Choose to Reuse: An Encyclopedia of Services, Business, Tools, and Charitable Programs That Foster Reuse by Nikki and David Goldbeck has tons of creative tips and tricks for breathing new life into old items. The book is printed on recycled paper with an environmentally friendly printing process.

Field Trips

Learning about reuse in the community may take some research. In larger urban areas, there may be local artists that reuse items or even larger entrepreneurs who reclaim materials and then sell them (this is especially common with building materials). Wherever you are, the following options should fit the bill.

Behind the Secondhand Scenes

Arrange to take your students to a local thrift store for a behind-the-scenes look at how it all works. Where do the items come from? How does the staff prepare them to be sold? How do they price them? What happens if something doesn't sell for a very long time? Wander around the store and see what types of items are there. How are they different from a regular store? Are the prices different? Is the packaging different? Does anyone see something they own? Does anyone see something they would want to buy?

For older students, you can add to the experience by visiting a regular department store first. Write down the prices of some common items you'll likely find at the thrift store, such as blankets, sheets, T-shirts, jeans, books, and plates. You can also ask where the items came from and where they end up if no one buys them. Examine packaging, too. Then go to the thrift store and compare prices, packaging, and the lifecycles of the same products. Ask where items came from, where they go, and how local products fit into the reuse equation.

Whatever you are doing and wherever you go, talk about where things come from and where they go. Embed in your students a habit of thinking of the big picture of stuff by repeating it as much as possible. This goes for activities that involve reducing, reusing, and recycling.

School Scrap Sculptures

Take your students to the local scrap or junkyard where old automobiles go to be picked apart by consumers looking for odd parts. In preparation, you can check out *Crashed, Smashed, and Mashed: A Trip to Junkyard Heaven* by Joyce Slayton Mitchell and Steven Borns to learn all about why there are junkyards and what happens there. It's appropriate for ages three to ten. After reading the book, have the class prepare some questions they'd like answered at the junkyard and list specific features they'd like to explore.

At the junkyard, have students pick out some random pieces for making a sculpture for the schoolyard. You can ask for monetary donations from parents prior to the trip or request in advance a donation of scraps from the junkyard owner. Select several pieces to bring back to the school. Have the students arrange the materials in different ways to make a sculpture. Use a nontoxic glue or wire to affix the pieces together. You can also ask around to see if someone who knows how to weld can help with the project; welding it will certainly give it the most permanence. Select a site on the school property, perhaps in a newly laid school garden, to permanently place the sculpture. You can dig a small hole, fill it with a little concrete, and place the sculpture in it. To give the process a little extra *oomph*, have a quick dedication ceremony and ask the principal to say a few words and make a commitment to reuse and protect the environment.

When dealing with any reusable materials—especially metal scraps—be particularly aware of sharp edges. You may want to have your students include a pair of work gloves in their school supplies. Between working with reusable materials and getting dirty with gardening and the other activities in this book, it'll be an investment in safety.

Take a Look at Better Books

One of the best reuse businesses in the world is a library. Make a list of questions about reusing books. Where do the books come from? How many times does one book get used? How do you repair worn books? What happens to the books after they are too worn for the library? Take a walk to your school or community library and ask to visit with the librarian. Go through your list of questions.

Human Health

Reusing materials is good for the planet, saves money, and protects human health. All these fantastic benefits in one fell swoop, but where's the connection? Step back to look at the big picture and you'll see how it helps.

Reusing Reduces Pollution

Every time you reuse something instead of buying something new, you eliminate all of the pollution created when something new is made and shipped to you. Reducing pollution means cleaner air to breathe, cleaner water to drink, and healthier people. Many new items also release chemical gases (that "new smell") that can be bad for your health, especially if you have asthma or allergies. When you buy something used, it's often already "off-gassed" most of the worst chemicals. Can you think of things that have a strong "new smell"? New cars, PVC shower curtains, plastic toys, carpet, and many other products all off-gas chemicals when they are new. That is why people often complain of headaches and sore throats in a new house or new building.

Don't Abuse Reuse

Some things are not meant to be reused and can actually endanger people's health if they reuse them. In most cases, these items are plastics that are used for food and beverages. Plastics are generally made of oil and synthetic chemicals. If the plastic becomes worn from scratches or heat, some of the chemicals can be released into the beverage or food. Plastic water bottles shouldn't be reused for drinking water. They quickly break down and end up polluting whatever drink you've put into the bottle. A healthier option for both you and the Earth is to buy a water bottle that is meant to be reused, like a stainless steel one. They're more expensive, but they last for years. Over time you save money by not buying single-use plastic water bottles. If you do buy a plastic bottle of water, get creative and use it for a flower vase, a bird feeder, or a container for collections of rocks or marbles. You can also fill it with water and keep it in the freezer to use on bumps and sprains or to keep your food cool when you travel.

There are literally tons of old tires waiting to be reused, and they have found new lives as ground covering around playgrounds and crumb infill for artificial turf. Many people are excited that they can teach kids about reuse and protecting the environment while providing a durable, low-maintenance ground for playing on. However, the tires have ingredients that may be unsafe for children's health. In addition, on hot, sunny days the tire pieces can heat up and burn children playing on it.

Take It Home

Let's hope your students have experienced so many moments of reuse at school that taking it home is a no-brainer. If you need a little help to inspire your students' families, try these two ideas to get things started.

There are currently more than 80,000 chemicals registered for use in everyday products, but less than 10 percent have been adequately tested for potential health impacts on children. It's better to be safe than sorry, so if a product contains ingredients that you are unsure of, avoid it.

Reuse Challenge

Make a math homework assignment by creating a graph with students' names on one side and reuse options on the other. Create coupons that say "Our family has completed_____to fulfill one Reuse Challenge" and send several home with each student. As students return their filled-in coupons, fill in the graph demonstrating reuse actions. Here are some examples of actions:

- Use reusable bags for shopping. They can be cloth, paper, or plastic as long as they are reused.
- Cut up old, unusable clothing for rags and use them in place of paper towels.
- Assign yourself a glass or cup and reuse it for the entire day.
- Use old jars for leftovers.
- Use your bathroom towel for one week.
- Wear your jeans at least twice before washing them (as long as they are visibly clean).
- Reuse sandwich bags at least twice by washing them and drying them.
- Don't use paper or throwaway plastic dishes for at least one week. Wash and reuse your dishes.
- Go to the library to get books instead of buying them.

Provide these examples, but also encourage the students and their families to come up with their own ideas. It's fun to learn what families do!

Reuse 101

At home there are many ways to reuse materials instead of throwing them away, and there are also opportunities to buy secondhand items in order to protect the planet and human health. Ask your students about ways to reuse materials and make a list of their suggestions. Send home the list of all the children's suggestions plus a list of the following resources to buy used items. If you encourage students to buy reused items, they may become less preoccupied with the latest expensive fashion rage.

- **Local thrift stores.** Kids grow out of their clothes quickly, so their clothing is often barely used. Stop at the thrift store first when you're stocking up on seasonal clothing needs.
- **eBay** (*www.ebay.com*) is a vital resource for finding almost anything you can dream up. It is a very trustworthy community of people selling products to other people. Buy there. Sell there. Use it and love it.
- **Craigslist** (*www.craigslist.com*) is another, more localized version of eBay where people can easily post items they want to sell. You can actually go visit the seller and see the item for sale before buying it.
- **BookMooch** (*www.bookmooch.com*) allows you to sell your own used books to earn points to buy other people's books. It's a virtual book swap for people who love to read.
- **Freecycle** (*www.freecycle.org*) is an international community of people looking to get rid of and find products for free. You can find free couches, clothes, gardening supplies, and much more.

With the power of the Internet, people's ability to find used items is nearly limitless. Take some time before you run off to the department store and find what you need used. It's easier than ever and it's completely affordable.

CHAPTER 5

Recycle

As the planet's natural resources decrease, it becomes more and more important to recycle the resources that have already been taken from the Earth. The World Population Institute has determined that as of 2005, the population of the Earth is growing at a rate of 80 million people per year. Some things, like wood from trees, can only replace themselves if they are given enough time. In order to not run out of our resources entirely, it is vital to find ways to keep them out of the garbage.

What It's All About

Recycling means giving materials a second life. It is the final effort after reuse to keep something out of a landfill. Unlike reuse, which tries to keep the material in use with only small changes, recycling transforms the material into a new product. Recycling requires more resources than reusing.

Rudimentary Recycling

People have found ways to recycle many different materials, including aluminum, paper, glass, and some plastics. Paper and cardboard are chopped up, de-inked, and processed into new pieces of paper and cardboard. Aluminum is melted down and then reformed into new aluminum products. Glass is washed, broken up into small pieces, melted, and molded into new glass products. Some plastics are washed, chopped up, melted, and made into new plastic products. Recycling, while not as efficient as reusing, still saves resources and conserves energy when compared to making products out of virgin resources. For example, it takes 95 percent less energy to make recycled aluminum cans, 60 percent less energy to make recycled paper, and 30 percent less energy to make recycled glass than it would using new resources.

SOURCE

Check out *www.kidsrecyclingzone.com* for an online learning adventure for your students. With games, fun facts, magic tricks, and even training to be a recycling superhero, your kids will have a blast. It even has a list of additional links for more fun and learning through sites like PBS and Disney.

Downcycle Versus Upcycle

Recycling is meant to reuse resources by creating new products that are just as strong and useful as the original. Glass (which is made from sand) and metal (which is made from mineral ores) can be recycled an infinite number of times and still be just as strong as when they were first created. Paper (mostly made from trees) and plastic (mostly made from petroleum), on the other hand, become weaker and less useful when they are recycled. For example, nice white office paper cannot be recycled into nice white office paper more than a couple of times. The wood fiber just gets too weak. Instead, it gets recycled into cardboard and other paperboards, but after six or seven times of being recycled, it can hold up no longer and ends up trashed. Plastic has a similar story but a shorter lifespan. When a material cannot be recycled into an equally strong and useful product, it is called downcycling.

FACT

Recycling one aluminum can saves enough energy to run a television for three hours. In the United States, people use more than 80 trillion aluminum soda cans every year! Luckily, beverage cans are some of the most widely recycled items.

The opposite of downcycling is upcycling. Upcycling is when someone takes something headed for the trash and turns into something more useful than it was originally. It's a lot like reusing, but the main difference is that it's meant for designers to think about upcycling options at the end of a product's life instead of downcycling options. When someone invents a new package or product, they immediately think of how to design it so it can easily be upcycled when it's done being used. You can try a fun upcycling project by folding a newspaper (preferably one that used soy inks) into a pot for a seedling. You can find directions at *www.geocities.com/newspaperpots*. The reason it's upcycling instead of recycling is that it doesn't require any energy or resources (other than your own labor) to make it into something else. Another added bonus is that when the plant is ready to go in the ground, you can put the whole pot in because it will naturally decompose in the soil. No waste at all!

Global Picture

Recycling is not something that is just done in the United States. People recycle everywhere, but they recycle in different ways and in different amounts.

Outside over There

The United States creates more waste and more recyclable material per person than anywhere else. What happens to all of it? While we don't recycle as much as some other countries, we do export recyclable materials to other countries. In fact, by cargo container load, the number one export from the United States is waste paper. Almost all of it goes to China to be recycled into shoe boxes, newspapers, and other cardboard boxes. Why? China simply doesn't have enough trees to make all of the paper it wants.

When you teach your students about recycling, remind them that reusing and reducing are more important for protecting the Earth than recycling. It's great to recycle, but it should only be an option if there wasn't a way to reduce or reuse.

The United States also exports e-waste—computers, television, cell phones, and other electronics. Poorer countries accept the e-waste because there are valuable metals and other reusable materials in the products. However, in addition to the valuable materials, e-waste also contains many dangerous materials that can make people sick. As the workers break the electronics apart, they let out these dangerous materials that can make them sick or pollute their community's water and air. Critics are trying to get the people who make cell phones, computers, and other electronics to take them back when people are done with them and safely take them apart to reuse and dispose of the materials.

How Do You Compare?

In the United States, people recycle about 32.5 percent of solid waste. How do other places compare? In Switzerland, people simply refuse to throw away some materials, like glass and paper. Every grocery store has glass recycling bins, and once a month there is free paper and cardboard collection. All lawn and garden waste is picked up every two weeks and people can bring aluminum cans, batteries, and oil to special drop-off places. Almost everything has a place and little ends up as waste. Why does it work so well? It's not because they feel much stronger about protecting the environment. It's because recycling is free, but they have to pay to throw away garbage.

In Senegal, recycling is not so coordinated; it's just a daily part of life for resourceful individuals. These imaginative people find a way to reuse almost everything, from plastic bags to fruit peels (which are used in perfumes). Old cans find a new life as drinking cups. Old papers are used to wrap food that is purchased at the local market. Artists collect metal waste to construct their creations. They even use plastic bags to make shoes.

Research other countries to discover the innovative ways they recycle and reuse materials. How does it compare to the United States?

For the Classroom

Let's hope your school has a recycling program. If it doesn't, be sure to check with your garbage pickup to see if you can set one up. You can teach your students some important concepts about recycling no matter what your school's recycling program looks like. With their own hands-on recycling projects, children can begin to picture the recycling loop.

What Is Plastic?

There isn't just one kind of plastic; there are many. There are seven that are most common and can usually be identified by a number enclosed in a chasing-arrow symbol on the bottom of the product. Not all of them are recyclable everywhere. Check with your local facility to see which plastics it will recycle. The numbers denote the following categories:

- **#1 polyethylene terephthalate** (PETE or PET) is mainly used for clear bottles. They can be colored, but they are always transparent.
- **#2 high-density polyethylene** (HDPE) is mainly used for "cloudy" milk and water jugs, opaque food bottles, laundry soap containers, bleach bottles, and shampoo bottles.
- **#3 polyvinyl chloride** (PVC or V) is used in some cling wraps, soft plastic containers, shower curtains, flooring, plastic pipes, soft plastic toys, and more.

- **#4 low-density polyethylene** (LDPE) is mainly used in food storage bags, plastic grocery bags, and some "soft" bottles.
- **#5 polypropylene** (PP) is mainly used in rigid containers, like yogurt tubs and some cups and bowls.
- **#6 polystyrene** (PS) is mainly used in foam clamshell-type containers, meat and bakery trays, clear take-out containers, and some plastic cutlery and cups.
- **#7 all other plastics** is mostly a plastic called polycarbonate, but as more and more plastics are developed, the #7 category also includes newer plastics.

Yes, some plastics are made from plants like corn and potatoes. Since most plastic is made from oil, scientists have been inventing new kinds of plastics made from renewable resources like plants.

Some plastics have been shown to leach chemicals. People should avoid using them for food or drinks, and children shouldn't play with toys made from them. These plastics are PVC, PS, and PC. For almost every product made from these plastics, you can find safer alternatives. Learn more at *www.healthychild.org*.

Not all plastics can be recycled, even if they have the chasing-arrow symbol on them. What plastics are recyclable in your community? Bring in examples of a variety of plastics and challenge your students to figure out which ones can be recycled and which ones cannot. You can do this in a variety of ways, but one way is to have two piles of the same assortment of plastics and split the class into two teams. Have a race to see who can separate the recyclables from the nonrecyclables the fastest.

Positively Paperific

Get down and dirty with hands-on recycling by making your own pretty papers from discarded paper. If you want the paper to be specific colors, make sure to keep the construction paper pieces organized by color.

You'll need:
- old paper
- a small tub
- frames with screens stapled over them
- a blender
- an old bed sheet
- some sponges

1. Have the children cut the paper into small one-inch squares.
2. Fill the tub about halfway with water and lay the screens at the bottom.
3. Put some paper in the blender, add water until the paper is completely immersed, and blend it into what's called "pulp." For colored paper, add a handful of newsprint or office paper with a handful of construction paper.
4. Pour the pulp into the tub of water on top of the screen. Quickly pull the screen up out of the tub. Pull it straight up so it captures a good deal of pulp. Turn the screen pulp-side down onto a piece of sheeting about the same size as your frame (it works best to have some towels under the sheeting to capture excess water). Use a sponge to soak up more of the excess water. Gently pull the frame away from the sheeting; the pulp should stick to the sheeting.
5. Hang the sheets of paper up to dry overnight. pull the sheeting off and—voilà!—paper!

You can make the papers even more decorative by adding crushed flower petals or bits of confetti or colored thread. You can even put seeds into the pulp so the paper can be planted and grown. This can make a nice gift. Homemade papers tend to bleed when you write on them, so use pencil, pen, or crayon instead of markers.

School Projects

Schools are a natural place for recycling because so much school waste is recyclable. Paper, which is the easiest to recycle, makes up most of the waste. Aluminum, glass, and plastic bottles are also easily recyclable. If your school already has a recycling program, try to add to it; if it doesn't, it's time to start.

So many of the crafts described in this book are fun, easy, and educational. Instead of just doing them with your own class, consider having an eco-craft table at your school carnival or open house. Make sure to describe, or have a poster describing, why the craft is good for the planet.

Lunchroom Brigade

School cafeterias are incredible opportunities for recycling. You may be able to recycle some of the products your school already buys, but other products may have to be switched so you will be able to recycle the packaging. Take some time with your students to assess what's in your lunchroom garbage and how to increase recycling.

You'll need the help from lunchroom staff and custodial workers to examine the garbage, but choose one day when you collect and separate the waste. You might also want to ask parental permission, as well as asking for parent volunteers. Separate the trash into piles of compostable organic waste, plastic, paper, glass, aluminum, and waste. Could your school compost the organic waste? Small schools may have the capacity to compost items on site. If not, is there a local place that might compost your waste? There are sometimes organic-waste compost facilities or else farmers looking for organic waste to feed pigs. Generally when students do this project, they weigh each type of material to figure out how much they could keep out of the landfill if they recycled. Weigh each and multiply by how many days of school there are.

Starting from Scratch

If you don't have a recycling program, build support for the effort by petitioning. Petitions are a fun, strong way to tell people in power that you support a particular issue. If your school doesn't recycle or if your community doesn't pick up recyclables at the curbside, it is about time they did! Recycling is one of the easiest ways people can save energy and protect precious resources. Have your students create a petition form with a statement about the recycling issue at the top. Be sure to have plenty of lines for everyone to sign if they agree with your request. When you have collected all the signatures you can get, put the petition form in an envelope and send it to the leader of your choice. It may be your principal or it may be the president of the United States.

You can also present your petition in person. Call your city's mayor and ask if your class can meet with him or her to discuss an environmental issue that you are concerned about. You may want to present this during a city council meeting or take it virtual by using *www.thepetitionsite.com.*

ALERT!

Starting a new recycling program or expanding an existing one can be challenging at first. Get expert help by calling your local or state government solid waste office. They often have recycling staff that can come to your community and help with all the logistics of establishing a program that works for your city and your school.

Recycling Receptacles

Help your school with recycling by ensuring that there are enough bins and that they are clearly marked. Place bins in easily accessible areas, especially areas that generate a lot of recyclables, such as classrooms, lunchrooms, teacher lounges, staff offices, and copy rooms. You can use old copy-paper boxes, plastic storage containers, or your community's curbside recycling bin to collect the materials. Have your students make signs to post by recycling areas that show why it's so important to recycle and protect the planet. Have them make other ones that clearly label what goes into each bin.

Next, educate the school's students, staff, and parents about the recycling program and what can be recycled. Make sure staff, students, or volunteers regularly empty the bins. You can even weigh them and set some goals for the future. Create a chart and fill in the weights of recyclable and solid waste once a month for six months. How much are you recycling? Can you increase recycling rates by having classrooms compete? Are the bins in the best locations? Take your story on the road and teach other schools how to start or strengthen a recycling program.

FACT

More than 20 million Hershey's Kisses are wrapped each day. Sounds sweet, but it uses 133 square miles of aluminum foil. It's all recyclable, but most people throw it away. How big is 133 square miles? Plot it on a map of your state. Next time you have a Kiss, recycle the foil.

Get out and about to see how recycling works in your community. It's one thing to take on the smaller projects at school, but seeing it on a grand scale is very impressive and is sure to generate ideas and action.

The Full-Size Facility

If your school has a recycling program, you can call the company they contract with to find out about field trips to their facility. Otherwise, you can call your local government office of solid waste management or look up recycling in the yellow pages to find a facility to tour. Your students can learn about the different equipment used to sort the materials, how it's packaged for shipping, where it goes, and what its second life will look like. They can also learn about how much each material is worth and how much the facility processes every year. Has the amount gone up or down over the years? What are some of the obstacles to getting the community to recycle more? What can kids do to help?

New Stuff from Old Stuff

It might take a bit more research on your part, but you can try to find a local business or artist who does his or her own small-scale recycling. You can also look for a local business that sells products made from recycled materials. Green building supplies are especially interesting and are becoming common in most major home renovation stores. You can look at lumber or carpet made from old plastic bottles, countertops made from crushed colored plastic, tiles made from old glass, and much more. The variety of different products being made from recycled materials grows each day and serves as an inspiration for creating more. If you can, compare the recycled-content product with its conventional counterpart. How does lumber made from recycled plastic look and feel compared to wood lumber? How does recycled paper look and feel compared to virgin paper? How does carpet made from recycled plastic feel compared to other carpets?

Human Health

As with reducing, reusing, and any type of conservation, less waste translates into less pollution, a cleaner planet, and better health.

Dropping Pounds of Pollution

Using products made from virgin materials instead of recycled materials creates much more pollution. Pollution is created from mining or logging and from shipping, processing, and packaging. Seventy-one garbage cans of waste and pollution are created from the extractive and industrial processes necessary for making new products for every one can of garbage you put at the curb. Keep that 71:1 ratio in mind. Making paper from paper, aluminum from aluminum, glass from glass, and plastic from plastic is much easier on the Earth than drilling for oil, clear-cutting a rain forest, or mining for ore. Two more statistics to keep in mind as examples:

- Recycling 1 ton of paper saves 60 pounds of air pollution.
- Recycling glass reduces mining waste by 70 percent and air pollution by 20 percent.

The garbage you create leaves a long trail of garbage and pollution that are contaminating the air you breathe, the water you drink, and even the food you eat.

Household Hazardous Waste

Almost everyone has household hazardous waste. This includes things such as cleaners, nail polish, paint, and oil. They are materials that can make people very sick if they are used incorrectly. With the rise in allergies and asthma, many families are trying to steer clear of products that are considered hazardous waste. If you have products that are considered household hazardous waste, it's important to know how to safely dispose of them.

Children should never handle hazardous waste. As you learn about these products, remind your students to be good label readers and to stay away from products that have label warnings. If their parents have to use something that has a warning label, children should avoid the area, and windows should be opened for proper ventilation.

Guess what! Some of them can be recycled! For example, used motor oil can be cleaned and reused. Don't ever pour it down a drain or onto the ground because it ends up polluting drinking water. According to the U.S. Environmental Protection Agency, "you pour it, you drink it!" Another common household hazardous waste that can be recycled is old paint. You can call the local solid waste office to find out how to dispose of household hazardous waste safely and to drop off products to be recycled. Also, you can use these locations to pick up paint or other supplies (like varnishes and glues) that you may need for a project.

Learn to identify hazardous products by learning the meanings of the signal words found on them.

- **Poison** is the most hazardous level. It means a product is extremely toxic. Poisonous materials can cause injury or death if ingested, inhaled, or absorbed through the skin.
- **Danger** means that a product is highly toxic, highly flammable, or highly corrosive.
- **Warning** and **Caution** both indicate that a product is toxic, corrosive, reactive, or flammable.

You can research the safety of things you have around your house by using the Household Products Database at *http://householdproducts.nlm .nih.gov/.* If you want to show the kids how to use it, bring in some of your own products or clip pictures out of magazines and then look up the safety of the product. This website and *www.healthychild.org* are great to share with parents.

Don't know how or where or if you can recycle something? Earth911 *(http ://earth911.com)* is the premier resource for finding the facts on recycling. It couldn't be any easier. Just enter your Zip Code or search by product type to find out if and where you can recycle. No more excuses!

Take It Home

Recycling is easy once you make it a habit, and it really cuts down on your garbage fast. Your students' parents will be surprised at how little they really throw away once they start separating out what can be recycled. Remind parents to close the recycling loop by buying recycled products, too!

Recycle Detector

Have your students be waste watchers at home. Ask them to answer the following questions with their parents' help:

- What's in your garbage at home?
- Do you recycle? What do you recycle? How much every week?
- If you don't recycle, what's stopping you? Could you recycle?

Give some advice for parents who are new to recycling. Tell them to take small steps to start recycling, like just sorting out paper at first. After that becomes a household habit, start recycling glass as well. Keep adding to your household recycling habits until you're recycling everything your community will take. Sometimes there is no curbside pickup, so you'll have to find where to drop it off. The bright side? Drop-off stations often pay you for your recyclables. Parents can think of something the whole family would enjoy and set aside a jar to save their recycling money. They can challenge students to guess how long they think it will take to reach their goal. This may encourage them to find more recyclable products in the house or start recycling campaigns at church or in the neighborhood.

Close the Loop

Buying items made from recycled materials closes the recycling loop. Luckily, recycled products are becoming so common that often people buy them without even knowing they're recycled. Have your students go on a shopping scavenger hunt with their family and find twenty items that have recycled materials in them. This will be marked on the label. Have students write down the products they find so they can bring the list to school and compare with the other students. A good place to start is with paper products. For example, a major manufacturer of paper plates, Chinet, now has a version made of recycled paper that is also compostable. When students bring their lists to class, talk about the experience. Did the number of products they found surprise them? Was it easier or harder than they thought it would be? Encourage children to talk with the store manager to tell him or her how much they appreciate being able to buy products made out of recycled material.

CHAPTER 6

Composting Counts

Composting is the breakdown of organic materials like food and plants into nutrient-rich soil. It's a process that happens all the time in nature, but people speed it up by using heat. Composting counts because it keeps useful material out of landfills, helps people replenish the Earth's soil, and even helps prevent global warming. Teaching children about composting helps them understand the full cycle of organic life: from yucky table scraps to divine dirt that grows more food for your table.

What It's All About

Composting is becoming an issue of increasing interest across the country. As landfills fill up and solid waste generation increases, people are looking for news ways to divert materials. Composting keeps organic materials out of the garbage and turns it back into rich, healthy soil.

The Dirt on Soil

What is dirt anyway? You can use it to make mud pies and grow plants, but if you look at it closely, you'll find that dirt is actually made up of many different parts. Dirt actually starts out as rocks, but over time the rocks break down into smaller and smaller pieces until they become dirt. What makes dirt different from sand (which is also tiny bits of rocks) is that there are more organic material bits mixed in, like tiny bits of plants. Dirt is also made up of living creatures like ants, worms, fungi, and bacteria. These three parts—rock bits, organic bits, and living creatures—make up about half of the dirt. What's the other half? Air and water.

One acre is about the size of a football field minus the end zones. Between five and ten tons of little bugs, bacteria, and creatures live in one acre of soil. They work tirelessly to make the soil healthy for people to grow food and for plants and trees to thrive. You can help them in return by not spraying poisonous chemicals on lawns or fields.

Each ingredient in dirt plays a special role in creating an environment for plants and trees to grow in. The tiny bits of rocks hold everything in place. The tiny bits of plants add the vitamins and nutrients to help grow healthy plants. The living creatures turn the tiny plant bits into even tinier bits so the plant roots can absorb them. They also dig little tunnels through the soil that helps air and water move through it more easily. The air provides oxygen to both the plant roots and the living creatures, which would suffocate without it. The water helps break down the nutrients and is vital for the survival of the plants and the creatures.

Worm Wise

What is vermiculture? It's a worm culture! Worms are very simple creatures, but they are essential to healthy soil. Go outside and dig up some worms. Look at their bodies. They are only one tube inside another, and the inner tube is the digestive track. If you look closely, you'll see it because it is a dark brown color. That's the food they're eating almost all the time.

They have no eyes because they spend their life underground where it is dark. Earthworms dig tunnels by eating the dirt in front of them. Then they excrete the dirt with a little mucus (worm snot) to keep the tunnel walls in place. Eat and excrete, eat and excrete. A worm's life is simple indeed. These simple tunnels help oxygen and water get into the soil for the plants and other organisms.

SOURCE

The essential guide for teaching kids about worms and vermiculture in the classroom is *Worms Eat Our Garbage: Classroom Activities for a Better Environment* by Mary Appelhof, Mary Frances Fenton, and Barbara Loss Harris. This engaging book includes more than 150 worm-related activities that teach children about the environment and promote problem-solving and critical-thinking skills.

The other important thing that worms do is create what are called "castings" (also known as worm poop and worm manure). Castings are excreted waste and dirt clumps, and you can often find them on the top of the ground in moist places. They look like tiny bunches of grapes and they fertilize the soil. Can you find any castings around where you found your worms?

You can make your own mini–worm world for your classroom with a large jar and a couple of worms.

1. Place some pebbles at the bottom of your jar.
2. Add about four inches of soil on top (preferably soil from wherever you found your worms).
3. Welcome your worms by gently placing them into the jar.

4. Feed your worms. They like fruit and vegetable scraps, coffee grounds, eggshells, and bread. Take some small scraps and place them under a thin layer of soil so fruit flies don't stop by to snack.

5. Cover the jar with black paper or cloth; since worms are used to the dark, this will make them feel more at home. Don't cover it too tightly; you want air to be able to circulate.

6. Spray the soil with water to keep the mini–worm world moist (but not wet). Feed the worms a little more food every few days.

7. Watch through the glass to see the tunnels the worms dig. How fast do they eat the food? How quickly can they dig a tunnel? Do the worms grow?

For a variation on this project, you can have several worm worlds and feed them each different types of food. Regular earthworms should do the trick for this kind of small-scale experiment; however, for best results, purchase some red wigglers from a bait shop or online. They are the premium worms for digesting waste. Feed one jar with food scraps, feed the next jar with newspaper clippings, and feed the final jar with grass clippings and leaves. What happens to the soil? What happens to the worms? After keeping the worm worlds for a few weeks, set the worms free and use the soil for the next experiment.

After you release your worms, keep track of which soil is from which worms if you fed them different diets. Get seedlings and plant each one in different soil. Which one grows the biggest?

Global Picture

Happily, composting practices are beginning to increase in the United States, but many other countries throughout the world have either been composting as communities for much longer or are doing it on a much bigger scale. People all over are starting to recognize the value and importance of composting. You can help spread the word, too!

From the City to the Farm

All big cities in India are legally required to compost organic wastes for rural farmers to use to restore soil and protect it from drought. Countries across Europe have been doing the same thing since the 1960s, and many developing countries in places like Africa and Asia are also working on increasing what is known as urban-rural nutrient recycling. A nutrient is anything that provides nourishment. Food is a nutrient for humans. Compost is a nutrient for soil. Turning the food waste into compost is a form of recycling. It's a great form of cooperation because the people in the city need the food from the farmers in the country. Likewise, the farmers in the country need the food waste from the city to create compost for healthy soil to grow more food.

Global Warming: Composting to the Rescue!

Composting isn't just a great way to reduce waste and help restore nutrients to the soil; it's also a super solution for preventing global warming. Here's how:

1. When waste decomposes in a landfill, it does it anaerobically (without oxygen) because everything is squished in so tightly the oxygen can't get in to help the material break down as it would in nature. Anaerobic decomposition creates methane gas, a strong greenhouse gas. Landfills are the number-one source of human-created methane. The more waste we keep out of landfills by doing things like composting, the less methane gas is created.

2. Planting trees helps prevent global warming because plants help keep greenhouse gases out of the atmosphere by doing something called "carbon sequestration." It's a fancy term that just means they hold or store carbon dioxide. It may be hard to believe, but dirt can hold twice as much carbon as plants. Healthy soil has a lot of organic material in it. It's the organic material that helps hold all the carbon dioxide, but many current farming practices strip the soil of the organic material and saturate it with synthetic chemicals and fertilizers that further weaken the soil. Putting compost back into the soil helps make it strong and healthy again. It also quickly increases its ability to hang on to the carbon dioxide and protect the planet from global warming. Super Soil to the rescue!

It's time to "Keep Compostable Organics out of Landfills" (Keep COOL). If your community isn't composting paper and organic waste, it is totally un-COOL. Write letters to your mayor and city council letting them know how smart it is to compost. You can learn more about the issue, how cities can start composting, and more at *www.cool2012.com*.

For the Classroom

Classroom composting holds a wealth of learning opportunities. From this one activity, you can integrate lessons of environmental stewardship, Earth science, biology, nutrition, math, and language arts. This is the shortest list of ideas, but I hope it inspires many more from you and your students.

To Rot or Not to Rot

Some things rot and some things do not. You can only make compost from things that rot. Can your class come up with a list of items they think will rot and a list of things they think will not? Gather small, similar-sized samples of these items (which may include paper, cardboard, a leaf, a banana peel, an eggshell, a plastic wrapper, a piece of aluminum foil, a small glass trinket, etc.). If at all possible, find a space on school property where you can dig a small hole for these items and they will not be disturbed. If not, you can also do this in a plastic container or even a small aquarium in the classroom. To facilitate the process, you may want to make it a worm bin.

Place your samples in the hole or the container. Have students guess what will happen to the items. What will rot? How long will it take? What will happen to the items they think won't rot? An interesting material to add is plastic made of corn or soybeans. Find a synthetic plastic that looks and feels the same. Compare what happens to them.

Soil Sleuth

Examine the makeup of soil using wet and dry methods. The dry method is taking a couple of tablespoons of soil and spreading it out across a large white piece of paper. Use a magnifying glass to look closely, or even a microscope if you're working with older children. You can also fill a jar about one-third full of soil and then add water to explore it in a different way. Shake it up and wait a day. The sand and mineral matter will sink to the bottom in layers, leaving the organic material floating at the top. Compare soil samples from different locations like a fertile garden bed, exposed dirt on a playground, and the soil under grass. How are they different? What's in the dirt?

FACT

Planet Earth is teeming with life. For example, there are more living individual organisms in a tablespoon of soil than there are people on the Earth. Everyone, including the organisms in that tablespoon of dirt, does their part to keep the world healthy and promote life. What have you done today?

School Projects

Composting at school is an invaluable hands-on way for students to learn about waste, nature, and the cycle of life. In addition, the school saves money on waste disposal costs and can save additional money by using the compost instead of purchased fertilizers to boost the health of garden beds or other plants. Schools can even earn money by selling finished compost or food waste.

School Composting Programs

There are four different ways schools can compost:

1. If your school is small enough and has large enough grounds, you may be able to compost all of your food waste on-site.
2. If your school is larger, you could just compost some of your food waste on-site.
3. You can collect all of your food waste for a commercial composting facility. They will come and pick it up just like your garbage collector.
4. You can connect with a local farmer to use the food waste either as compost or as pig feed.

Any way you go about it, you'll need a lot more help than this book can offer. Composting programs are very rewarding and a brilliant thing to do for the Earth, but they take coordinated, long-term commitment. There are a variety of resources available to you, and here are a few to get you started:

- The Mansfield, Connecticut, school district started a composting program and wrote a fantastic, comprehensive manual to help other schools do the same. You can find it at *www.ct.gov/dep/lib/dep /compost/compost_pdf/schmanual.pdf.*
- TetraPak, makers of aseptic packaging like milk cartons, wrote its own quick guide to school composting with success stories and tips. It even has its own staff person to help schools get started with composting. Learn more at *www.aseptic.org/Composting .pdf.*
- The Illinois-based Greening Schools program has compiled a thorough list of composting resources for schools. Check it out at *www .greeningschools.org/resources/view_cat_teacher.cfm?id=73.*

There are some health issues to consider when dealing with compost. First of all, never compost any type of manure or feces or any animal byproduct such as meat scraps, bones, or dairy products. Without high enough temperatures, these materials can generate dangerous pathogens and bacteria. Also, people with asthma, allergies, or suppressed immune systems should not deal with the compost directly. Always wash your hands well after working with compost.

School composting programs are gaining popularity across the country. Do a little research online, call people who have experience with composting, and contact your local government's solid waste offices. You're sure to find a treasure trove of information to begin a successful composting program at your school.

Reading, Writing, 'n Wriggling

Your whole school can reap the rewards of a worm farm. It will save your school money, reduce waste, and teach your students a variety of different lessons in a hands-on, unforgettable way. Vermiculture is most successful when it's a student-driven program, so start early in the school year by following these simple guidelines:

1. Identify who will be in charge of making sure the worms are being cared for properly. Maybe this is someone already familiar with vermiculture or someone who'd like to learn.
2. Create a worm volunteer team. These volunteers can change throughout the year so more students can be involved. Have a sign-up sheet somewhere and check it regularly. Volunteer activities include collecting and cutting up food, collecting leaves, mixing the material, and collecting the worm castings and compost tea.
3. Assess how much your school can compost or how much your school wants to compost. You can always start small and expand as your school becomes more knowledgeable about the process and responsibilities.
4. Work with cafeteria and custodial staff to figure out how to best collect waste. What will you collect? How should you do it? How often should you do it?
5. Decide on bin size and location. Set up the bin and enjoy!

Getting the program started is definitely something that older students will have to tackle, but once the bin is built and in place, everyone can participate and learn.

SOURCE

The Worm Café: Mid-scale Vermicomposting of Lunchroom Wastes by Binet Payne is the classic guide to school vermiculture. It includes the true story of how a teacher and her students saved their school $6,000 annually by composting, and it also has worksheets, a model letter to parents, quizzes, and a thirty-page annotated guide to useful curricular material.

Field Trips

They say composting happens. That's because it's an essential part of life. There's no stopping it; it's happening all the time. Whether it's people or nature in charge of the compost pile, get out and check it out to learn how compost happens.

Commercial Composting

Not every community has a commercial composting facility, but more and more are springing up across the country. You can look up *compost* in the yellow pages or call your local government office of solid waste management. Ask if your community composts and what the rules are if it does. If there is no composting program, ask why not. Hopefully, you do have a local facility to visit. Compost facilities are happy to teach students about the process. An educator can often come to your classroom prior to a field trip to teach your students all about the basics of commercial composting. Then they'll take you on a guided tour of the facility to show you the dirty details of composting!

FACT

According to Resource Recycling, if people composted the 21.5 million tons of food scraps created every year instead of sending it to the landfill, it would result in the same decrease in greenhouse gas emissions as taking more than 2 million cars off the road.

Nature's Recycling Program

Take a field trip to a nearby forest or woodland and check out how nature handles composting. Have the students examine the forest floor to see how leaves, twigs, and other organic material are decomposing. Bring small hand trowels, large white sheets of paper, and magnifying glasses so the children can dig and discover. Placing small amounts of material on the white paper makes it easier to identify what's happening. Have them discuss what they see and think about the process of decomposition. Help facilitate the breakdown of materials with a decomposition craft.

Each child will need a small piece of white cloth (a sturdy cotton linen works best). Get permission to have them gather plants in a variety of different colors from the forest. Then you'll need a hard surface, like an asphalt path, and each child will need a good-sized rock that they can easily hold. Each child should put their fabric down on the hard surface and then place a leaf or flower on the fabric. Using the rock to hit the plant, they can create a "painting" using the pigment that comes out of the plant when it is struck. What colors do the different plants leave behind? What happens to the smooshed plants? Sprinkle all the leftover compost back onto the forest floor. It is well on its way to decomposing!

Human Health

What does dirt have to do with health? A lot more than you'd ever guess! Once you start digging into the details, you'll uncover unexpected connections. Start with the following two connections and then try to dig up your own!

ALERT!

According to the U.S. Environmental Protection Agency, burning brush, leaves, and other yard waste can release a variety of hazardous air pollutants, some of which can cause cancer or other adverse health effects. Compost instead!

Don't Treat Soil Like Dirt

Soil is a vital part of life, and healthy soil is necessary to support all of the life below and above ground. Have you ever read *Horton Hears a Who*? Remember how it turns out that there's a whole thriving village of Whos that live on that one tiny flower? The soil under your feet is home to millions of tiny creatures that you can't see. And when it comes to composting and farming, tiny creatures are the key. Sometimes these tiny insects and bacteria are called the "microherd" because these minute organisms are the most important livestock on a farm. People need to protect the microherd because they work hard to make the food we eat healthy and strong.

Have your students make up their own imaginary underworld picture. What do the tiny creatures look like? How are they bringing nutrients to the plants? What other jobs might they do? How does composting help take care of the critters in your underworld and help strengthen the soil? Take care of the dirt and it will take care of you.

SOURCE

The National Gardening Association coordinates the website *www .kidsgardening.org.* It has a wide variety of resources for teachers and parents to help start gardening projects. There are resources for funding and a network of schools that are gardening to help ensure your success. Get growing and sprout a youth garden!

Soil Helps the Sick

Have you ever gotten sick and had to take antibiotics? Some illnesses are caused by bacteria that your body can have a hard time fighting. Antibiotics help your body kill the bacteria, but where do antibiotics come from? They come from a variety of places in nature, but most come from the microorganisms living in healthy soil. Scientists believe the microorganisms make their own antibiotics because they have to compete with so many other microorganisms to stay alive. By composting, we are helping build and strengthen the population of microorganisms in the soils. They, in turn, help us get healthy when we're sick by providing us with the "recipe" for antibiotics.

Take It Home

Small-scale composting is much easier than many people imagine. If you're a gardener, the end product is pure gold. If you don't garden, use the compost on indoor plants or give it to a friend or neighbor who gardens.

Quick Guide to Composting

Yard trimmings and food residuals make up 23 percent of the U.S. waste stream. By composting, you significantly reduce the amount of waste that goes to the landfill, and you also create the single most important thing you can give your soil. Your students should be totally wise to the benefits of healthy soil by now. Have them write an illustrated guidebook to composting that they can take home and share with their parents and other adults they know. Here are the basics to include:

1. Write an introduction about what composting is and why it is important.
2. The first step in composting is buying or building a bin. You can build one out of wood and chicken wire or cement blocks stacked on their sides so the holes are exposed. It's essentially just a big box with no top or bottom.
3. Fill your bin with a balance of the following materials: green stuff (grass clippings, vegetable and fruit scraps, coffee grounds, tea bags, plants) and brown stuff (fall leaves, dead plants, old flowers, straw, hay, cardboard, sawdust).
4. You can also add (in moderation) eggshells, paper, paper towels, hair, and even old cotton clothing.
5. To jump-start the process, you can sprinkle garden soil in between layers to introduce the soil organisms that will digest your scraps.
6. Turn the pile regularly with a pitchfork to aerate the pile, which speeds the process. It also keeps the process happening aerobically, which should be odorless.
7. Keep the pile damp but not wet. Food scraps might keep the pile damp enough, but it depends on the climate. You may need to spray it here and there.

8. Never compost the following items: meat scraps, bones, fish, plastic or synthetic fibers, oil or fat, feces, weeds that have gone to seed, diseased plants, glossy magazines, or coal ash.

9. Harvest the compost from the bottom of the pile. Use it on your gardens or give it to a friend or neighbor who gardens. They'll love you for it!

Generally, if you bury your scraps in the center of the pile instead of just throwing them on top, you can prevent much of the odor, which draws bugs and animals. Make sure the bin is snug to the ground or add chicken wire around the bottom. If need be, use natural repellants like predator urine or peppermint extract.

Are there any other tips that you can add to your guidebooks? Not only is this book helpful for educating others, it would make a great gift for any beginning gardeners you know.

Pumpkins to Pigs

How many pumpkins do you think get thrown out after Halloween? Enough to make a hungry pig cry! Find a local farmer who could use all the past-prime pumpkins as a delicious gourmet feast for his livestock. Work with your class to make collecting the pumpkins as easy as possible.

CHAPTER 7

Plain as Water

Water is necessary for all living things. This chapter explains what water is and focuses on people's relationship with it. People use water for drinking and preparing food; cleaning their bodies, homes, clothes, and cars; and partaking in recreational activities such as swimming, surfing, and boating. Whether it's for survival or for fun, people use water all the time.

What It's All About

The planet Earth is unique in the solar system because of its abundance of water. It is one of the reasons that this planet can support life while others cannot. Where does the water come from? Where does it go? What's the story of water?

Water, Water, Everywhere

Water covers 70 percent of the Earth's surface, but 97 percent of it is salt water in oceans and seas. People cannot drink salt water, so even though it seems as if there is an unending supply of water to support human life, only 3 percent of the water on Earth is the fresh water that can actually help people survive. More than two-thirds of the fresh water is frozen at the North and South Poles, which means that the 6 billion people who share this planet have to share less than 1 percent of the water on it.

SOURCE

Project WET (Water Education for Teachers) is an online resource for teachers with interdisciplinary curricula to help kids learn all about water. It has great curricula, materials, and products that are kid tested and approved. It also offers workshops regularly across the country and has an awards program to recognize your efforts. Check it out at *www .projectwet.org*.

Create a visual picture of just how little 1 percent is. You can draw a pie chart and color it to look like the Earth. You could use a chart of ten squares by ten squares or a jar with 100 marbles or dry beans. For each method, start with the whole and ask the students how you would go about showing 1 percent. When all of the methods correctly show 1 percent, return to the water discussion. Look at the globe and how much water is covering it. Look at your diagrams and demonstrations that show how much water covers the planet. Then look at how tiny the 1 percent is compared to the 99 percent. It's not very much, is it? That's why people have to take care of the fresh water and make sure it's not polluted or wasted.

Water Cycle

Water is the only substance that can be found in three forms: a liquid (water), a solid (ice), and a vapor (clouds or steam). Water is usually in its liquid form. It turns into a solid when the temperature drops below freezing—32°F or 0°C. Water becomes a vapor when it is heated and escapes into the air. Water constantly cycles among these three forms.

The water cycle involves three stages: evaporation, condensation, and precipitation. Every day, sunlight warms the water in oceans, rivers, lakes, and streams. Once the water warms to a certain point, it vaporizes and floats up in the air. This is called evaporation. The gaseous water molecules float higher and higher, and the air gets cooler and cooler. Once the air gets cool enough, the water vapors turns back into liquid droplets. This is called condensation, and that's how clouds are made. More and more droplets float up into the cloud until it becomes too heavy to float anymore. Then it rains, which is also known as precipitation.

Have the children sing a fun song about the water cycle. You can make up your own or use the following song written by Lori Ann Phelan:

Water Travels in a Cycle
(Sing to the tune of "She'll Be Coming Around the Mountain")

Water travels in a cycle, yes it does
(use pointer finger to make a big circle)

Water travels in a cycle, yes it does (repeat finger circle)

It goes up as evaporation (moves hands up to the sky)

Forms clouds as condensation (make a cloud overhead with arms)

Then comes down as precipitation, yes it does!
(sprinkle with fingers while bringing arms down in front of you)

Muckin' Up the Water

Have you ever been to a place where the water wasn't clean? Where was it? What did you see? Maybe that was garbage floating along a shoreline or oil in water. These are examples of water pollution, but you can't always see it when water is polluted. Most of the pollution mixes into the water invisibly. Where does it come from? Find pictures to illustrate this to your class to emphasize the message.

FACT

All the water on the planet today is all the water people will ever have. There is no way to make "new" water. People can only reuse the existing water. The water you drink today is the same water the dinosaurs drank millions of years ago.

Farms that don't use sustainable practices are one source of water pollution. If chemicals are sprayed on the plants, rain can cause the chemicals to soak through the ground and into the groundwater. If it rains so hard that the soil can't soak it up fast enough, the water runs off and carries the chemicals with it to the nearest water body. If a farm uses sludge as a fertilizer, the runoff can include manure that can contaminate nearby water sources.

Factories are another source of water pollution. They often have large pipes that lead from the factory to a nearby water source. The factory uses water to make a product, and when they're done with it, it flows down the pipe and out into the water, carrying the toxic leftovers with it. Sometimes the water that enters into the lakes, rivers, and wetlands is too warm for the plants and animals that live there.

Another source of water pollution is from people's garbage and sewage. Cities have water treatment facilities, and they collect a lot of the pollutants from the water—but not all of it. Certain pollutants such as antibacterial soaps pass through the treatment process. The water that is discharged into a local stream or river still has some pollutants in it, and this makes an unhealthy habitat for the plants and animals that live in the water.

One way that people's garbage ends up in water is from storm drains. Storm drains prevent streets from flooding when it rains. Just like a drain in a sink, they let the water drain away from the street and take the rainwater to a local body of water. The problem is that anything in the street gets washed away with the rainwater. That can mean litter, pet waste, pesticides, salt, oil and gasoline from cars, and anything else people leave in the streets.

ALERT!

It is important for children to understand they shouldn't drink water from rivers, lakes, or streams. The pollutant is usually somewhat invisible to the naked eye, so you can't tell simply by looking at the water if it's clean enough to drink. Even when swimming, children should keep their mouths closed so they don't unintentionally swallow the water.

Global Picture

Water has many stories to tell. Some are beautiful and some are sad, but in the end the moral of all of the stories is the same. People need to respect water and to take better care of it.

World Water Day

The population of the planet increases rapidly every year. The more people there are, the more water is needed to support life. On top of human demand, climate change impacts the water cycle. Droughts and floods place stress on the water cycle. There's enough water for everyone on the planet, but people need to manage it better. Do a class research project on what water issues affect different parts of the globe. How do people get water in the very dry regions of Africa? What about water usage in very cold places like Antarctica? How much do people use? Do they use it for different things than you? How do they move it from the water source to their home?

Once you've learned about some of the water issues and water usage practices from around the world, join in the global celebration on World Water Day. The United Nations designated March 22 as World Water Day in 1993. Every year, thousands of people from all over the globe celebrate water for life on this very important day. There is an international poster contest as well as educational events and walks for water in communities across the planet. Coordinate something for your classroom or your community to celebrate water and commit to taking better care of it. Visit *www* *.worldwaterday.org* for more information.

H2knOw

What do you know about bodies of water? What are the different types of bodies of water? There are oceans, lakes, rivers, streams, wetlands, natural springs, gulfs, and more. Divide the students into small groups and have each group research one type of water body. They should create an educational H_2knOw poster to teach other students about that type of water body. It should include a definition, a few interesting facts, and some pictures. To address the global concerns, you can also have them pick a specific, actual place in the world that represents their body of water and search for water quality issues. For example, if they were assigned lakes, they could research Lake Chad in Africa. Likewise, you can assign each student a water body and have them make their posters as a homework assignment.

It's not always important to have a set activity in mind to engage your students in hands-on learning. Sometimes, you can simply give them information, like the information about water pollution, and let them come up with ideas for projects. It's empowering and encourages them to be innovative thinkers.

For the Classroom

Water is a fascinating liquid that has a lot of secrets to tell. When you're studying water, remember to balance the lessons with information about usage and pollution because both issues are very important to protecting the world's fresh water.

A Closer Look at Leaks

Does your classroom have a sink? If not, maybe you can use the art room or a different room with a sink to conduct this experiment. Hopefully, the faucet isn't already leaky (if it is, tell maintenance). For this experiment, you'll need to simulate a leaky faucet by turning on the tap just the tiniest bit. Have the students guess how much water will leak out after one day of dripping. The drips are pretty small. You can hold up containers of different sizes to help them visualize. Will it be one cup? Will it be one quart? Will it be one pint? Will it be one gallon? Will it be more?

FACT

Approximately one in six people in the world, or 1.1 billion, do not have access to safe, clean drinking water. In the United States, people take for granted that clean water is readily available at any tap, but in some countries, people walk for miles simply to get to water. Learn how you can help at *http://water.org*.

For a younger class, you'll have to do the experiment yourself. For older students, you can pair them up and have them do it themselves. You'll need two paper cups, a teaspoon, and a timer. Follow these steps:

1. Have each pair of students write down their guess for how much water will drip after a day.
2. Have each pair of students approach the sink separately. One student should catch the water in a cup and the other should time it for two minutes.
3. After they return to their seats, they can measure how many teaspoons of water were collected in the cup, emptying the teaspoons into the second cup as they count.
4. Have them write down the number of teaspoons that dripped after two minutes. Then multiply it by thirty to find out how many teaspoons of water would drip in an hour. Then multiply by twenty-four to find out how many teaspoons of water would drip in a day.
5. Record all of the students' answers on the board. Find the average. Convert the number of teaspoons to tablespoons, cups, quarts, and gallons.

Did anyone guess this number in the beginning? How much would this end up being every month? How much in a year? What if everyone in the classroom had a leaky faucet? Leaky faucets are no laughing matter!

To help report water leaks in public places, go to *www.kidsforsavingearth .org* and click on "Water." List the name and address of the public place that has the leak and what the leak is. Kids for Saving Earth will send out a "Water Wasters" warning to remind them to repair their leaky faucets or toilets.

Many times, a faucet may not have a leak; it may not be all the way turned off. Children are especially prone to leaving the tap slightly open. Practice turning the tap all the way off. Make up a quick rhyme to remember to turn it all the way off.

Oil's Not So Slick

Water gets polluted when oil is spilled into it. Oil spills can be extremely difficult to clean up. How difficult? Try this:

- Place a pie pan on a table and fill it halfway with water.
- Pour about an eighth of an inch of vegetable oil on top of it.
- Try to remove the oil using a spoon.
- Try a cotton ball, aluminum foil, netting, or anything else you can think of.

What happens to the oil in the water? Have a discussion. If there were animals or fish in the water, what would happen to them?

School Projects

Schools are big buildings that use a lot of water every day. They use water for heating and cooling systems, restrooms, drinking fountains, water faucets, locker rooms, cafeterias, laboratories, outdoor playing fields and lawns, and sometimes even swimming pools. Schools can make a significant difference in the effort to manage water wisely.

Water Watchers

People in the United States expect that water will always be there whenever they turn on the tap, but water is a limited resource and people are using a lot of it every day. Consider these facts:

- It takes more than fifty gallons of water to make an eight-ounce glass of milk.
- It takes 115 gallons of water to grow the wheat for one loaf of bread.
- It takes 100 gallons of water to grow one watermelon
- It takes roughly fifteen gallons of water to make one gallon of gasoline.
- It takes 280 gallons of water to make one Sunday newspaper.
- It takes 39,000 gallons of water to make one new car, including tires.

It takes water to grow your food. It takes water to make your schoolbus. It takes water to make your notebooks and your textbooks. How can your school start to cut back? One way is for you to start being water watchers. Make signs for your school's restrooms that encourage people to turn off water while they're washing their hands. Report to maintenance whenever you see a leaky faucet or hear toilets running after they've filled. Make educational posters for your hallways. Ask people if they are water watchers or water wasters.

SOURCE

Many of the ways that a school can save water can only be controlled by maintenance staff and administration. It's a tremendous way to save money and protect the environment, so help them out and find the information they need at the National Clearinghouse for Educational Facilities' water resource site: *www.edfacilities.org/rl/water.cfm.*

Break Free from Bottled Water

Do you drink bottled water? Almost everyone does these days, but what happened to drinking tap water? Why do people think it's not okay anymore? Bottled water manufacturers want you to think that bottled water is better because they want to earn your money. Guess what? Bottled water isn't any better than tap water. It's also super-bad for the environment.

- Each year in the United States, 29 billion plastic water bottles are produced for use.
- Making all of these bottles requires 17 million barrels of crude oil.
- Nearly 90 percent of water bottles are not recycled and wind up in land-fills where it takes thousands of years for the plastic to decompose.

That's some pretty big numbers. Try to break them down so they are more understandable. Divide 29 billion by 365. How many bottles are made each day? How many each hour? What's 90 percent of this? That's a lot of garbage!

Some school districts have banned bottled water. Can you get yours to? Start selling reusable stainless-steel water bottles as a fundraiser to prompt the conversation and get people to act. You can even try to get your mayor or city council to try to reduce bottled water consumption by writing them and urging them to take the "Think Outside the Bottle" pledge. Visit *http://thinkoutsidethebottle.org* for more information.

You might wonder if your local school's water is safe to drink. Many schools across the country have lead pipes that leach lead into the drinking water. Lead poses a serious health threat to children and can cause perma-nent brain damage. Other contaminants could be present as well. Fortu-nately, there are many resources to ensure that your students are drinking safe water. First, ask your school maintenance staff if they have any past records of water tests.

You should also call your local water utility to get the most recent Con-sumer Confidence Report (CCR), which is a water test that must be con-ducted annually. Still, if your school has lead pipes, the CCR won't show it. The CCR only shows the water test results at the facility, not what comes out of your tap or fountain. Ask your utility if they will donate the resources to conduct testing at your school. Try to push for annual testing of the drinking fountains at your school to ensure the safest water. You can learn more and find a variety of resources for schools through the U.S. Environmental Protection Agency at *www.epa.gov/OGWDW/schools/guidance.html*.

Field Trips

There's water, water, everywhere and plenty of places to see it. Kids love the water, but they don't need to get wet to learn about it. Here are two ideas for examining water in its natural state and learning how humans treat it and use it.

Water Treatment

Call your local water treatment facility to organize a field trip. Generally, these tours include a discussion of your city's sources of raw water, water treatment methods, and water distribution, as well as a tour of the facility. Before you go, read *The Magic School Bus at the Waterworks* by Joanna Cole and Bruce Degen. Also, brainstorm questions your students may have prior to your visit. Where does the water come from? Is it filtered? How? How does it get to houses? What makes it come out of the faucet? Where does water go after it goes down the drain? What about when you rinse a paintbrush or wash the dishes? Where does your city store water? How much water does your city use every year? How much is that per person? What else would you like to know?

To expand on your lesson, find out if the facility will test water for you. If not, try to find a certified water tester who would donate his services. Gather one jar of rainwater and one jar of tap water from your school. What's in them? Compare the list of findings and research what those contaminants might mean for your health. The U.S. Environmental Protection Agency also provides communities with annual drinking water testing results. Ask your students to investigate the results in their community.

Beach Cleanup

Do your part to clean up the environment by having a field trip to a local body of water that's been abused by litterbugs. It can be an ocean beach, a creek, a wetland, or a lake. Make sure to have latex gloves for the children to wear. Get permission slips from parents and encourage them to come and help. Make sure you require that the kids stay on the shore and not go into the water. When you first arrive, stand far back and ask the students to describe what they see. Walk up to the shoreline and ask them again. It's a different picture up close.

Ask the kids what types of litter they see on the beach. Does any of the debris include products they've bought? How do they think the litter got there? Do they think people dropped it on purpose? Did it blow here from somewhere else? Whatever the story of the trash is, it doesn't belong here. Have the children collect the garbage. Warn them not to pick up broken glass; instead, they should ask an adult to pick it up. Weigh what you've gathered at the end. How much litter did you collect? How much shoreline did you cover? How much litter is that per foot (or square foot) of shoreline?

FACT

The U.S. Geological Survey has been testing streams and groundwater for PPCPs (pharmaceuticals and personal care products) for almost a decade after initial testing in 1999 found some startling results. Chemicals like antibiotics, hormones, steroids, and other drugs were detected in 80 percent of streams and 93 percent of groundwater. Learn how you can help protect groundwater at *http://groundwater.org.*

Human Health

When most people think of a body of water, they think of a river or lake, but people are bodies of water, too! Your body is approximately 70 percent water, so you need to be drinking plenty of fresh, clean water every day in order to maintain a healthy body and brain.

You Dump It, You Drink It

The United States has some of the cleanest drinking water in the world. Because of state-of-the-art filtration systems, people can generally trust that what comes out of the tap is totally safe to drink. Still, more and more pollutants are finding their way into the natural water sources, and treatment facilities are beginning to have a hard time keeping up. So many of the products people use every day can end up polluting the water, and pollution doesn't just disappear.

People pollute water at home by using pesticides on their lawns and dumping used oil into storm drains. There are also a variety of products that people use without knowing they can end up in the drinking water. What are some products that you use that end up going down the drain? Think of doing dishes, washing clothes, or shampooing your hair. What's in these products?

Bring some common products into your classroom to investigate the ingredients that may cause water pollution. You can bring in laundry detergent, shampoo, bubble bath, dishwashing liquid, and anything else that may get washed down the drain. Have students try to read the ingredients from the label. Does anyone recognize what any of those ingredients are?

ALERT!

Most adults are stunned by the potential health risks of many of the ingredients in everyday products. It can be very scary. It's very important to teach children to read labels, but it's equally important to make sure they feel like there's something they can do and that the world's not a poisonous mess. Be careful to control the information you're teaching.

Use the National Institutes of Health's Household Products Database at *http://householdproducts.nlm.nih.gov* and the Agency for Toxic Substances and Disease Registry ToxFAQs website at *www.atsdr.cdc.gov/toxfaq.html* to look up the different ingredients. For many types of products, manufacturers are allowed to sell a product before it's been fully tested for safety. It's up to consumers to research which ones they feel comfortable using. What do you think about what these government sites say about the safety of these chemicals? Does it sound as if you should use them? Does it seem okay for the environment?

The second part of this project is to find safer alternatives to the products that seem to have scary ingredients. Do some research beforehand to find alternatives. For personal-care products, you can find safer alternatives at *www.cosmeticsdatabase.com*. You can easily find products to safely clean your home or school. Carefully read the labels, but don't count on the word *natural*. Natural does not necessarily mean it is safe or healthy. Also, for most cleaners, you can find make-it-yourself recipes online. If you can find someone to donate carefully cleaned spray bottles, it's great to mix up your own safe-for-the-Earth (and human health) all-purpose cleaner for the children to take home.

Water is vital to good health. Plain water is much healthier than soda and juice. When you're going different places at school, make time for your students to take a drink at the water fountain. Encourage everyone to have one. By the time your brain actually registers thirst, your body is already dehydrated.

You can find recipes for environmentally friendly all-purpose cleaners online. They work on sinks, tubs, tiles, floors, countertops, and more. Cleaners that include vinegar and borax are effective at killing germs and bacteria. Best of all, they're safe for the environment and human health—and they're cheap! Have the students design their own eco-friendly labels with the recipe so parents can mix it again in the future.

Beach Safety Bonanza

Beaches are a favorite destination of children and adults alike. Unfortunately, with increasing water pollution, people need to be aware if the water is safe to swim in. You can go to the U.S. Environmental Protection Agency's Beach Advisory site at *http://oaspub.epa.gov/beacon/beacon_national_page.main* to learn about closings and advisories, but there are also some basic tips that everyone should know.

1. Don't swim after a storm. Heavy rains can stir up polluted sediment and storm drains can send new pollutants into the water.
2. If it's stinky or dirty, walk away.
3. Look for litter and dirty rainbow slicks (oil and gasoline).

4. Don't get it in your mouth.
5. Don't swim by a storm drain.

Can your class make up a poem to remember these rules? Discuss why each rule is important.

Take It Home

Household water use is so constant people rarely even think of it. It's important to recognize how much is being used and how your actions impact future water quality.

The average person in the United States uses about 80–100 gallons of water per day. The largest amount goes to flushing the toilet. Place a tightly sealed plastic bottle filled with water inside your tank and your toilet will run on less water. Every little bit helps!

Watching My Water

Have students monitor how much water their family uses at home for one week. It will be difficult to be completely accurate, but even an estimate is useful. Children will become more observant about how much water they use, which will help them look for ways to reduce. Brainstorm a worksheet of water usage. How does your family use water? It will likely include things like:

- Showers and baths
- Dishes
- Laundry
- Washing hands
- Brushing teeth
- Watering the lawn
- Washing the car

There are many other ways people use water at home, such as cooking food, drinking, and flushing toilets. Make your list as long as what your class can come up with. Have them monitor this use for one week as best as they can. They should write down what the activity is and, if pertinent, how long it took. Compare lists and add up water usage for the whole class after the week is over. If you want to get technical, research online how much water each activity uses on average. How much water are your students' families using? Can you think of ways to cut back?

To expand on this project, have the students pick some ways they will use less water. Then monitor their usage for another week and see how much they've cut back. Can they reduce their usage even more?

Don't Dump It

Household hazardous waste is anything that has a cautionary label. The average U.S. home has 100 pounds of these toxic concoctions stored in its basement, garage, and underneath the sink. All of these items need to be disposed of responsibly so they don't pollute the environment. Here are some things that should never be poured down drains:

- Oil-based paints or stains
- Medications
- Pesticides
- Used oil
- Paint thinner

Homeowners should be aware of how to dispose of these substances. They can call their local household hazardous waste office (find it by calling the local solid waste management office) or by using *http://earth911 .com*. You can have your students make a fact sheet for their parents or have them go home and look for products (with parental guidance) that have cautionary labels on them. What products do they have lurking at home in their basement, garage, or even under the kitchen sink? You can use the "House Inspector Checklist" found at *www.kidsforsavingearth.org /inspectorchecklist.htm* to do a full audit of products in your home.

CHAPTER 8

Clear the Air

Air pollution has been an issue for hundreds of years. All the way back in 900 B.C.E., an Egyptian king complained about stinky air by asphalt mines. In the 1300s, the air in England became so polluted from coal burning that King Edward I outlawed it and threatened to behead anyone caught burning coal again. Today, air pollution is outside and inside, and even though we often can't see or smell it, there's almost always something in the air that shouldn't be there.

What It's All About

Air is all around, but how often do you think of it? Maybe when it's cold or windy or something smells, but not as often as you inhale it (about 20,000 times a day)!

A Recipe for Air

Even though you can't see air, it is made up of trillions of microscopic molecules. Air is made up of mostly nitrogen and oxygen gases, but there are tiny bits of other gases, as well as particles like dust and ash, water droplets, and sometimes ice crystals. Make your students into air molecules to demonstrate visually what air is and what it does. You'll need five different colors of construction paper cut into strips that can be used as arm bands. Assign one color for each component of the air (nitrogen, oxygen, water vapor, other gases, pollution). Next, assign students to represent the different components of air in the same ratio as real life. In a class of thirty students, twenty-one students will be nitrogen (78 percent), five will be oxygen (21 percent), two will be water vapor (variable), one will be other gases (1 percent), and one will be pollution (variable).

Separate the children according to the color of their arm bands. Talk about the different components of air—what there's more of and what there's less of. Can you see these molecules of air? Which ones do people breathe? People inhale oxygen, but they also inhale pollution.

Are air molecules separated in the air like the students are standing in the classroom? No. Have the children walk around the room and randomly mix themselves up. This is what air is really like, but is the recipe always the same? What about the air right next to a busy highway? The air in a forest? The air above a factory smokestack? It's ideal if you have pictures to show and compare.

Air pollution is always on the move. Remember how China struggled with air pollution before the 2008 Summer Olympics? Their air pollution blows all the way across the ocean and ends up adding to air pollution in the United States. Likewise, air pollution from coal-burning power plants in the United States blows up to Canada and all over the world.

On a smaller scale, if trash is burned in someone's backyard, it can easily move to the neighbor's yard. Have you ever been able to smell when your neighbor has a fire in their fireplace or when they're doing their laundry? That's because smells, scents, chemicals, smoke, and pollution are always blowing in the wind.

Since air is invisible, it's tough to get children (and adults) to really think about it and the role it plays in life. Once you start talking about air, you may be surprised at how quickly kids make the connection. Ask open-ended questions about air to see what discussions are sparked. What do they think about air? What does air do?

In and Out

The air inside and the air outside are actually very different. Think about how people use heaters and air conditioners to control the temperature inside a building. In order to do this, they have to make buildings that keep the warm air inside in the winter and the cool air inside in the summer. They have to be sealed up tight. In most buildings and even in homes, you can tell that the indoor air is different from the outdoor air because it smells different.

Ask your students to take a walking tour around their homes and yards and make a list of the scents they smell. Where are the smells stronger? Ask them to decide if the smells are good or bad. What does it smell like outside on the lawn? What does it smell like in the parking lot or driveway? How about the garage? What does it smell like in the bathrooms? Which air is "fresh" air and which might have pollutants in it? In the driveway you might smell exhaust from cars or lawnmowers, which are major outdoor air pollutants. In the bathroom you might smell cleansers, which are major indoor air pollutants (they're usually made of toxic chemicals).

When your students return to the classroom, have them read out loud some of the smells they discovered. List the items that might be bad to breathe and discuss ways to make your home healthier. Order *We're Not Asking for the Moon . . . Just a Healthy Home and Earth* from Kids for Saving Earth (*www.kidsforsavingearth.org* and click on KSE "Green Shop") for your library and ask the kids to take it home to read with their parents.

Global Picture

The air all around you and all around the Earth makes up the lower part of our atmosphere. The entire atmosphere is made up of gas molecules, but as you get farther away from the Earth's surface, the types of gases change.

FACT

According to the U.S. Environmental Protection Agency, for every dollar spent on the Clean Air Act of 1970, Americans have received a $20 return on health care and pollution savings. In 1990 alone, vehicle and smoke-stack emission reductions saved an estimated 79,000 lives and resulted in an estimated 15 million fewer respiratory illnesses.

Blowin' in the Wind

Begin your discussion about wind with a simple poem written by Christina Rossetti:

Who Has Seen the Wind

Who has seen the wind?

Neither I nor you.

But when the leaves hang trembling,

The wind is passing through.

Who has seen the wind?

Neither you nor I.

But when the trees bow down their heads,

The wind is passing by.

What makes air move? What makes the wind? Have all the students stand on one side of the room. Then have them all walk across to the other side at the same time. That's what wind does to air molecules, but how? The wind's energy comes from the sun. The sun's rays hit the Earth and warm the air molecules closest to the surface. When that layer of air warms up, it becomes less dense, and it floats higher, allowing cooler air to come back to the ground. That movement creates the wind.

Split the class into two groups. One group should stand on one side of the classroom, which represents the North Pole. The other group should stand on the other side of the room, which represents someplace warm (you can use a globe and let them pick a tropical place) near the equator. The sun's rays warm the equator more than the poles. So what will happen when those air molecules at the equator warm up? They get lighter and are replaced by the cold molecules that are at the poles. Have the children switch places. Now the cold ones are at the equator. What's going to happen to them? They are warming up and the ones at the pole are cooling down. What happens when the ones at the equator warm up? They trade places again. The warm air and cold air are constantly changing places. These are global air currents.

FACT

When pollutants end up in the air, they sometimes connect to the water vapor that eventually becomes rain. When the rain or water vapor comes down attached to the pollutant, it creates acid rain. Acid rain is harmful to plants, animals, soil, and water bodies. It's even strong enough to eat away at buildings and statues. Ouch!

Air Currents and Pollution

What happens if one of the places produces a bunch of air pollution? Say the people in the warmer spot build a whole bunch of factories and start driving a lot of cars. Have some of the children in the current warm group hold gray and brown construction-paper clouds that represent air pollution. Except for a very few scientists or explorers, no one else really lives at the poles, and they are probably not making any pollution, so your North Pole group doesn't get clouds. What's going to happen to that pollution, though?

When the air heats up, it trades places with the cold air. The students switch places again. Now the polluted air is far away from where it was made. What's happening in the warm place? More pollution is being made, so give some of your equatorial students some pollution clouds. Then the air heats up and everyone switches places again. Then more pollution is made, more students at the equator are given clouds, and everyone switches again. What's happening? The pollution doesn't go away; it just keeps blowing around. Unfortunately for the polar bears, even though they don't make any pollution, they still have to breathe it.

Wind Power

For thousands of years, people have used wind power. The ancient Egyptians used wind power to sail boats down the Nile, Europeans used windmills to grind wheat and other grains, and American colonists built windmills to pump water up from underground. Right now, most of our energy comes from burning coal and oil, which are nonrenewable resources and will eventually run out. Wind is called a renewable energy source because it will never run out, and it's also a very clean energy source. Mining for coal and drilling for oil create large amounts of pollution, as does burning them. Make your own mini-windmills with a piece of paper, a push pin, a couple small beads, and a dowel or pencil.

1. Decorate an eight-inch square piece of paper.
2. Fold the square into a triangle, corner to corner, and then fold again. Open it up and you should have a big *X*. Make a pencil mark about a third of the way from the center on each line.
3. Cut along the fold lines, stopping at your pencil marks.
4. Bring every other point into the center (don't fold) and stick a push pin through all four points in the middle. The head of the push pin becomes the hub of the windmill.
5. Turn the windmill over to make sure the pin went through the middle. Give it a little wiggle so the hole opens up a bit to ensure the windmill will spin.
6. Put a couple small beads onto the sharp end of the pin and then stick the pin into a thin dowel or pencil.
7. Huff and puff and blow the windmill around!

For the Classroom

Have you ever thought about the air in your classroom? Here are a couple of easy ways for you and your students to keep the air in your classroom fresh and healthy.

Another great way to learn about air and wind while getting some great exercise is by flying kites. If you have an open playground, you have the perfect spot for harnessing the energy from the wind and making your kites soar. Search online for directions to make your own from reused materials!

Out the Window

Have you ever heard of VOCs? Volatile organic compounds are released as gases from a variety of chemicals and some are bad for health. VOCs are released by a wide array of products numbering in the thousands. Examples include paints and cleaning supplies, pesticides, building materials and furnishings, copiers and printers, glues and adhesives, and permanent markers. Levels of many VOCs are sometimes up to ten times higher indoors than outdoors. The logical solution to this problem is to open a window and let the outside air in and the inside air out. A few things to consider:

- Make sure the window is not next to an exterior vent. Schools sometimes have ventilation systems that draw especially bad air out of the building. If you open a window by one, it could pull the dirty air right back in.
- Don't open windows on heavily trafficked streets or near idling vehicles. Air polluted with exhaust is not good to breathe.
- Likewise, if your window is next to a stinky factory or some other polluting business, just keep it shut. If there's a high pollen count or dust, you may also want to be careful.
- Even if there's heating or air conditioning on, opening your window just a little bit for at least five minutes a day can significantly improve your indoor air quality. Designate a student to be a window watcher to make sure the window is only open for five minutes.

Opening windows is about as easy as it gets and it's free. You can't beat that. Even if you can't open your classroom's window because of heavily polluted air outside, spread the word to other people and try it in other areas of the school.

SOURCE

Toxicology, Risk Assessment, and Pollution (ToxRAP) may sound like the name of a college course, but it's actually a curriculum for young children to learn about outdoor and indoor air quality and pollution. The focus is on age-appropriate, hands-on activities that demonstrate the concepts of air pollution and give kids solutions. Visit *www.toxrap.org* to learn more.

Plant Purification: A Growing Experience

Plants are natural air cleaners. In fact, NASA studied plants' ability to purify the air so they would know the best ones to keep the air clean and healthy on tightly sealed spaceships and future space stations. The best air cleaners they found, according to the University of Minnesota Extension Services, were:

- *Hedera helix* (English ivy)
- *Chlorophytum comosum* (spider plant)
- *Epipiremnum aureum* (golden pothos)
- *Spathiphyllum "Mauna Loa"* (peace lily)
- *Aglaonema modestum* (Chinese evergreen)
- *Chamaedorea sefritzii* (bamboo or reed palm)
- *Sansevieria trifasciata* (snake plant)
- *Philodendron scandens "oxycardium"* (heartleaf philodendron)
- *Philodendron selloum* (selloum philodendron)
- *Philodendron domesticum* (elephant ear philodendron)
- *Dracaena marginata* (red-edged dracaena)
- *Dracaena fragrans "Massangeana"* (cornstalk dracaena)
- *Dracaena deremensis "Janet Craig"* (Janet Craig dracaena)
- *Dracaena deremensis "Warneckii"* (Warneck dracaena)
- *Ficus benjamina* (weeping fig)

Reuse and decorate a glass or plastic container at least 6 to 8 inches in diameter to use as a plant pot. Use organic potting soil if possible and don't use fertilizers or pesticides on your plants. Keep the soil surface clean and free of plant debris because microorganisms in the soil help clean the air, too, but they need access to it. Also, make sure to not overwater as it can cause mold growth, which is another form of air pollution.

Whenever you bring plants into your room, be sure to do a little research first to make sure the plant is not poisonous to children. Also, you may want to make sure there are no potential allergic reactions associated with the plant or, if it flowers, the pollen.

School Projects

News headlines often report on poor air quality in schools, especially portable classrooms. Sometimes the air quality is so bad it requires evacuation. More than 56 million people—one out of every five—spend their days in schools, so it's only right that the air quality is as healthy as possible.

Tools for Schools

The U.S. Environmental Protection Agency created the Indoor Air Quality Tools for Schools (IAQ TfS) program more than a decade ago, and it is one of the most widely used resources addressing the issue. Its aim is to help schools find and deal with air quality issues for the well-being of students and teachers.

The IAQ TfS program provides resources and even software to schools at no cost to help implement a successful plan. It includes information for school officials, teachers, students, facility staff, parents, health care professionals, and the media that cover a wide range of air quality topics like mold remediation, asthma management, and renovation projects. They also host an annual symposium, as well as offer five awards that schools can apply for to gain national recognition for their efforts. The IAQ TfS kit should be used by every school; you can find it at *www.epa.gov/iaq/schools*.

ALERT!

Exercise might be bad for your health if you exercise outside on days that have bad air quality. Make sure that it's safe to run and play outside by checking out *http://airnow.gov,* the federal government's website for air quality alerts. You can even sign up to receive e-mail alerts so you don't need to remember to check the website.

Nonscents!

Everyone likes to smell fresh and clean, but sometimes people unknowingly wear so much perfume or cologne that it irritates others around them. Beyond simple annoyance, strong fragrances can give people headaches, set off allergies, or even trigger asthma attacks. The fragrances used in perfumes, colognes, shampoos, lotions, and other body-care products are usually chemicals. Some fragrance recipes contain up to six hundred different chemicals!

Small children don't usually wear a lot of scented products, but they pay the price when adults around them do. Clear the air for your students by starting a Nonscents! awareness program at your school. Make signs to hang around the school to talk about how scented products like perfumes, colognes, and lotions can contain chemicals that trigger asthma attacks, headaches, and other health impacts. Ask that employees and visitors reduce or avoid wearing scented products to school in order to protect the young lungs around them. You can direct them to *www.cosmeticsdatabase .com* to find safer personal-care products.

Field Trips

Air is everywhere, but where can you go to really get a good understanding of it? It sure would be fun to go into outer space and watch global winds pushing clouds around! Until that's possible, here are a couple of different ideas.

Indoor Air Adventure

Teachers are always looking for field trips that get them out of school, but one of the best field trips for learning about indoor air is one that explores your school building. People spend up to 90 percent of their time inside, so indoors is like the natural habitat for humans. Just as a beaver builds a den or a bird builds a nest, people build buildings to live in. You and the students can explore your school just as you would explore the habitat of another animal. Some of the tools the students will need for your Indoor Air Adventure are:

- Flashlights
- Notebooks and pencils
- A large ostrich feather
- A long stick or pole
- A narrow ribbon
- Scissors
- Tape

The students can use the flashlights for checking out dark spaces and record what they find in the notebooks. They can hang the feather or the ribbon in front of vents or other air sources to gauge air movement. Taping a feather or ribbon to the stick allows them to check vents in high places. Here are some things they can look for that can impact indoor air quality:

- **Water problems.** Stained or cracked ceiling tiles, plaster, wallpaper, and flooring can indicate problems.
- **Ventilation.** Have the kids use their noses to find areas that are stinky or stuffy, and use their eyes to look for dusty areas. Ask them to note areas that are too warm or too cold in their notebooks.
- **Overall cleanliness.** Examine floors for food or drink spills, and check for garbage cans that are too full.

How does your school rate? Is it a healthy habitat for all the humans who spend all day in it? If you find any issues of concern, have the class write a polite letter to the principal and custodian to let them know what you found.

FACT

Children are much more vulnerable to air pollution, both inside and out. Their lungs are still developing. They inhale more air per pound of body weight than adults. They play outside more. They are shorter and play on the floor where contaminants are more prevalent. Help kids breathe easier by following all the tips in this chapter.

Wind Farming

Do a little research to find out if anyone in your area either has a wind farm or even just one windmill on their property that they use for an energy source. Learning about wind power shows how people can use the air for energy in a way that doesn't pollute the air. Some interesting facts about wind power according to the American Wind Energy Association:

- By the end of 2008, wind farms in the United States will generate enough energy to power more than 5.5 million homes.
- To generate the same amount of electricity as today's U.S. wind farms, people would have to burn 23 million tons of coal or 75 million barrels of oil every year.
- In 2007, the pollution-free energy produced by wind farms prevented the emissions of about 28 million tons of carbon dioxide.
- Making wind power does not require any mining, drilling, transportation of fuel, or water usage, and it does not generate radioactive or other polluting waste. It's clean as a whistle!

The power of wind power is positively perfect! After your field trip, have your students come up with an advertising campaign for wind power. Can they make a catchy phrase? What pictures would be best? If the students are older and you have access to a video camera, try making a commercial. Does your utility company offer wind power if customers pay a little extra? Look into it and promote it as part of your campaign. A great printable handout on wind power can be found at the Kids for Saving Earth website (*www.kidsforsavingearth.org*). It's called "News That Will Blow You Away," and you can find it on the "E-Pal News" link by clicking on "Wind Power."

Wind Watching

Take a walk on a windy day. Be prepared with umbrellas, scarves, and paper planes. Use a compass to determine which way the wind is blowing. Enjoy experimenting with and watching all the things wind can do. Record your experiments.

Human Health

As you can see from reading through this chapter, it's tough to talk about air without considering how it affects human health. Whether inside or out, poor air quality can cause everything from headaches and allergy attacks to life-threatening conditions, such as carbon monoxide poisoning and severe asthma attacks.

Crabby Kathy

In 1998, the children of Kids Making a Connection (KMAC), wrote a true story called *Crabby Kathy* that was then illustrated by third and sixth graders. It is the story of a teacher named Kathy, who loves living in the country and looking at the stars (among other things that don't make her crabby). Unfortunately, whenever she comes to school she gets a headache, she starts coughing, and she gets crabby. The KMAC kids decide they'd better solve the mystery of why Kathy gets so crabby at school. They find a wide variety of indoor air pollutants and then they find all the ways to improve the air. Kathy is no longer crabby at school and everyone has learned a very important lesson. You can read this story online or print it up and make a nice cover for it. Then share the storybook with other classrooms and teachers. Find *Crabby Kathy* at *http://kids.niehs.nih.gov/kathy.*

Get Acting on Asthma

Asthma is on the rise and it's important to know what it is, how to prevent asthma attacks, and how to deal with it if someone has an attack. Kids for Saving Earth has a fact sheet for kids that talks about all of these issues. It also has action steps for kids, including:

1. Ask to see a doctor or tell your school nurse if you think you have breathing problems.
2. Check out your home and school environment to find asthma triggers. You can go to the KSE website to print out a "Toxic Tour Guide for your home." Use it with your parents to make your home a healthier place.
3. Write or e-mail letters to KSE explaining your concerns about asthma, and KSE will send them to government and corporate leaders.

Go to *www.kidsforsavingearth.org/programs/kidsasthma2.htm* to download the fact sheet and share it with your class. It's also important for you and your students to know what to do if someone starts having an asthma attack. Have your school nurse visit your class to offer advice and create an emergency plan.

FACT

Asthma is the number-one reason kids miss school. Nearly one in thirteen students has asthma, so it's important to follow the steps in this chapter to prevent asthma and asthma attacks.

Take It Home

Most people have no idea how polluted the air in their homes is. People only think of smokestacks and exhaust pipes when they think of air pollution, but there are many smaller sources that have a big impact on our environment and our health.

Clean Up Your Air at Home

After everything your students have learned about air pollution and air quality, they should have some good ideas for how to improve air quality and prevent air pollution at home. Have your students design a handout to take home to parents. Brainstorm different tips as a class. They could include:

- Open windows.
- Reduce the use of products that have chemical smells, such as cleaners, perfumes, and air fresheners. You can find information about safer alternatives to these products at *www.healthychild .org*.
- Grow plants.
- Dust and vacuum regularly.
- Don't idle your car in the garage.

What else can your students come up with? What about ideas for preventing outdoor air pollution? Driving less is one of the biggest ways people can act on outdoor air pollution.

After you've come up with all of your easy steps, have each child write them on a piece of paper and then decorate it either by drawing pictures on it or cutting pictures out of magazines. Give it more punch by having a line on the back of the handout that says "Our family commits to _____" and a line for a parent signature.

Burn Barrels

Some people, especially in rural areas, burn their trash in pits or barrels. It seems an easy way to get rid of your garbage, but the smoke it creates has a lot of really unhealthy toxic chemicals. Burning things like foam cups, plastics, and colored and bleached paper in backyards or even fireplaces causes smoldering toxic smoke that can spread throughout the neighborhood. It's not like municipal garbage incinerators because the big burners have fires so hot that many of the toxic chemicals are virtually eliminated. They also have big filters at the tops of their smokestacks that catch a lot of the other bad stuff. The U.S. Environmental Protection Agency estimated that between the years 2002 and 2004, backyard burning released more chemicals into the air than all other sources during that time period. When people burn trash at home, they have no way of capturing the pollutants. Backyard trash burning is a common method to dispose of garbage, but what can be done? This is a perfect issue for a letter-writing campaign.

Learn more about this issue by going online and searching for backyard burning. Have your students write letters to your state legislators asking them to make laws banning backyard burning. Also ask them to find ways to help farmers and ranchers dispose of their garbage safely.

CHAPTER 9

This Land Is Your Land

People live on the land, but it's one of those things that's easy to overlook. You walk on it, drive on it, play on it, build on it, and dig in it, but how often do you stop to think about it? The way people choose to use land has big impacts on the planet.

9

What It's All About

Land is shaped by many factors. Natural processes that shape land include volcanic eruptions, earthquakes, and erosion. People also shape the land by building on it, farming it, and extracting natural resources from it.

Land the Way Nature Intended

What is land? It's more than dirt and rocks. People are surrounded by and live on very different types of land. The land was formed by many factors over time, and today it supports vastly different types of life and cultures. The eight major types of landforms are:

- Mountains
- Plains
- Plateaus
- Valleys
- Hills
- Forests
- Deserts
- Tundra

Assign small groups to each type of landform. Depending on how many students are in each group and what age they are, have them research what the landform is, what natural processes may have created it over time, what types of vegetation and wildlife inhabit the area, and what types of communities live in each area. To make it easier, they can pick one community to explore, such as a specific nomadic tribe that lives in the desert. They should work together to make a poster about their landform and then do a class presentation explaining the different areas they researched.

SOURCE

Go to *www.enviroliteracy.org* and click on "Land." You'll find a wealth of information about natural land formations and land-use issues ranging from forestry to mining. The website has many ideas and resources, most of which are adaptable to any age group.

Buried Treasures

Inside the land are gems, jewels, veins of coal, and pools of oil. All of these resources are valuable to people, but the local environment and communities pay a high price as the land is stripped and mined in search of its buried treasures. People have mined for ages, but has it become a thing of the past? Is there a better way to either find these resources or live without them?

Study the Appalachian Mountains to learn about mountaintop removal and the animal and plant life that is threatened by it. Children may wonder why such practices continue to be used if they are obviously destructive. Discuss the reasons mountaintop removal is still popular, and research alternatives. Draw pictures of the threatened animals and include them with a letter to coal-mining companies. Ask them to protect these animals by stopping mountaintop removal. You can find videos about this issue at *www.ilovemountains.org*.

Each year the world population increases by about 90 million people. How should we be planning cities in order to accommodate all of these new people? How long can the population increase before the planet simply can't support everyone?

Global Picture

For centuries, people mainly lived on farms. In the late eighteenth and early nineteenth centuries, more and more people started to move into the city. It happened first in the United States and Europe, but now it's happening the world over. What does it mean for the environment and its inhabitants?

Building It Bigger and Bigger

Land is used for many reasons—for buildings, farms, parks, stores, houses, and more. People in the government plan how to use land; when buildings are constructed, they are often referred to as our built environment.

Planning how to use land is like putting together a jigsaw puzzle. Planners have to find the best balance between places for residential developments, commercial developments, and industrial developments.

When people build a house—or any other type of building—it is called development. When big cities become overdeveloped, it's often called urban sprawl. Urban sprawl eats up natural green spaces like forests and wetlands, wildlife habitats, and even farms. Sprawl also increases traffic and pollutes the air and water. Flooding damage is often more severe as well. If there are so many negative consequences, why do communities keep spreading outward? Part of the reason is because of population growth. Another is because cities often offer the best job opportunities, so people from rural and small communities sometimes move to the city to make a better life for themselves.

FACT

It's very important to build in the right spot. Places like fire stations, schools, and government buildings are generally placed in convenient locations so they are easily accessible. You wouldn't want to build the only fire department on the edge of a community because it would take too long to get to a fire on the other side of town.

Use the Internet to look for images through time that show evidence of global development. An easy term to search for is *global light pollution*. You can find maps of the world at night to see where the major light pollution comes from. Over time, the skies have gotten brighter and brighter, and they will continue to do so as urban sprawl continues. Another way to examine development over time is by looking at your own region's development. Your local library will usually have books of old maps so you can see how your region has been developed over time. What was it like ten years ago? Twenty-five years ago? Fifty years ago?

A Peek into the Future

City planning in the future is bound to be different than it is now. People are getting smarter, technology is changing, and urban engineers must keep the Earth in mind if we are to have healthy places to live. This is called sustainable development. One example of how new cities are being planned is Masdar, a planned community in Abu Dhabi, in the United Arab Emirates. The plans for the city include:

- Creating all of the electricity from the sun and other renewable sources
- Reusing or recycling all materials so the city creates zero waste
- Banning cars and only allowing personal rapid transit systems and other public transit within city limits
- Creating a wastewater plant that reuses water as many times as possible (like using old dishwater to irrigate plants)

What would your perfect eco-city look like? Have your students draw pictures of a dream green city. They should label their innovations for reducing pollution, reducing traffic, maintaining green spaces, conserving water, and anything else they'd like to add.

For the Classroom

Your classroom is on one tiny piece of land, but you can have big impacts on the land around you by learning about how to protect it. Simple activities can teach students about the importance of land use and planning.

Landopoly

In the traditional game of Monopoly, people buy properties and are then allowed to charge others when they land on them. In real life, it's not just about buying properties. Community planning involves a wide range of decisions and each one has its own set of consequences. Michigan State University Extension developed a new board game called Landopoly to teach young students about what types of decisions must be made when planning communities and what their real-life consequences can be. It also shows the importance of civic engagement in ensuring that development reflects the desires of everyone in the community. Print up the instructions, board, and game pieces at *http://web1.msue.msu.edu/cplanner/jcp/landopoly.pdf.*

Kids' Community Planning

Use colorful construction paper and assign students to design and cut out school buildings, police departments, office buildings, churches, and homes. Piece the buildings together in a collage on mural paper to create the perfect community. Don't forget to include wetlands, parks, rivers, and other green areas. You might want to add rain gardens to the tops of buildings.

Everyone learns better through repetition. Play games several times if you have time. Invite your students to lead the class discussion. They can even ask the same questions you've already discussed. Simply repeating it and owning it will make it much more memorable. And they might come up with entirely new ideas.

School Projects

Schools are a piece of city planning. It's not easy to decide where to build a school, so most communities think long and hard before selecting a location. By their very nature, schools have rather large carbon footprints. The size of the building and playground and parking lots cover a large amount of natural space. Here are some ways to balance out that impact.

Adopt a Green Space

A good steward is someone who takes good care of things. When kids take care of toys and clean up messes, they are being good stewards of their homes. Likewise, it's important for kids to understand how to be good stewards of the Earth by taking care of it and keeping it clean. Really good stewards of the Earth leave spaces cleaner than they found them. For instance, if you go to the park, you should make sure to put your garbage in the garbage can, but what if someone else littered? Do you just walk by? Be a good steward. Pick it up and throw it away.

As a class or a school project, you can research your community and find a local space you can adopt. Maybe it's a local park or a local trail. Select a few ideas and have students vote on which one they want to adopt. They can also choose actions, goals, and a project name. Some project ideas include:

- Pick up trash around your school or at a nearby park and reuse the trash to create posters or signs about littering.
- Work with local park and recreation or land managers to clean up a recreation area or plant trees.
- Design flyers (on the reverse side of used paper) to educate people about land stewardship.

It can be a one-time community event or an ongoing school commitment through which different classes do the cleanups or other projects each month.

Whenever you choose to do park or playground cleanups, make sure you have parental permission and plenty of adult volunteers on hand to supervise the children. Some types of litter are not safe for children to touch. It's best if you can get trash grabbers (the poles with claws at the bottom), but protective gloves will also work.

Playground Planning

Whether you're in the position to build an entirely new playground or to spruce up an existing one, get students engaged in the process. It's a fantastic learning opportunity, and children are your number-one customers! Here are some eco-friendly ideas:

- Use play structures made from recycled plastic, metal, or sustainably forested woods.
- Given the current lack of long-term health impacts of using recycled tires as a playground surface, and the fact that the mining processes for pea gravel are not eco-friendly, it seems right now that wood chips may be the most environmentally friendly option to provide good cushioning if a child falls.

- Get creative when you "decorate" your space. Use discarded paving stones for paths, reclaimed wood for decorative fencing, or whatever other reusable materials inspire you.
- Make it a living space by incorporating native plants or even a small vegetable garden. If the space is fully paved, put your plants in raised boxes.

What do the kids want? Make sure you respectfully consider all ideas and invite students and parents to help with construction. One last thing: Don't forget to make your playground a pesticide-free zone. Children deserve to play somewhere safe and free of chemicals. Celebrate the opening of your playground with an outdoor environmental concert. The Kids for Saving Earth "Rock the World" concert has reproducible sheet music and scripts about creating an eco-friendly playground.

Field Trips

Step out your door and you'll see land, so your field trip options are limitless. Here are two that reinforce the important concepts of planning and public ownership of land.

SOURCE

Kids and Community was developed by city planners to engage children in the process of planning and help them understand it better. Visit *http:// myapa.planning.org/kidsandcommunity* to get in on the action.

Who Plans Your City?

Kids have probably never thought about the people behind the planning of your city, but they make a big impact on life in your community. They get to decide where everything goes and help develop long-term visions for what the city hopes to look like in the future. Take your students to the city planning offices to meet the people behind the plans. Go prepared with questions about the layout of your city. Ask to see maps of the city and learn about how things are zoned. What is the comprehensive plan for the city's future? What projects are they currently working on? You might be surprised at how interesting it is to get inside the action of mapping.

ESSENTIAL

Part of the reason that people litter or pollute is that they don't realize that so much of the land is theirs. When people start claiming ownership of the land and this country, it will naturally lead to greater civic engagement and a more vibrant, successful democracy. Make your kids understand that this land is their land.

This Land Really Is Your Land

Do you own any land? Yes, you do! Did you know there are millions of acres of land in this country that belong to you? There are 600 million acres of federal land alone—that's one-third of our country! Then there's state land, like state parks and nature reserves and county and city land, such as parks and trails.

Visit a local nature reserve or state park. When was it first designated as public land? Was there one person or a group of people who donated it or fought to protect it? How is it maintained? Is the area suffering from any major environmental issues right now? What can you do to help? How many people visit this place each year? Is it home to any endangered species or unique geographic features? Park guides are very experienced tour guides and nature interpreters. They are accustomed to working with school groups and will provide a memorable day for your students. When you return to the classroom, have each student draw a picture of their favorite part of the field trip and write one amazing fact they learned. Also, choose one thing you can do to protect the land. After all, it is yours!

Human Health

The way people use the land is the way they build an environment around them. From cutting down trees that cleanse the air to constructing buildings, each of these decisions has an impact on human health.

FACT

According to the U.S. Environmental Protection Agency, more than 40 million tons of hazardous waste are generated in the United States every year. It comes from factories, chemical manufacturers, petroleum refineries, and even smaller businesses like gas stations and hospitals. How much is that every day? How can people reduce that amount?

Superfund Ain't So Super

The absolutely grossest, stinkiest, yuckiest, most toxic places in the country are known as Superfund sites, and there are more than 1,300 of them across the nation. They are typically left over from factories and army bases where tons of toxic muck has been unloaded into the soil and water. Some have been cleaned up and are considered land that is safe and usable. The U.S. Environmental Protection Agency and the Agency for Toxic Substances and Disease Registry are working together to help protect everyone from these hazards. Still, there are many sites that can cause health problems, from asthma to cancer. There are two very important things you can do right away to terminate toxic waste:

1. Visit *www.kidsforsavingearth.org* to learn easy pollution solutions through the "What Is a Toxic Waste Site?" program (choose the link from the drop-down list at "Air"). Encourage students to tell their parents not to buy toxic chemicals like pesticides and heavy-duty cleaners.
2. Visit *www.scorecard.org* and enter your Zip Code. You'll get a list of your community's worst polluters and the name and address of the head of the company. Have the kids write them a letter asking them to clean up their act.

Your voice matters and your actions add up. You are the leaders of the future and the future starts now!

Healthy Home Survey

Create a survey to send home to parents. Engage your students to help you decide on questions. Do you use pesticides on your lawn? What do you do with your toxic waste? If you are gardening, do you use pesticides? Do you recycle? After the parents have completed the survey, create a chart to demonstrate the results. Calculate the percentages, and as a group, write a letter that you can distribute to the parents. In the letter, also include suggestions about how to take healthier Earth-saving actions.

Take It Home

Homes are the most personal space of land ownership. Most people only think they own land if they own a house, but since everyone owns the public spaces around our states and communities, it's important to recognize the small steps we can take to understand our space and how to protect it.

Kid Cartography

A person who makes maps is called a cartographer. For this assignment, all of your students will be kid cartographers. First, there are two things every cartographer needs to know:

1. A map is a "bird's-eye" view, which means it's a picture of what a place looks like from the air.
2. Maps have legends—collections of symbols that represent different features of the map. They can be letters, numbers, colors, shapes, or symbols. The legend also includes a scale, which says how much space on the map (usually an inch) equals a mile in real life. It also includes a compass rose so people know which way north, south, east, and west are.

The first map your students should draw is a map of their neighborhood from memory. They'll need to make symbols for houses, other types of buildings, and any other prominent features that may be in their neighborhood. You can work together as a class to generate these symbols. Write them on the board so students can copy them onto their maps if they need them. As an example, draw your neighborhood on the board. These don't need to be exact; just be sure to capture any favorite places and major features like parks, rivers, and highways.

Have the kids imagine they are flying above their neighborhood in a helicopter. What would it look like? Where is their home? Do they regularly walk anywhere? Where and what is it? Put it on the map. Make sure to include a legend that explains any symbols used in the map and label the names of streets and natural features like lakes and rivers if you know them. The second part of this project is to take the map home and walk around the neighborhood. Is anything missing? Look for signs and write down the names of streets. Now look at the maps from an environmental perspective. How many parks, wetlands, or forests are there? Where does the wildlife live?

You can expand on this assignment by using a local street map to compare the children's maps. You can also use a mapping tool on the Internet to see how maps are different.

Rain Gardening

In any city, a rain garden can be very helpful to create a space for water to drain so it doesn't end up running off onto paved surfaces, into storm drains, and then into surrounding water bodies. This can save your local waterways from being polluted with all the chemicals and debris the rainwater would collect if it were allowed to go its own way. Rain gardens are built to have the water drain to them instead of natural waterways. Healthy soil and special plants are placed in the rain garden in order to filter and drain the water into the soil safely, naturally, and healthily. You can get started with instructions and printable guides at *www.raingardennetwork .com*. This site has basic instructions, but charges for regional details. If you don't want to pay for your regional specifications, contact your local Cooperative Extension office. You can find the contact info through the U.S. Department of Agriculture at *www.csrees.usda.gov*. Teach the children about rain gardens and their importance so they can go home and teach their parents.

If you want to be more involved, send information home and ask parents to volunteer to be a part of a rain garden club. Everyone who's interested can have his or her name placed in a hat. When a name is drawn, the whole group goes to that person's house to work together to build the rain garden. Many hands make light work. The more you do, the faster you'll all get at making a garden. Don't forget to get the kids involved! They love digging holes and planting flowers! Please remember that small residential rain gardens are fairly simple to make, but a larger garden like one for a school will need professional help and planning.

CHAPTER 10

Walking, Rolling, and Moving

If you use something other than the energy of your own legs to get somewhere, you are most likely creating pollution. Cars create a lot of air emissions; buses and trains do create pollution, but not as much. Whether you walk or bike, any type of transportation that is self-propelled is a totally Earth-friendly way of moving.

What It's All About

There are many ways to get around. Some methods create pollution and some do not. Walking, biking, and sailing are Earth-friendly ways to transport yourself, but you cannot always get by with these methods. How can we make the other ways more environmentally friendly?

Planes, Trains, Boats, and Automobiles

Cars, trucks, some trains, planes, and buses burn gasoline to make them go. When gasoline is burned, it releases exhaust that pollutes the air. In fact, vehicle emissions are the number-one source of air pollution. Vehicles cause land and water pollution when they leak oil, gas, brake fluid, engine coolant, and other chemicals. These vehicles also need roads to drive on and parking lots to park on. Building roads and parking lots means covering natural green spaces with concrete, which destroys natural habitats for bugs, birds, and animals. It also means using up other natural resources like gravel and oil. Noise pollution is another harmful by-product of these modes of transportation.

E FACT

More than 8 million miles of roadway crisscross the United States, taking up about 17,375 square miles of land—an area about the size of Maryland and Delaware combined. Using a large local map, cut a piece of paper scaled to the map that would represent 17,000 square miles. How much of your region would it cover?

Roads are necessary for getting around, but all that driving leads to a lot of roadkill. Roadkill is the number-one way that humans kill wildlife in the United States. According to the Defenders of Wildlife, more than 1 million animals are killed on the nation's roadways every single day.

Have your students design a small postcard to tape to a dashboard to remind drivers to slow down and look for wildlife. Not only will it prevent roadkill, but slowing down also increases gas mileage, which protects the planet and saves money! Put the kids in charge of keeping a watchful eye out for wildlife on the road while they are riding in the car.

Eco-Travel

Since people now know that transportation can be hard on the environment, they've begun to come up with new ways to travel. Hybrid cars run partially on gasoline and partially on electricity. Diesel cars are being turned into biodiesel cars, which means they run on plant oil instead of fossil fuel oil. Some people run their biodiesel cars on used vegetable oil from restaurants. There are even cars that run on solar power and water. These vehicles are still test cars, but they may be what most people drive in the near future.

For shorter distances, bicycles are the most efficient form of transportation. There are many types of new bikes that help make pedal power more feasible for everyday activities like getting to work and running errands. The Xtracycle, or sport utility bike, has an extended frame so there's room to haul things safely. From surfboards to furniture to kids, the SUB can haul almost anything. Electric bikes have small engines that help propel them. They are powered by small batteries and pedaling. A Twike seats two people side-by-side and is a three-wheeled cross between an electric car and a bike. The battery powers the car and the driver can assist by pedaling, which makes the battery last even longer.

All that pedaling can make you thirsty, so make sure you carry a water bottle with you! There are many reusable eco-friendly water bottles that will keep you hydrated without generating more trash for the landfills. You can choose from aluminum and plastic bottles in all different shapes, sizes, and colors.

Have your students invent their own Earth-friendly transportation. First, brainstorm all the different ways to get around. Some ideas to get you started include roller skates, cars, buses, trains, planes, all-terrain vehicles, helicopters, hot-air balloons, and rockets. How many can you come up with? Once you have your list, have the students create their own unique mode of transportation by drawing it on a large piece of paper. They should come up with what it would look like and also how their invention would be powered.

Global Picture

Everybody everywhere has places to go. You'll be amazed at the innovative methods people use to get around. Looking at the different ways people travel helps people better understand how to solve local transportation problems.

Transportation Around the World

Why do you think people might use different ways to get around? Do you think weather would make a difference? If you live someplace that's covered in snow a lot, which do you think you'd ride: a bike or a dogsled? If you lived in the desert, would you ride in a boat or on a camel? Here are some of the different ways people use to get around in foreign countries:

- **In Thailand,** people ride around in *tuk-tuks*, three-wheeled motorized vehicles with room for a driver in front and two to three passengers in back. The *samlor* is like the *tuk-tuk*, but it doesn't have a motor and is pedaled like a bicycle.
- **In Venice, Italy,** many roads are actually waterways. People ride in boats called gondolas, steered by a gondolier who stands at the back. Gondolas are like taxis, but they go on water instead of land. A larger boat that acts like a bus is called a *vaporetto*. These large boats hold many people and have certain routes and stops throughout the city.
- **In Southwestern Asia,** people use a horse-drawn carriage called a *tangah*. The carriage has two big wheels and is attached to the horse with two long bamboo poles.
- **In China,** transportation forms are changing rapidly. Some people still ride in rickshaws or velotaxis around the cities. A rickshaw is a two-wheeled carriage that seats one or two people and is pulled by one strong person. A velotaxi is similar but is like a large tricycle that moves by pedaling.

Use the Internet to learn about more forms of transportation around the world or check out the book *Transportation* from the *Around the World Series* by Margaret C. Hall. Have the students explore options and choose their favorite. They can draw a picture of themselves riding their favorite one and label it with the name of the vehicle and the country where it is primarily used.

Public Transportation

Most people use private transportation, like their own cars. Public transportation is when a larger vehicle has a set route and is open to everyone at a set cost. Public transportation is very useful in big cities, where thousands and even millions of people have to get around all day long. It benefits people who may not have the money to have their own car or simply don't want to have one. It also has a smaller environmental footprint per passenger because more people are using one vehicle. It lessens traffic jams by keeping cars off the road. Public transportation includes buses, trains, subways, trams, trolleys, and ferries.

Here are some more interesting public transportation systems from around the world:

- **Shanghai, China**, has one of the only operating magnetic levitation trains, or maglevs. It is a high-speed train that is suspended and guided along a track using magnetic forces instead of wheels. Maglevs can reach speeds nearing 600 miles per hour (similar to an airplane)! Countries all over the world are exploring opportunities to build their own maglevs.

- **Aerial tramways**, also known as cable cars, carry people high above the ground or water in small cabins attached to large cables suspended high in the air. Maybe you've seen small ones used at tourist sites, but there are also larger ones used for public transportation. The Vanoise Express cable car carries 200 people per cabin at a height of 1,250 feet over the Ponturin gorge in France. There is also the Roosevelt Island Tramway, which can carry up to 125 people and connects Roosevelt Island to Manhattan.

- **Personal rapid transit systems** are one of the most efficient and convenient forms of public transportation. They consist of small cars that can hold two to three people and run on elevated tracks through cities. They are completely computer controlled, so traffic jams are impossible. They run on electricity and there is no schedule or fixed route. Passengers select when and where they want to go and only need to go to a station where vehicles are waiting. These systems are currently in planning or construction phases in several locations in the United States, the United Kingdom, and the Middle East.

Explore your own local public transportation. The following activity outlines a train trek, but you could easily substitute a transit bus ride or trolley—whatever is available to you. How often do you see trains? Trains are a great environmental choice and their quality is continually improving.

In most parts of North America, kids don't have much exposure to trains. To appreciate the value and Earth-saving aspects of traveling by train, a short adventure from one end of town to the other and back would be an inspiring experience.

- Prepare for your trip by studying about the history of trains. You'll find an abundance of information about train history for kids online, including short quizzes.
- Check out your library for books about trains so students can draw pictures of their favorite type of train. Is it the engine, a coach, or a freight train carrying new automobiles? Cut them out and attach them to each other on a bulletin board in the classroom.
- Add a map-reading session to your preparation. Determine how many miles you are going to ride and then determine how many miles that would be if each family in the class drove that distance instead of riding on the train.
- Prepare train travel notebooks in advance for the kids to take notes about the trip. For example, they could list at least ten interesting things they saw while traveling on the train. Be sure to keep track of how long the trip takes and to find out how fast the train is traveling.

Again, even if you don't live by a train, adapt this project to any sort of public transportation. When you return to the classroom, have each student share the ten things they saw. Keep track on the board. Were there things that many students noticed? Were there things that only one or two students saw? Did they think riding on public transportation was more fun than a car?

For the Classroom

Park your students at their desks and get them buckled in to learn some basic driving education. Teaching them the concepts of eco-friendly driving should get them prompting their parents to be Earth-safe drivers, and maybe, just maybe, they'll remember these issues when they drive someday.

The Great Car Comparison

Gas mileage is a term used to describe how many miles a car can go on a single gallon of gas. Car manufacturers are trying to make cars that get better gas mileage, and people are looking for ways to increase gas mileage. Have each student find out from their parents what the make, model, and year of their car is. Using *www.fueleconomy.gov*, enter each car's information to find out gas mileage, greenhouse gas emissions, energy impact score, and air pollution ratings. Each child should draw a picture of their family's car and write the year, make, and model at the top. Designate a corner, and perhaps an icon, for each of the numbers you find from *www .fueleconomy.gov*. Have the children rank the cars. Which one will get the farthest on one gallon of gas? Which one releases the fewest greenhouse gases and air pollution? Which one has the smallest energy impact? Is it always the same car?

Travel Through Time

People have not always had cars, trains, and planes. In the United States, people first rode horses or walked long distances. How has transportation developed since then? Can you make a timeline showing the progress of travel? When were bicycles invented? When was the car invented? How about the motorcycle? Look up trains, planes, submarines, and any other type of transportation your students are interested in. Assign one method of transportation to each student. Ask them to write a report and to present their information to the class. Their report should include information about the type of fuel used and the environmental efficiency of the method of transportation. Place a timeline on the bulletin board and give each student a bar-shaped piece of paper to write the name of the transportation form and the approximate date it was invented. As each student gives a report, ask them to help you pin the bar on the timeline.

School Projects

Whether it's school buses, parents dropping off kids, staff driving to work, or delivery drivers dropping off supplies, there is almost always a constant stream of traffic to and from schools. Here are some ways your school can help ensure that all that transportation is as Earth-friendly as possible.

No Idling, Please

School buses, supply trucks, and even cars often sit idling near schools. Not only is it noisy, it releases unnecessary pollution into the air, wastes fuel, and causes wear and tear on the engine. If children are outside or if there is an air-intake vent or window located near the idling vehicle, kids will end up breathing the exhaust. Diesel exhaust contains particulate matter that can aggravate lungs and trigger asthma attacks. The U.S. Environmental Protection Agency has also determined that diesel exhaust is a probable human carcinogen.

ALERT!

Children's lungs should not be blown off! Since kids are more susceptible to air pollution, it is up to you to keep them from breathing in potentially noxious gases if your school does not have a no-idling policy. Protect students' lungs by not letting them play or line up by idling school vehicles and by closing windows or doors when vehicles are idling nearby.

Make a no-idling policy at your school to protect children's health, prevent pollution, and save money. You can find all of the tools you need to successfully implement a program by visiting the U.S. Environmental Protection Agency Clean School Bus program website at *www.epa.gov /cleanschoolbus/antiidling.htm*. You can find a prewritten press release, fact sheets, tips for teachers and staff, certificates, posters, case studies, and more. While it's great that it's all packaged and ready to go, empower your students to enforce the policy (and encourage other adults) by having them design the campaign posters and materials.

SOURCE

It All Adds Up to Cleaner Air is a program of the U.S. Department of Transportation that has dozens of ideas for helping people drive smarter and cleaner. There are materials you can use for handouts, as well as resources for conducting community-wide campaigns. Visit *www.italladdsup.gov* for more information.

School Car-nival

Most schools host an annual school carnival to raise funds and get the community together. How about adding in a little environmental transportation education for all of the adults who drive to it? Have every parent who participates get a number that's entered into a drawing for a prize. Find a local car repair business to donate a free tune-up as a prize. Set up several simple ways to improve car efficiency and reduce pollution. Some examples:

- Have an air compressor and fill tires.
- Contact your local department of transportation to test gas caps for cracks or leaks. Ask a local vendor to donate or discount replacement gas caps for those who need them. Leaking gas caps release 200 pounds of emissions and thirty gallons of gas per car each year.
- Ask a local vendor to donate window shades. The cooler a car stays, the less air-conditioning it needs and the less pollution it creates.
- Ask parents who own the latest environmentally friendly cars or trucks to bring them to show off at a green car show section of the car-nival

You can also share materials you may have created in class about not idling and driving slower to look out for wildlife. Get creative, make it fun, and you'll make a big difference in the community as you help influence drivers to take care of their cars so they create less pollution!

Field Trips

People are constantly in motion, and wherever you go you'll be surrounded by a variety of vehicles. Take notice of transportation and start thinking what could be changed in order to better protect the planet.

Can You Keep Count?

There are a lot of cars, trucks, buses, and other vehicles on the road every day. How many and where are they in your community? For this field trip, you will either need to split the class up into small groups and have volunteers take them to different locations, or else have a way to get all of the students to several locations in one day. Choose several locations you know will have different levels and types of traffic. Some transportation-viewing spots include next to the school, near a shopping mall, near a major intersection, and out in the country.

ESSENTIAL

> For any location that has heavy traffic, try to find a place indoors away from the exhaust where the children can watch the road. For instance, you can watch the road from the skywalk in the mall. This will help you keep kids safe from harmful exhaust and any flying debris the vehicles may kick up.

Assign children different categories of vehicles to count. Some can just count cars; some can count buses; some can count trucks or construction vehicles. Set a time limit; usually about fifteen minutes is as long as you can keep them interested. Reconvene in the classroom with your data sets and create a simple map of the locations you measured.

How many of each type of vehicle were counted at each location? For the areas with heavy traffic, are there places that children learn or play nearby? How can you prevent exposure to the exhaust? If it's a building, you could close windows when traffic is heavy. If it's a park, you can choose to go there when the streets aren't so busy. Did you see any trains? If so, how many people do you think they are carrying? Did you see any tugboats or barges? What were they carrying? How many trucks do barges take off the roads?

Walk and Run

Take a two-mile loop though the school neighborhood. Before you head out, check the mileage in your car. Mark the one-mile point. Head out with the kids; at times, run for a short distance and discuss how much more energy it takes to run fast. Explain that cars are the same. The faster the car goes, the more energy they use.

It's great to get kids to bike more, but you want them to bike safely. Contact your local bicycle patrol police or a local bike shop to organize a Bike Rodeo. At Bike Rodeos, kids have their bikes tuned up, learn helmet and biking safety, and play fun games for prizes. Make a Bike Rodeo an annual event at your school.

Human Health

Since vehicles are a major source of outdoor air pollution and a major contributor to global warming, it's imperative that people find transportation methods that are better for human health and the environment.

It's Cool to Walk (or Bike) to School

Walking and biking are great ways to travel that don't create any pollution and are also better for your body. National Walk-to-School Day is celebrated in October to kick off the school year. It helps kids figure out how to walk or bike to school and promotes safe routes to continue these activities throughout the year. You can visit *www.walktoschool.org* to find events in your area, register your own event, and download promotional and educational materials for hosting an event. You'll also find information about the national Safe Routes to School program, which helps schools implement comprehensive plans to help kids walk and bike to school safely year-round.

Biking and walking are extremely beneficial to children's health, and the overall community benefits from decreased traffic congestion and better air quality. Because of this, the federal government offers funds to states and communities to start programs that promote these activities. Get started transforming your community today!

Take It Home

Drive the environmental issues surrounding transportation home with these easy projects. Fortunately for parents, when it comes to greening how they get about town, it also means more green in their wallets.

Hypermile

Every little step counts, especially when it comes to driving. Send tips home to parents and ask them to gauge their exact gas mileage before they try some of the following tips. Then, have them report back after two weeks of following the steps. To get their car's exact gas mileage, they should check the odometer before filling their car with gas. The next time they fill the car they should write down the new reading on the odometer to find out how many miles they have gone since the last time they gassed up. Then they should divide that number by the number of gallons of gas they put in their car the second time. This will tell them exactly how many miles they are currently getting per gallon of gas.

Have them try some of the tips from the following list of tips to get better gas mileage:

- Go easy on the pedals by easing into acceleration and stops.
- Avoid idling by turning off the engine whenever you know you'll be sitting for more than thirty seconds. It's harder on your car's engine to idle than to stop and start again.
- Dress warmer and reduce your car's warm-up time in the winter.
- Keep your trunk as empty as possible because extra weight decreases gas mileage.
- Slow down. Gas mileage increases about 15 percent when you drive 55 miles per hour rather than 65 miles per hour.
- Open windows or air vents instead of using the air conditioning.
- Keep tires properly inflated.
- Get regular tune-ups.

Ask parents which steps they took and if their gas mileage increased. If it did, hooray for them! Well done! If it didn't, it may mean that two weeks just wasn't enough time to see a difference. Encourage them to keep trying and report back later in the year if they'd like.

No one likes to be told what to do and no one likes to feel as if they are being judged. When you send eco-assignments home, be sure to discuss the issues in a light and friendly way. Always be encouraging about every small act and be sure to talk about how it directly benefits them. Emphasize activities that save money and protect their family's health.

Eco-Travel Challenge

Get your students' families involved in reducing pollution by choosing Earth-friendly transportation. You can set up the challenge to last one month, the entire school year, or anything in between. Have the students brainstorm all the different ways to eco-travel. This can include walking, biking, riding public transportation, and carpooling. It should not include options such as driving a hybrid because not all families have access to one. Make up a symbol for each of the eco-friendly methods of moving. Make a chart that has each child's name and rows of boxes for the dates your challenge will cover.

Send home a notice saying you will be having a class Eco-Travel Challenge and you would like the families to try to choose Earth-friendly options as much as they can for the duration of the challenge. Any time they choose an eco-friendly mode of transportation instead of driving, the student gets to mark it on the chart using the appropriate symbol. Don't let them know until the end, but everyone who tries at least once is a winner. Every little bit helps, and being supportive of all efforts will hopefully promote more efforts in the future. Make awards to send home with the students.

CHAPTER 11

Power to the People

People can turn their electricity on and off with the flick of a switch. It's used for heating, cooling, cooking, lighting, and powering all of the gadgets of modern society. Schools, homes, cars, roads, toys, food, and clothing all require energy. Energy is as much a part of everyday life as water and air, but where does it come from? How does it impact the environment? How can people create it and use it more responsibly?

What It's All About

Energy is invisible, but you can see all of the wonderful things energy makes possible. From making your body move to powering computers, energy is life!

Energy, Energy, Everywhere

Sources of energy are all around us. In fact, almost everything has hidden energy potential, and the different forms of energy serve different purposes. Energy for a person is different than energy for an automobile. Can you think of some sources of energy? Here are some examples:

- The light from the sun is pure energy, and many other sources of energy originally got their energy from the sun. For example, plants turn sunlight into leaves, flowers, and fruits. Animals eat the plants, changing the energy in the leaves and fruits into body mass. When animals die, they decompose; after a very, very long time, their energy turns into oil, coal, or natural gas. That's why these sources of energy are called fossil fuels. Sunlight is also used to charge solar cells. These panels are like batteries that are charged by sunlight.
- Food gets its energy from the sun, but then people eat it to get their own energy. Food is digested and then the energy in it is used to make the heart beat and the blood pump, which keeps the whole body working.
- Where does wood come from? It comes from trees, which are big plants that have absorbed energy from the sun. When wood is burned, it releases its energy as heat.
- Coal, oil, and natural gas are the most common sources of energy. All of them are burned to create heat, electricity, or fuel for vehicles. But they take thousands of years to create. People are using them much faster than they can naturally form. Consequently, they are limited in supply and are running out. These fuels can also be hard to find or mine, and they cause a lot of pollution.
- Water is used to create energy. The flow of water is used to push turbines that create electricity. This is called hydroelectric power.
- Wind can be used to turn windmills, which generate electricity.

- Nuclear power comes from a radioactive ore called uranium. Radioactive materials store more energy than any other source, but radioactive waste is extremely dangerous. Exposure to radioactive materials can result in mutations, illness, or even death.
- Garbage can be burned at waste-to-energy facilities. The fire warms pipes of water, which create steam to generate electricity.
- Chemical reactions can create energy. For example, batteries create energy through chemical reactions, but after a while the reactions stop and the battery dies.

Since people are using energy all the time, it easily goes unnoticed. Try to get your students thinking about when they use energy. Even when you are done with your energy unit, you may want to sprinkle in energy awareness and energy conservation tips throughout the year.

Almost everything has energy or can be used to help create it. It's just hard to get the energy out and put it to work. Explore energy sources even more by making a potato battery. You will need:

- One low-voltage LED clock
- Two zinc-coated galvanized nails
- One large potato, halved
- Two short pieces of copper wire or two pennies
- Three long pieces of insulated copper wire

Here is how you generate power from the potato:

1. Remove the battery from the clock.
2. Poke a nail into each half of the potato.
3. Poke a piece of copper wire (or penny) into each potato. The wire and nail should not touch.
4. Use a long piece of wire to connect the copper wire of one potato to the positive (+) terminal of the clock's battery compartment.

5. Use another wire to connect the nail in the other potato to the negative (–) terminal in the clock's battery compartment.

6. Use the third wire to connect the nail in one potato to the copper wire in the other potato.

Voilà! Set your clock. Try the experiment with other foods like lemons or pickles. Can you light a light bulb? What else could you try to power?

The kind of energy the human body runs on is called caloric energy. How many calories a day do you need to be healthy? Can you find where calories are listed on food packaging? Can you keep track for one day and see if you are eating too much or too little?

Energy Alphabet

Depending on the grade level you teach, you may already have a science unit on energy as a part of your annual curriculum. If so, try to integrate concepts of energy conservation and renewable energy into your existing curriculum. If not, try this crash course in energy. Select several books about energy to read with your class. Some fun options include *Charlie Brown's Encyclopedia of Energy* by Charles Schulz, Dorling Kindersley's *Eyewitness Books: Electricity*, Dorling Kindersley's *Eyewitness Books: Energy*, *Why Should I Save Energy* by Jen Green and Mike Gordon, and *Energy and Power* by Rosie Harlow and Sally Morgan.

Have your students write an ABC book that can be shared with other classes and kept in your school library. First, have the class brainstorm energy-related words or concepts for each letter of the alphabet. For example, *A* is for alternative energy, *B* is for battery, *C* is for circuit. You may need to provide examples for some of the harder letters. *Q* could be for quit wasting energy, and *Z* could be for zap. Assign one page for each student. They should first draft the text and show it to you for editing. Each page should include the letter and what it stands for, as well as an explanation of the word or concept. Once you have approved what they have written, they can write it on their page along with a colorful drawing illustrating the word or concept.

Global Picture

Between 1850 and 1970, the number of people living on Earth more than tripled, and energy use increased twelvefold. All over the world, people are plugged in. With population growth and increasing ways to use energy, people are really straining the Earth's resources.

> When teaching young children about energy, be sure to remind them about the dangers of electrical outlets and exposed wiring. They should never touch anything electrical without adult supervision.

The End of the Age of Oil

Oil is the world's number-one source of commercial energy. It powers almost all machines that move. But oil is a fossil fuel and it will run out. People have to find new sources of energy, as well as learn to better conserve energy. Consider these facts:

- The United States consumes 25 percent of the world's oil, and 70 percent of that is imported.
- Over the years Americans have driven larger and less fuel-efficient cars and bought bigger homes with more appliances. As a result, U.S. oil use increased in the last decade by nearly 2.7 million barrels a day—more oil than is used daily in India and Pakistan combined, which together contain more than four times as many people as the United States does. Recently, that trend has slowed due to the lack of and the expense of oil.
- In the early 2000s the average American consumed five times more energy than the average global citizen, ten times more than the average Chinese, and nearly twenty times more than the average Indian. If the average Chinese person used as much oil as the average American uses, China would require 90 million barrels per day—that's 11 million more than the entire world produced each day in 2001.

It is a very similar story for coal, the number-one global source of electricity. What's the world to do when the oil and coal run out? Assign small groups of students to explore alternative fuels and ideas that countries around the globe are creating to address the end of fossil fuels. For example, the European Union is talking about using a small section of the Sahara Desert for a solar field. It is an intensely sunny place with such vast unused space, so it is an ideal spot to harness solar energy. Supporters of the plan believe the Saharan solar panels could harness enough solar energy to power all of Europe! Almost all of Iceland's energy comes from geothermal power and hydroelectricity. How do they get so much power from these renewable sources?

According to the U.S. Department of Transportation, Americans drove 1.4 billion fewer highway miles in April 2008 than they did in April 2007. Discuss why this happened. Is it because more people are trying to reduce exhaust emissions? Is it because oil prices went up? How much does a gallon of gas cost you now compared to one year ago?

A Wave of Energy

Oceans cover three-quarters of the Earth's surface. There is tremendous energy in ocean waves. Waves are caused by the wind blowing over the surface of the ocean. There are methods for harnessing the action of waves to generate energy production. Small, onshore wave-energy sites can produce enough energy to power local communities. Japan and Scotland have active wave-energy programs.

Demonstrate the power of waves by using a large pan of water and an electric fan. What do your students think will happen to the water after you turn on the fan? Can you make things move in the water because of the movement of the water (not because of the wind)? Try objects that lie flat on the top of the water, such as small pieces of wood or cardboard. Can you predict what will happen?

For the Classroom

Do you leave your computer on all day at your desk? Do you keep the lights on even when there's plenty of sunshine to brighten your classroom? How many things are plugged in? Do they have to be all the time? Start thinking of energy use in your classroom and the habits will naturally spill over into the rest of the school and students' homes.

Energy Hogs

What would your day be like without energy? Have a discussion about how many things you use each day that require energy. Energy is very important, but it's even more important to not be an energy hog. Energy hogs use old, inefficient appliances and leave electronics on. They don't fix energy leaks in their buildings. The energy hog challenge is a fun approach to energy conservation and your students will love it. It is a set of classroom activities that includes lessons about sources of energy, energy use, and energy conservation. Each student can become an official energy hog buster upon completion of the lessons. The energy hog website (*www .energyhog.org*) has online games for children, printable classroom activities and guides for teachers, and even a portal for parents.

As an extension on the project, have your students draw pictures of energy-hogging appliances and then add a hog face, legs, and tail. Then they can write something like "energy hogs waste energy and money." You could also make a hog face, legs, and tail that could be taped to actual appliances.

Energy Audit

Do a classroom audit to find all the ways you use energy. Then identify ways to reduce your use. You can do the audit as a group, have all the students do their own audit, or assign separate areas to small groups. Here is what you'll be looking for:

- **Lighting.** How many lights are there? How many light bulbs do they use? What is the wattage of each bulb? What type of light bulb are they? How long are the lights on each day?
- **Energy "vampires."** Appliances and electronics can suck energy even when they are not being used, which is why they are sometimes called energy vampires. Vanquish your vampires by unplugging things when they are not in use or plugging them into a power strip and then turning off the power when you aren't using them. For this part of the audit, write down all the different electronics and

appliances, estimate how much they are used, and look at whether they are left on, put into sleep mode, turned off, or unplugged. If you can, find the wattage of the appliance or electronic either by looking on the backside or looking it up online.

- **Heating.** Measuring how much heat you use just in your classroom is near to impossible. Instead, record what type of fuel is used to generate your heat, the number of windows in your classroom, the number of doors, and the location of any drafts. You can look for drafts by holding a wispy peacock feather or other light, flexible material that would be easily moved by the slightest air movement, near window and door frames. Also, does the classroom have a controllable thermostat? If so, at what temperature is it set?

After you've conducted your audit, have the class brainstorm ideas for how to reduce your energy use. For example, closing and opening windows or doors can help moderate your room temperature so you don't have to rely on the HVAC system so much. You could also turn out the lights, or at least a section of the lights, when the sun is shining bright enough to light the room. Make sure you unplug your vampires at the end of each day. What else can your students think of?

School Projects

Schools spend more money on energy than on textbooks and computers combined. Implementing effective conservation programs can lead to reductions of as much as 25 percent in utility bills. In addition to saving your school money, you'll also be providing a unique opportunity to create a new generation of energy-smart citizens.

You can empower kids by giving them responsibility. Rotate the responsibility of watching for ways to reduce energy use by designating a different student each week to make sure unused electronics are unplugged and that lights are turned off when they are unnecessary.

Lights Out!

Design a Lights Out campaign with your students. In essence, you want to remind everyone in the school to turn out lights any time they leave a room or when there's enough sunshine to light up a space. Every little bit counts.

First, find out from your facilities manager how much electricity your school uses each month. Then you can check again when your campaign is in full swing to see if you're having an impact. Next, make clever signs that can be posted by light switches. Finally, devise a way to reprimand and reward people and put the students in charge of watching for people who have forgotten to turn off lights and people who remember.

For older students, you can make this about more than just lights. Spearhead a comprehensive energy conservation program at your school. Invite someone from your local utility company to visit the school and do a comprehensive audit with your students. Identify the ways in which your school could quickly and easily make changes to conserve energy. The best way to conduct a broader conservation program in your school is to make it a schoolwide effort. Teachers, students, facility staff, and administrators should all play a role. Try to convince your school district to reward a percentage of the savings back to the school—providing an added incentive for everyone to do their best to save energy.

VendingMiser

Vending machines are often overlooked, but they are among the most insidious energy vampires. The VendingMiser is the answer to the silent suckers. By installing a VendingMiser, each vending machine will use about half the energy. You can also install them on coolers and other snack machines. Learn more by going to *www.usatech.com* and clicking on "EnergyMisers."

Either encourage your school to find it in their budget to buy Misers (they generally pay for themselves in the money you save in one year), or host a fundraiser to buy them. You could have families or classrooms adopt vending machines to get them Misers and save energy to protect the planet! Don't forget to make signs that talk about the Misers and how much energy you're saving so everyone who uses the machines can learn from your efforts.

Field Trips

With energy all around us, making a field trip is almost as easy as stepping out your front door.

SOURCE

Watt Watchers *(www.wattwatchers.org)* is a Texas state program that has resources for schools to start energy conservation efforts. They have clever posters and "tickets" for students to give to teachers who forget to turn their lights off. The materials can be used in any school across the country and can also serve as a model for developing your own program.

Go to Your Source

Where does the power for your school come from? Major power generators are often located far from the places they power, but if you are close to your facility, call and set up a tour. If you are far away, at least discuss with your students what type of energy your school uses. Is it nuclear? Is it from burning coal? Look on a map and see how far it has to travel to get to you. Then try to find a local source of energy that might provide smaller amounts of electricity to your community. Is there a dam? Maybe a public building that has solar panels?

Energy for the Future

Research your community to find out if there are any alternative fuel sites like wind farms or solar fields. You can also try to find a local organization or college that is researching new energy sources like biofuels. Generally, people who are creating or inventing the energy of the future are extremely passionate about their work and will welcome the opportunity to talk to your students about it. If you're having a hard time finding someone, contact a local environmental organization that works on energy issues.

Human Health

Using electricity may seem like it doesn't have a health impact, but creating energy often also creates pollution. Just as with any other type of pollution, it eventually ends up impacting human health. Most energy currently comes from fossil fuels, which create a lot of pollution. People need to look for new energy sources because fossil fuels are running out, but also because it's important to reduce pollution.

Pollution from Power

In the United States there are more than 400 coal-fired power plants, and they emit more toxins into the air than any other single source—about 42 percent of all U.S. toxins; according to the 2002 U.S. Environmental Protection Agency Toxic Release Inventory. In addition, half of all Americans live within thirty miles of a coal-burning power plant. Coal-burning power plants release huge amounts of mercury (which is toxic to brain development), as well as more than 361,000 tons of other toxins, including vanadium, barium, zinc, lead, chromium, arsenic, nickel, hydrogen fluoride, hydrochloric acid, ammonia, and selenium.

Divide your students into small groups to research the potential health impacts of each of these toxins. One of the most informative websites for learning about toxins is the Agency for Toxic Substances and Disease Registry's ToxFAQs at *www.atsdr.cdc.gov/toxfaq.html*. Have your students explore their toxin using this site and any others they find. They should compile basic information about what the toxin is and the potential health impacts. When they are done studying it, they should prepare a presentation for the class. How do they feel after learning about these pollutants created from burning coal? What does it make them think about finding cleaner energy sources? What about more ways to conserve energy and reduce pollution?

Learning about toxic pollutants is always overwhelming. Remember to remind your students that everyone can create change and even small ones count. Every time they turn out a light or unplug electronics, they are a part of the solution. They are helping protect the planet by reducing pollution.

Take It Home

There are more and more people living on this planet every day, and each new person will cause an increase in the use of energy. With energy prices starting to increase, people are just beginning to reduce their use, but there is still a long way to go in order to be responsible energy users.

Personal Power

How much energy are students' families using? Take a close look by having students conduct an audit in their homes. Have younger children write the words or draw pictures of all the things around their homes that use electricity. Have older students conduct an audit with their parents' help, to assess how many appliances and electronics they have and how much they use them. Using the survey at *www.ase.org/uploaded_files/educatorlessonplans/howmuch.pdf*, you can also determine an estimate of how much it costs to use all of the energy. How does it compare to an actual utility bill? Are there any energy hogs or vampires sitting around? Ask the families to commit to taking at least one step to reduce their energy consumption. You can have them take the Green Ribbon Pledge at *www.greenribbonpledge.org/pledge/index.html*. The pledge will help them identify a specific action and calculate how much of a savings they will see. Their pledge will be added in to the entire campaign's pledge and you can see how much energy is being saved overall. The numbers add up fast, showing every little bit helps!

Drafts Are Daft

One way people waste energy is through drafty homes and poorly insulated walls. While you can't ask people to invest in insulation, you can show them where energy might be slipping away through a simple draft test. A side benefit to this project is that it will help keep out rodents and insects.

First, make a draft tester by taping a small sheet of used (cleaned) plastic wrap to a pencil. It should be affixed so that when the pencil is held near a draft, the plastic wrap will move from the airflow.

Next, check locations around the house that could be drafty and rate each location as a three (strong draft), two (moderate draft), one (weak draft), or zero (no draft). Here are the most common locations for drafts:

- Windows
- Exhaust fans in bathrooms and kitchens that vent outside
- Dampers in fireplaces and woodstoves
- Exterior doors
- Light fixtures attached to exterior walls
- Window air conditioners
- Mail chutes or slots in walls or doors
- Cracks in the foundation in basements or exterior walls
- Holes where pipes come into the house
- Where your clothes dryer vents
- Where porches and steps meet the house

What did the students find? Are their houses drafty or pretty well sealed? For many of the leaks, parents can simply caulk the area to plug the cracks. You can also have the kids make draft guards from fabric and rice. They are essentially long snakes that sit at the base of doorways or windows to block drafts. You can presew the cloth tubes and leave one end open or use old tights or even children's pant legs as material for the snakes. Fill each snake with about 2 pounds of rice. Have the students fill the snakes outdoors because the rice will end up all over the place. Use fabric glue or fusible webbing to close the end after the snake is filled. You can even turn them into "real" critters by having the students glue or paint on eyes and faces.

CHAPTER 12

Things Are Warming Up: Curbing Climate Change

You've read it in the headlines and heard it on the news, but what can you do? And, more importantly, what can kids do? It's been called the most pressing issue of all time and some predict dire ecological collapse unless we act immediately. The issue of climate change can be daunting. The key is to keep it simple and find the smallest acts that create the biggest impacts.

What It's All About

Climate change, also known as global warming, means the whole world is warming up. The planet regularly goes through periods of warmth and cold, but this time things are heating up too fast. Scientists who have been studying it for a long time have determined that it's not a natural warming like in the past. People are making the world warmer, but how and what does it mean?

We Live in a Big Greenhouse

If you've ever been to a greenhouse, maybe you remember how warm it was inside. That's because the seedlings and plants need a stable, warm environment to grow. The greenhouse keeps the plants protected from the weather and makes sure the temperature doesn't get too cold. The Earth lives in a greenhouse, too, but you can't see it. It's called the atmosphere, and it protects the Earth from the cold, harsh environment in outer space while still letting in heat from the sun to keep us warm and letting out any extra heat we don't need.

SOURCE

Hippo Works *(www.hippoworks.com)* makes funny, short cartoons about a variety of environmental issues, including a series on global warming. Episode 4 is about methane gas and has an especially catchy tune called "The Power of Poop." It injects laughter into a very serious subject.

The atmosphere is made up of gases. Extra gases are created from things like exhaust from cars and pollution from smokestacks. These extra gases are making the greenhouse stronger; while that may sound good, it's not. A stronger greenhouse means the extra heat from the sun gets trapped in our greenhouse.

You can see how this works by taking two jars and putting a teaspoon of water into each. Put a lid on just one jar, and place them both in a sunny spot. Wait a few hours and see what happens. The open jar won't change, but the closed jar will be steamy inside. Why? Just like the greenhouse effect in our atmosphere, heat from the sun could not get out of the closed jar.

FACT

The United States, European countries, Japan, and China emit the largest amounts of greenhouse gases. It's unfair, but the places releasing the least amounts, like Africa and South America, are where people are suffering the most from the impacts of climate change. Droughts are making lakes and rivers dry up, and it's becoming difficult to grow crops for food.

What a Difference a Couple of Degrees Makes

You might be wondering what the big deal is. Why does it matter if the Earth gets a little warmer? Well, each thing in nature depends on each other. When the Earth heats up, the natural balance is upset and things can go wrong. For example, global warming is slowly melting the ice at the poles. What happens when ice melts? It turns into water and makes the ocean levels rise all over the world. People who live near the ocean will have to move inland as the water creeps up. You can see how this happens by placing a bowl upside down in the middle of a cake pan. Pour in some water to create an "island." Place a small glob of clay near the water's edge; it can represent a house or a city. Now slowly pour in more water to simulate the melting polar ice caps and watch as the water level goes up and the clay ends up in the water. Dropping ice cubes into the bowl and waiting for them to melt takes longer, but it illustrates the point even more clearly.

Scientists also believe global warming is making the weather change. There are more heat waves. There are more severe storms and droughts. There is more lightning, which can spark forest fires. None of this is good for people or the plants and animals of the Earth.

Global Picture

People have it pretty good here in North America, but what Americans do here is impacting other people all over the world. The United States releases more greenhouse gases per person than any other country, and those gases don't just stay above the United States and cause global warming here; it creates global warming for everyone.

Global Warming Around the Globe

It's important to understand that global warming impacts everyone, everywhere, in many different ways. Glaciers around the world are shrinking. You can find before and after pictures online or refer to Al Gore's book *An Inconvenient Truth* for some striking images of how places used to look and how they look now. While the corresponding movie is certainly overwhelming for a child, the book offers some compelling images of how things are changing around the world. For instance, there are pictures of lakes and rivers that have dried up and images of flooding. In addition, for older children, there are charts and graphs with statistical data of the changes over time.

ESSENTIAL

Try to get your students thinking about emissions at every opportunity. How did they get to school? Bus? Car? Bicycle? When are you using electricity or heating or air conditioning? Listen for when the HVAC system kicks in. Much of being a good steward of the planet is getting into the habit of always thinking about it.

Who's Making Gas?

Greenhouse gases are released from burning gasoline for fuel for our cars and other vehicles, from burning coal for electricity for our homes, and from the burps of cattle, pigs, and chickens. You can do a quick comparison of who's creating the most gases by comparing pictures of different places around the world. For instance, by looking at a picture of a big city like New York City or Tokyo, you can see streets filled with cars and lights and signs that need electricity all the time. In the picture of Tokyo, you may see many more people riding bicycles, which don't release greenhouse gases. Compare these images with some from a village in Africa or South America.

You'll probably have a hard time finding any sources of greenhouse gases in these images other than small fires that people may use for cooking food.

In the same vein, you can have children go through old magazines and find pictures of air pollution. Make a collage of the images they find. Make another one showing clean air images.

For the Classroom

It's easy to bring this big issue into your small classroom when you consider how many small actions have led to this problem. Get creative about not only teaching the concepts but walking the talk. Do whatever you can to reduce your classroom's carbon footprint.

Climate Versus Weather

Climate is how warm or cold or wet or dry a place normally is over a long period of time. You can talk about climate by discussing the typical seasons in the place where you live. What is summer usually like? What is it like in the winter? Weather, on the other hand, is what happens every day. It is fickle and can change unexpectedly. You may not know what the weather will be, but you know what the seasons typically bring.

Plants, bugs, birds, and animals are used to dealing with whatever weather and climate they live in. They've grown and lived through it for thousands of years. If the climate is changed, they may not be able to live in it anymore. Think of putting a cactus in the rain forest or moving a polar bear to the desert. They wouldn't be used to the climate and wouldn't be able to find the right kind of food to eat or homes to raise their babies. It's easier for people because we can change from jeans into shorts if it gets a bit warmer or go inside and turn on a fan, but the plants, bugs, birds, and animals can't do this.

To demonstrate this on a smaller scale, take two identical small plants and place thermometers in the pots. Place a glass bowl or a small greenhouse over one. The one that has the greenhouse should be placed in a sunny spot or near a heating vent. The other plant should be placed in a location that is appropriate for it to thrive. Read the thermometer in each pot regularly so you can see how much warmer the "climate" is for one compared to the other. Over time, watch the growth (or lack of growth) and discuss how the climate is impacting the plant.

ALERT!

There are a lot of tough words in this book. It's more memorable and a better learning opportunity if students are in charge of defining new concepts. Encourage them to raise their hands when they hear a word they don't know and then have them look it up and read the definition aloud.

Another variation is to use two different plants like a cactus plant and another typical houseplant. Read the directions for the cactus and do what is expected. Read the directions for the other houseplant and do the opposite of what is expected. Don't water it and don't give it the sunlight it needs. See how long it lasts.

What's Your Climate and How Has It Changed

Everyone loves talking (and complaining) about the weather. For a week or a month or even the whole school year, you can chart the weather for each day on your classroom calendar. The most important thing to watch is daily temperature; older students can also chart precipitation.

Look at a comparison over time by researching historical averages. Go online and search "historical temperature averages" for your city. How warm was the average for this time of year five years ago? Twenty years ago? Fifty years ago? Likewise, you can compare precipitation averages over time. Is it getting wetter? Drier? You can also chart storms and extreme weather like tornadoes. Are there more than there used to be?

School Projects

Schools release a large amount of greenhouse gases through the energy they use just to keep the building working the way it should. Add in the gases that are created just to get everything—from the students to the lunches— onto the premises, and you've got a lot of potential to cut back on these emissions. Some of them, such as how to cut overall energy use, are covered in other chapters, but here are some more concrete ideas for tackling global warming as a school.

SOURCE

Get your classroom a copy of *The Down-to-Earth Guide to Global Warming* by Laurie David and Cambria Gordon. It is a comprehensive resource for ages eight and up that clearly describes the science and has ideas for how we can work together to stop it. It's informative, inspiring, and has enough great photos to keep any young reader engaged.

Design an Awareness Campaign

It's wonderful to let kids use their own creativity to develop awareness campaigns. They can design posters that offer tips for reducing greenhouse gas emissions that they can hang on your school's walls. They can offer ideas to school boards and other school officials for reducing emissions. You can also work with your students to assess your school's carbon footprint. Do an online search for "school carbon footprint," and you'll find a variety of resources to walk you through the process. For the best experience, start the effort in the fall or winter and reassess in the spring or summer. It takes people time to make changes, and it motivates students when they see they've made a difference.

Classroom Contests

School carbon-footprint calculators let you look at how much your school's greenhouse gas emissions are, and individual carbon-footprint calculators do exactly the same thing. Have each student do an assessment of his or her home and then aggregate the results for the whole class. Have a contest with other classrooms to see which one can bring their overall footprint down over a given period of time. The natural spirit of competition can create enormous changes (and it's a great way to get the kids to bring the issue home).

Field Trips

Exploring climate change out in the world is no easy task. It's not something that's readily apparent like pollution or recycling. The key is to draw every experience back into the global picture of what people are doing to the planet that creates climate change and highlight how things will change if people do nothing.

Since so many of the school projects in this book can play into reducing your greenhouse gas emissions, take the opportunity to tie the pieces together. It's always encouraging to learn that your actions impact a variety of things. Our world is all about interconnections. The more you can emphasize that, the better.

Gobble Up Greenhouse Gases

Trees absorb carbon dioxide, one of the main greenhouse gases. Planting trees is one of the cheapest and most effective ways to reduce the amount of greenhouse gases in the atmosphere. Take a walk around your schoolyard and determine how many mature trees you have. Multiply them by fifty to determine how many pounds of carbon dioxide you are taking out of the air. Then decide how many more trees you can plant and where they should be planted. Do some fundraising to earn money to buy trees or ask your local garden store to donate a few trees. Invite parents and have a planning party.

The Zoo as a Global Picture

Zoos are an amazing collection of species from all over the world. To prepare for a field trip to the zoo that focuses on the impacts of global warming, research some of the species you will see. Do some of the animals come from an area where their natural habitat is threatened by global warming? How? One of the clearest examples is the polar bear. With ice flows melting, they have no landing pads for catching fish.

Zoos also offer an opportunity to examine the different climates and ecological systems that are necessary to support various animals. Look at the vegetation. Discuss which animals must have controlled indoor climates compared to those that can live in the climate you live in. What would happen if you moved a lion into a penguin's space? All of these creatures need a specific climate with specific vegetation to thrive.

When you take field trips, think of the most Earth-friendly way of getting there. Can you walk? Can you take a light rail? Which mode of transportation will release the fewest greenhouse gases? If you take a school bus, remind the driver not to idle. Maybe you can calculate your emissions and plant trees to make up for it.

Tired Tires

Cars release enormous amounts of greenhouse gases into the air from burning gasoline. Accordingly, it's important for people to try to get the best possible fuel efficiency. One easy way to do this is simply by keeping the tires inflated. It takes less energy to propel a car with properly inflated tires. A simple experiment to show kids how important this is (so they can remind their parents) is to take a booby-trapped bicycle ride. Have everyone let some of the air out of their bicycle tires and ride around the playground. Then fill the tires back up again and ride again. The students will see how much less energy it takes to move the bike. From this experiment, students will learn how much less energy or gasoline it will take to move a car when the tires are well filled.

Human Health

The issue of climate change doesn't hit home for many people, but government agencies and other credible institutions are increasingly showing how climate change will seriously impact human health.

Climate Change and Bugs

Mosquitoes and other insects love warm weather. While a mosquito bite can be an annoying itch, it can also carry harmful bacteria. By making the Earth warmer, people are creating a world in which mosquitoes are happy and can live in more places for longer periods of time. With more mosquitoes, people not only get more itchy bites, they also have more of a chance of getting sick from the diseases they spread. It's the same story for other bugs because bugs generally do not like the cold. Creating a warmer world is like inviting the bugs to bug you even more. Who wants that?

SOURCE

The U.S. Environmental Protection Agency hosts two websites that let you know when the sun's rays are harshest and when the air quality is poor in your area. It's especially important to be aware of these days when you're planning long outdoor activities with children. Visit *www.epa.gov/sunwise/uvindex.html and www.airnow.gov.* You can even sign up to get e-mail alerts.

Hot, Hot, Hot!

Global warming is causing more heat waves, and high heat can impact health in many different ways. The most obvious is heat exhaustion, when a person's body simply cannot cool down and becomes dehydrated to the point that the person becomes very ill. The fatigue and nausea can make it seem like the stomach flu.

Warmer temperatures also impact the quality of the air you breathe. While you cannot always see dirty air, global warming makes the air dirtier by increasing ozone and particulate matter levels. The invisible pollution in the warmer air can affect your ability to breathe, especially if you have asthma.

Take It Home

Taking global warming issues into every individual home is the key to preventing further devastation. Just like many of the school projects overlap with other issues covered in this book, the home issues do, too. Still, it's important to give parents an easy way to deal with one of the most pressing issues of all time. Empowering people through easy tips is the key to success.

Prevent Global Warming at Home

You can help to reduce global warming by using energy more wisely. Here are five easy actions your students' families can take at home to help reduce global warming.

1. **Reduce, reuse, recycle.** Do your part to reduce waste by choosing reusable products instead of disposables. Buy products with minimal packaging. And whenever you can, recycle.

2. **Control your climate naturally.** Instead of relying upon your heater or air conditioner all the time, watch the temperature outside and open and close your windows accordingly. Open the windows when the temperature outside is what you want inside and close them when you don't. Adding insulation to your walls and attic and installing weather stripping or caulking around doors and windows can reduce the amount of energy you use and lower your heating and cooling costs more than 25 percent. Turn down the heat while you're sleeping at night or away during the day, and keep temperatures moderate at all times. Setting your thermostat just two degrees lower in winter and higher in summer could save about 2,000 pounds of carbon dioxide each year.

3. **Change your light bulbs.** Replace incandescent light bulbs with compact fluorescent light (CFL) bulbs. Replacing just one 60-watt incandescent light bulb with a CFL will save you $30 over the life of the bulb. CFLs also last ten times longer than incandescent bulbs, use two-thirds less energy, and give off 70 percent less heat. Note: CFLs contain a small amount of mercury and should not be disposed of in the trash. Go to *http://earth911.com* and enter your Zip Code to learn where you can bring yours for recycling.

4. **Drive smart.** Less driving means fewer emissions. Driving less will help you save money on gasoline, and walking and biking are great forms of exercise. Explore your community's public transit system and check out options for carpooling to work or school. When you do drive, make sure your car is running efficiently. Every gallon of gas you save not only helps your budget; it also keeps 20 pounds of carbon dioxide out of the atmosphere.

5. **Embrace energy efficiency.** When it's time to buy a new car, choose one that has good gas mileage. Home appliances now come in a range of energy-efficient models. Visit *www.energystar.gov* for more information on energy-efficient products and home improvement ideas.

Work with the students to develop a plan of action. Choose a couple of things to do right away and revisit the list to continually curb your energy consumption and reduce global warming.

ESSENTIAL

Always try to find ways that your students' homework assignments can have a longer impact. Keep a list of activities that you have sent home readily available so that you can send reminders to parents asking how things are going. Celebrate successes and have the students brainstorm ways to overcome obstacles.

Tune-up the Earth

From having regular car tune-ups to driving slower, you can do many things with your car to help prevent global warming. Go to *www.kidsforsavingearth.org*, click on "Air," and choose "Tune Up the Earth Challenge." Print up the materials and send them home for your students to share with their parents.

CHAPTER 13

Flying Feathered Friends

What do birds have to do with a green classroom? Every part of nature is important. All of the life on this planet works together and serves some purpose in keeping the Earth healthy. It is a web of life, and everything is connected. Watching and learning about birds can help you better understand the ecosystem and begin to hear the warning signals the birds are sending.

What It's All About

Birds are beautiful creatures. Have your students ever watched them and yearned for the ability to soar through the sky? Do your students know the names of any birds? Does anyone have a bird as a pet? Does anyone have a favorite bird?

Bird Basics

Not all flying creatures are birds, and not all birds can fly. Are bats birds? No, they're flying mammals. Are butterflies birds? No, they're insects. Can your students think of any other creatures that fly that aren't birds? Does anyone know any birds that can't fly? There are actually many birds that fall into this category, but some of the most common ones include penguins, ostriches, and kiwis.

Two things that make birds unique are their feathers and their hollow bones. Both of these features help give them the ability to fly. The major parts of a bird include the crown, bill (beak), eyes, throat, breast, belly, foot, tarsus (leg), tail, rump, wingbars, back (mantle), nape, and eyebrow. Using a picture of a bird, can your students guess where all of these parts are?

FACT

There are about 10,000 species of bird and they come in all colors, shapes, and sizes—from the tiny bee hummingbird—which is only two and a half inches long, to the huge ostrich—which can grow up to nine feet tall!

Birds play an important role in controlling the insect population, spreading seeds, and, in the case of the hummingbird, even pollinating flowers. Using a variety of bird books or the Internet, have the students look through the birds and pick their favorite. Younger students can draw or paint a picture of their favorite and write the name of it. Older students can research a few facts to add to their picture or even write a short report.

Name That Bird

Ornithologists, the people who study birds, use a variety of observations to help them identify different species. Here are the basics for bird identification:

- **Category:** Is the bird a swimmer, flier, wader, or bird of prey?
- **Field marks:** Does the bird have spots of color, eye-rings, or other distinguishing characteristics?
- **Size and shape**
- **Behavior:** How does the bird eat, mate, fly and/or swim, walk, flock, and climb?
- **Wings and flight:** What shape are the bird's wings when it is flying? How does it fly? Does it soar or swoop or dip up and down?
- **Range of habitat:** Where is the bird? Is it in a tree? Is it on a cliff? Is it on the ground?
- **Special features:** Is there anything extra-special about the bird? Does it have a very distinct beak or legs?
- **Birdcalls and birdsongs:** What does the bird sound like?

Gather photos of a variety of birds. Assign one bird to each student or create small groups and have them answer all of the identification questions. Then place all of the pictures on a wall and play "Name That Bird." Each student should read their answers as if they are the bird speaking. For example, "I like to swim. I have an orange breast." Have the other students try to guess what bird is being described.

SOURCE

Learning birdsongs is fun and easier than you'd think. Birders use mnemonics to remember a bird's song, which means they come up with a phrase that sounds like what the bird says. For example, an Eastern towhee says "hot dog, pickle-ickle-ickle!" Have fun learning birdcalls by visiting *www.learnbirdsongs.com*.

Bird Business

Birds are busy little creatures doing their part to create a healthy, thriving planet.

- Birds eat bugs. Songbirds eat bugs that can damage crops.
- Birds eat rodents. Owls eat mice and rats that can carry disease.
- Some birds pollinate flowers.
- Some birds, like vultures, eat just about anything, acting like the Earth's garbage disposal.

People all over the world have come to rely on birds. In southern India, farmers watch the skies for flocks of birds that signal imminent rainfall. In Colorado, whitewater rafting guides have trained homing pigeons to deliver photos back to home base. Beyond the business of birds, they are also simply enjoyable. Do you know any songs about birds? Any poems? A story or fairy tale? Have you ever seen a painting of a bird? Bird photographs?

Have your students go home and try to find a song, poem, story, movie, painting, or photo of a bird. When they return, have a bird show-and-tell and discuss the importance of birds and what they mean to your students.

Global Picture

People become very used to seeing the types of birds that live in their neighborhoods, but there are so many more species to explore. There's a whole world of birds with a rich history to tell.

Great Migrations

Many birds migrate to different areas each year. They need to go where their food is and where the climate is most welcoming at a certain time of year. The Arctic tern is the farthest traveler and logs an incredible round trip of about 20,000 miles per year going from the Arctic to the

Antarctic and back. Even tiny little barn swallows are capable of flying more than 6,000 miles annually. How do they find their way?

- They follow dominant geographical features like mountains and rivers.
- They watch the stars and sun (just like sailors on the ocean).
- They use the Earth's magnetic field to guide them, relying on tiny grains of a mineral called magnetite in their heads.
- Many simply go with the flow, flying in large flocks.

Using a large map or globe, different colors of yarn, and a removable adhesive, chart the migration paths of different birds. You can name the bird and then tell the student what the two destination points are. Who flies the longest? Who travels the shortest distance? Do any birds migrate through your area? When could you watch for them?

You can also participate in International Migratory Bird Day (IMBD). Visit *www.birdday.org* for education materials for bird festivals and events and a directory of bird education resources.

FACT

Ever wonder why migrating ducks and geese often fly in V-shape formations? Each bird flies in line of its neighbor's beating wings, and this extra bit of supporting wind increases lift, thereby saving each bird a little energy. The leader is the only one that doesn't get this benefit, but the group switches leaders so everyone gets a chance.

Here Today, Gone Tomorrow

What happens to the birds when the forest they live in is cut down so people can build houses and furniture with the wood? What happens to the birds when a marsh is filled in with soil to build a shopping mall? What about the birds of the grasslands when the grasslands are tilled under to create farms? What happens when you can no longer hear the birds sing in the morning? People need to have farms and houses and places to buy clothes and other necessities, but the world needs birds. Discuss how the students feel about the competition for land between people and nature. Would they be willing to give up having so many stores if it meant there would be more forests for the birds? What else would they trade? Are there other ways to cohabitate?

All over the world, there are species of birds that might disappear forever if people keep taking over the land and polluting the air and water that all creatures share. Assign each student an endangered bird to study. They should draw a picture of it, write the name of it, note where it lives, explain why it's endangered, and give one tip for helping protect it. You can find a watch list of endangered birds on the Audubon Society's website at *www.audubon.org/bird/watchlist*.

For the Classroom

Let your students' imaginations and passion for the Earth soar by bringing birds into your classroom. It would be especially exciting if someone had a pet bird you could observe for a while.

Being a Birder

Birding requires patience and the ability to be still and quiet. Birds are naturally skittish, but your patience will pay off. You'll need binoculars, a bird field guide, and a blank notebook. For older children, you can borrow a few pairs of binoculars and have the students share. For younger children, make binoculars out of old toilet-paper rolls, tape, and string. Before you go outside, study your field guide to find out which birds live in your area and which ones would most likely be found nearby. If your school is in the middle of the city, you won't be seeing any marsh dwellers. Know where you are and what you are looking for.

The best time to see birds is generally first thing in the morning. Have the children watch for birds and take notes in their notebooks. They can write down or draw things to help them remember the bird to look it up in the field guide later. What color is it? Does it have any distinctive markings? How big was it? What was the beak shape? Wing shape? What was the bird doing? What is the bird saying? Can you mimic its call?

After taking notes, look through the field guide to find out what kind of bird it was. You can also discuss the differences between the birds you've seen. Which one was biggest and which one was smallest? Which one do the students think was the prettiest? Which one was the strangest? Did any bird have a particularly memorable birdcall or song? Which one was the fastest flier? Depending on where you are located, you can also discuss why you may not have seen very many birds. Are there places around for them to land or build nests? Where would they find food? How is the air quality?

Eating Like a Bird

Birds use a lot of energy when they fly, and they need to eat a lot of food to power their flight. Seeds (especially sunflower and millet seeds) and suet or peanut butter are high-energy bird foods. Students can make a variety of simple bird feeders, but one of the easiest is a pinecone feeder. Attach a piece of string or yarn to a pinecone. Using a spoon, cover the pinecone with suet, lard, vegetable shortening, or peanut butter. Roll it in seeds, hang it from a tree branch, and voilà! Fast food for flying friends!

To make the feeder a bit more gourmet, you can create a more flavorful, energy-boosting fatty mixture for the base. Mix ½ cup suet, lard, or vegetable shortening with 2½ cups raw oats or cornmeal until well blended. You can even mix in chopped dried fruit or chopped nuts for extra oomph.

ALERT!

Always be sure you are aware of any peanut or nut allergies your students may have. For the extremely sensitive, even touching peanut butter can cause a serious allergic reaction. Know your students and always have emergency plans of action that are available for your own reference and for substitute teachers.

Build a Bird's Nest

Just like people build different types of homes in many types of locations, so do birds. Birds build nests just about anywhere you can think of with a wide variety of materials. They are creative architects! Some owls raise their young in burrows underground. Birds live in chimney hideouts, mud homes, and even small depressions in the sand. They build nests with branches, twigs, leaves, mud, saliva, trash, string, and even their own feathers.

Discuss the types of material birds might use:

- What would make a nest strong enough to hold up to storms and wind?
- What could be used to hold all the pieces together?
- What could make the nest soft and cozy?

Look closely at pictures of different types of nests to try to identify the different components. Have students bring nest materials from home, collect them from your schoolyard, or use things that you supply. Either alone or in pairs, have students try to build their own nests.

Any time you handle materials from nature or even craft materials in your classroom, you should make sure that your students are very careful about not touching their faces. Children should wash their hands well, using a plant-based soap and singing the ABCs twice as they scrub between their fingers and around their fingernails.

School Projects

Creating a welcoming environment for birds on your school grounds is a great way to initiate ongoing learning experiences. Get everyone birding by providing a living, outdoor classroom for everyone to enjoy.

Feed the Birds

Just like people love going to events with free food, birds will flock to your school grounds if you leave out some munchies. First, you'll need to know what types of birds are native to your area and what they like to eat. Next, you'll need some bird feeders. You can make simple bird feeders out of milk cartons or two-liter plastic bottles simply by cutting small windows in them, sprinkling seed in the bottom, and tying them to a branch. These are cheap and easy, but they need to be refilled very often. A better choice is to ask a local hardware or garden store to donate bird feeders or hold a small fundraiser to buy some. At your fundraiser, sing the song "Feed the Birds" from *Mary Poppins*.

When you select a location for the feeders, choose someplace that is relatively quiet. Outside a window is nice because the children can watch them without scaring them off. Be patient after you've put up your feeder; birds will take some time to decide if it's a place they feel safe visiting. You can make it extra inviting by having a birdbath nearby as well. Just be sure to change the water frequently so you don't create a breeding ground for mosquitoes. Have the students help with refilling the feeders and changing the water. For extra learning engagement, post a sheet of paper where you can write down what type of birds your students see visiting the feeders and when.

> Bird feeders can lure other animals you might not want on your school grounds, like rodents. To keep them away, clean up spilled seed and hulls from the ground regularly. Slather the underside with Vaseline and cayenne pepper and place the feeder about ten feet from any squirrel jumping point. You should also take feeders down over vacations.

Rebuilding Bird Habitat

The land where your school stands probably used to be bird land. Help rebuild the community by providing landscaping that the birds can thrive in. It's not quite as simple as just putting up birdhouses. Birds would rather live in places that closely resemble their natural habitat. Six basic principles for bird-friendly landscaping include:

- **Food.** Know what type of birds you are inviting and what type of food they like to eat. You can provide bird feeders, but it's more sustainable to know which types of plants, flowers, shrubs, and trees provide the food that local birds prefer.
- **Water.** Just like people need water, birds look for sources of water. Having a birdbath, water garden, or pond will create a more inviting atmosphere for birds.

- **Shelter.** Birds are naturally skittish and need plenty of spaces to hide from activity, predators, and harsh weather. Trees, shrubs, tall grasses, and birdhouses are the best hiding spaces for birds.
- **Diversity.** Including a variety of plants, trees, flowers, and shrubs creates the most optimally inviting natural space for birds.
- **Seasons.** Make sure your plants provide year-round habitat for birds. For example, plant deciduous and evergreen trees and shrubs, as well as plants that provide year-round food sources.
- **Protection.** Make sure there are plenty of places for birds to hide from storms and natural predators. Don't use herbicides and pesticides in your yard. They are poisonous to both the birds and the insects they may feast on.

It takes some thought, time, and money to invest in landscaping for a bird-friendly schoolyard, but the rewards are immeasurable. Not only is it wonderful to see and learn about the birds that inhabit your yard, it's also a lesson in cohabitation. Teaching children how to live in cooperation with nature is an invaluable lesson for life and a wonderful way to help protect the Earth.

Field Trips

Birds are all around us, but rarely do people take the time to actually watch for and learn about their flying feathered friends. Given birds' skittishness it's difficult to get a true sense of their beauty, but making it a priority in your curriculum will instill in your students a lifetime skill and appreciation for these creatures that are so important to planetary health.

Ogling Ornithologists

Look into ornithology programs at your local college or university. Even if it doesn't have a nature reserve or structured facility to teach people about birds, it will definitely have people who are passionate about birds and will welcome the opportunity to teach your students what they know. If there isn't a learning institution in your area, maybe there is a local Audubon Society or other natural conservation organization that has a bird specialist on staff. Even if they don't have a prescribed field trip that they regularly offer students, they will have an abundance of knowledge to share with your students. Contact them and develop an idea for a field trip where they can show off everything they know about the local bird population. If you help them develop a field trip program that didn't exist before, you can help establish a learning opportunity for more students in the future.

SOURCE

Audubon Adventures from the National Audubon Society is one of the top ten science programs for schools. Get your Audubon Adventure resources today by visiting *www.audubon.org/educate/aa.* Your local chapter of the Audubon Society can also be an invaluable resource.

Au Naturel

Take a field trip to a local nature reserve or even a local state park. Any sort of natural setting will definitely provide many opportunities for seeing local birds. Make sure to study field books beforehand so you know what to look for. Create a list of the birds you might see and have each child check them off if they see them. Discuss how these birds differ from the birds you saw on school grounds. Repeat the bird-watching activity you did at school and compare the different birds you saw.

Human Health

Birds are extremely sensitive to pollution and chemical contamination. They are quickly impacted by climate and other changes in the environment. Birds can alert us if something is wrong—but only if we're watching them. By protecting birds' health, people are protecting their own health.

Canary in the Coal Mine

People used to bring caged canaries into coal mines to gauge the air quality. If a canary was singing in the mine, the air quality was okay. If a canary tipped over and died, everyone evacuated the mine. Birds still serve as warning signals for pollution. They are very sensitive to chemicals and other contaminants in the environment, and if they get sick, it means that soon people will get sick. By watching the health of birds and how contaminants affect them, people can get a clearer picture of how to protect themselves.

Human activity impacts bird populations through the use of pesticides. Sometimes when planes apply pesticides to farmland from the air, flocks of birds are covered with the poisons and either get sick or die. Other times, birds that have encountered pesticides are not able to reproduce or lay eggs with weak shells that leave babies vulnerable. It has become increasingly clear that using pesticides is also bad for human health. Visit the American Bird Conservancy at *www.abcbirds.org/abcprograms/policy/pesticides* to learn more.

Whether you buy chicken and turkey from the supermarket or hunt your own pheasants or ducks, it's important to know what contaminants might be in the meat. If you purchase poultry from large factory farms, you may be supporting farms that release pollution into the environment.

Silent Spring

The book *Silent Spring* by Rachel Carson was named one of the twenty-five greatest science books of all time by the editors of *Discover* magazine. This book has been widely credited for assisting the launch of the environmental movement. In particular, it deals with how the environment impacts human health. The book documented the effect of pesticides on the environment, especially birds, describing a future spring in which there will be no birds to sing. Rachel Carson was an extraordinary writer, ecologist, and biologist. Have your class do a group project on her life. You can do it as a bulletin board display, a short book, or even a play.

Take It Home

If you watch long enough from any window you will eventually see some birds. You can get your students' parents involved in birding with some simple homework assignments. They can provide enriching learning experiences for both parents and children, as well as promote quality family time. Who could ask for more?

Become a Bird Buddy

Kids for Saving Earth promotes a Bird Buddy program where kids can select a bird they are trying to protect. Visit *www.kidsforsavingearth.org /programs/birdbuddies.htm* to learn about all of the ideas for protecting birds. In addition to what is listed, you can also have your students do a homework assignment based upon whatever type of bird or birds they regularly see from the windows in their homes. They should watch for birds and then pick one to research. What is it? What is its natural habitat? Where did it live before buildings were all over? What does it eat? How can you help it be happier?

Your morning cup of coffee might be bad for the birds. Sun-grown coffee requires the destruction of forests that are homes to birds, as well as many other plants and animals. Buy shade-grown coffee because a shade-grown coffee farm is a mini-ecosystem.

Families can develop an action plan for befriending birds and helping to create a happier habitat. Have students report their action plans in class. They can decide to create a landscape for birds or write letters to the mayor about preserving bird habitats. Have each student go online and find a photo of the bird they will help. Print it out and place it on a poster board. Write the bird's name on the back and use it as a flash card in your classroom.

Backyard Birding

Have your students watch for the different birds that visit their neighborhoods for one week. They should write down a description of the bird they saw and what it was doing. At the end of the week, compare and contrast which birds were where, what they were doing, and why they might be there or not. Ask your students how their neighborhoods might invite or inhibit bird visits.

CHAPTER 14

Underwater World

There is something magical about life underwater. Plants sway as if dancing. Fish in schools move in perfect unison. The colors, the shapes, the diversity— it's a world beyond imagination. Even the smallest aquarium has a hypnotic beauty. It's hard to imagine being able to impact a world even bigger than the one on land, but that's exactly what's happening. Human actions have repercussions for the underwater world.

What It's All About

There are two main types of aquatic ecosystems. One is freshwater and the other is saltwater. Freshwater systems include rivers, streams, wetlands, ponds, and lakes. Saltwater systems, also know as marine ecosystems, are the large bodies of water surrounding the continents, oceans, and seas. Different types of fish, animals, and plants live in each type of water.

Sweetwater Seas

Fresh water makes up only 3 percent of the Earth's water, but it is home to 41 percent of the world's fish species. It also supplies all human drinking water. The Great Lakes—Superior, Michigan, Huron, Erie, and Ontario—and their connecting channels form the largest surface freshwater system on Earth. They are also known as the Sweetwater Seas; they're so large, they're like seas, only they're not salty. Some interesting facts:

- The Great Lakes contain 90 percent of the freshwater supply in the United States, equaling approximately 6 quadrillion gallons of water. They provide drinking water to 30 million people.
- If you stood on the moon, you could see the lakes.
- If you dumped out the lakes and spread them evenly across the forty-eight contiguous states, the water would be about 9.5 feet deep.

These lakes are big, big, big—but not so big that people cannot affect them. Despite their size, their ecosystem is just as fragile as any other, and all the species that live in this vast underwater world are suffering from pollution, invasive species of fish, and the diversion of water.

FACT

While Lake Superior is the largest freshwater lake as far as surface area goes, Lake Baikal in Russia is the deepest freshwater lake. More than 300 streams feed it, and it is home to the world's only freshwater seal, the Baikal seal.

Make your voices heard and let polluters know you want them to protect water. There is nothing like a letter from a kid to sensitize individuals and companies to environmental issues—and a drawing with the letter really helps. Investigate the companies near water areas in your community. Send them letters to ask them what they are doing to help protect the water in your neighborhood. For an easily printable handout for upper-elementary students, go to *www.kidsforsavingearth.org* and click on "Water." Check out "Wonderful World of Water."

A Salty Underwater Home

Covering three-quarters of the Earth's surface, oceans are as diverse as they are large. These saltwater havens are home to the tiniest plankton and the largest creature on Earth, the blue whale. The oceans are full of bizarre and fascinating creatures that have adapted to extreme and unusual conditions, but people still know very little about them.

SOURCE

The Monterey Bay Aquarium makes a memorable field trip if you live in California. For those of you who don't, visiting the website is the next best thing to visiting in person. Visit *www.mbayaq.org.* There are great activities under the "Teachers" tab, and you can use their webcams to see what's happening at the aquarium.

Create classroom "Fish Stories" books. To understand the importance of the oceans, it a good idea to learn a bit about the fish that call this habitat home. You can create a list of animals of the sea and have the kids draw names from a hat. The list can include pictures of these animals as well. You can go to *www.enchantedlearning.com/coloring/oceanlife.shtml* to help you find marine life and drawings for your list.

Assign students activities to research and write about. You can show the diversity within one animal family by assigning each student a different type of species. For example, there are more than 375 known species of sharks. Many people think sharks are scary, cranky carnivores, but not all of them are. Sharks come in all sizes, from the massive whale shark to the tiny dwarf shark; they have babies in all different ways; some like deep waters and some like shallow; and some eat fish and some eat plankton.

Have each student draw a variety of different pictures of the fish for their book, maybe showing development from baby to adult. Include the name of the fish, habitat information, food, what pollution dangers the fish faces, and finally one action that can be taken to help protect the fish. Bind the book pages together and pass the book around the class to take turns reading fish stories. Take turns sending it home to read with parents.

Global Picture

Waters the world over are suffering from pollution, global warming, over-fishing, and a variety of other harmful human activities. From the smallest streams to the biggest oceans, the plants and creatures are sending signals to people that all is not well and it's time to change.

Where Are All the Fish Going?

Freshwater and saltwater fish are disappearing at alarming rates. People love eating fish, but are too many being eaten? How often do you eat fish? What kind? Where does it come from? Have you ever gone fishing? How do you think fish are caught? Most kids think of pole fishing, but some might know about net fishing. Here are some different ways fish are caught to be sold in stores or at restaurants.

- **Dredging** is when fishermen drag a large metal frame that has teeth that act like a rake along the floor of the ocean. The frame has an attached mesh bag that catches bottom feeders like scallops, clams, oysters, and other shellfish.
- **Gillnetting** is using large nets that are suspended in water by floats and weights. The size of the holes in the nets vary according to what size fish the fisherman wants to catch. The fish's head can go through the net, but not its body. When it tries to back out, its gills get stuck.

- **Harpooning** is a traditional way of catching fish. A fisherman watches for fish and then throws or shoots a spear into the fish. The spear is connected to a rope so the fisherman can reel the fish in.
- **Hook and line fishing** is the fishing method most people are familiar with. Fishermen use a rod, reel, and bait to catch fish.
- **Long-lining** uses a long fishing line that ranges from one to fifty miles long. Many smaller lines with bait and hooks are attached. A boat pulls the line all day and then pulls it in to collect the catch.
- **Purse seines** are a big wall of net that are used to scoop up schools of fish. They are most often used to catch tuna.
- **Trolling** is hook and line fishing, but the fisherman props numerous poles around the boat.

Can you guess which ways of fishing are environmentally friendly? Have the students draw a picture of an underwater scene. Make sure to include a wide variety of sea life, coral, shells, and plants. Have a collection of aquatic life books that they can refer to for drawing the pictures. Now, read through the fishing methods again and imagine what happens when each method is used. They can use their hands to pretend they are using the fishing method on their picture. When fishermen dredge, they rake the bottom of the ocean. What happens if you rake across the bottom of your pictures? How would it affect the habitat? Imagine if these different practices were used on land. What if a giant net came through your neighborhood all of a sudden?

Dredging is not ocean-friendly because the rake disrupts the ocean floor and all the critters, plants, and habitats on it. It also ends up catching creatures that the fishermen don't want. These creatures, known as bycatch, are usually killed through the fishing process and then tossed overboard as waste after they've been separated from the catch. Gillnetting and purse seines both use nets that accidentally catch far more creatures than the fishermen really want. Long-lining attracts seagulls that get caught in the line, as well as other creatures that are curious about the bait. Since the line is so long, the fishermen have no control over what they're catching until they draw it in at the end of the day, often with a lot of bycatch.

Trolling, hook-and-line, and harpooning are ocean-friendly ways to fish. The fishermen have complete control over what they're catching and they cause minimal disruption to underwater habitats.

Save Our Seas

Everyone can do something to help protect all of the bodies of water that provide people with food and fun. Small acts each day add up over time to make a big difference. There are so many ways to help protect the saltwater and sweetwater seas, it's hard to know where to start. Here's one way to get started.

Learn whatever you can about aquatic ecosystems. Start by picking one creature that's being harmed by pollution or overfishing. Learn everything you can about that creature and tell everyone you know, every chance you get.

Make up a short story or poem about that creature and how it is sad because people are hurting it and its family. Have ideas for your readers to help protect this creature and aquatic ecosystems in general. Illustrate your story and then start reading it to everyone who will listen. Likewise, you can write a short skit, have a puppet show, or even record a short video. Use your imagination to teach the world.

Everyone can do something, and every little bit helps. Make that a classroom mantra and repeat it whenever you're discussing the dismal and depressing facts about how badly humans are damaging the planet. There's always a solution and it starts with you!

For the Classroom

Bring the magic of the underwater world into your classroom and inspire a new generation of conservation-minded marine biologists! The more your students learn about all life on Earth, the more inspired they will be to protect it.

Deep-Sea Diving

The deep sea is the largest environment on Earth—but it is the least explored. It is difficult for people to venture to the great depths because the water pressure becomes crushing, temperatures are near-freezing, and there is no light. This extreme environment is host to a variety of unique animals that scientists are just beginning to learn about.

One of the most interesting features of some of the creatures that live far beneath the sea is that they glow in the dark, or are bioluminescent. Just as a firefly creates its own light, these creatures rely on their own ability to make light in order to survive in an environment that is always dark. Look up loosejaws, black dragonfish, siphonophores, blackdevil anglerfish, and other bioluminescent water creatures. What do they look like? Why do they use bioluminescence? Do they use it to attract mates or prey? Do they use it to see?

Pollution this, pollution that. Your kids might start to get bored with always talking about pollution, so try to mix things up by discussing how different ecosystems or species would be impacted by global warming or water shortages.

After you have learned about these amazing glow-in-the-dark creatures, have each student pick their favorite and use wax color crayons to draw a picture of it. Be sure to have the kids press very hard with their crayons so that all the drawing is filled with color EXCEPT in the spots where the creature glows. Next use black tempura paint to paint over the entire drawing. It should leave the crayon exposed but make it nice and dark around the fish, just like it would be in its natural habitat. When the pictures have dried, give them the big surprise. You're going to make them bioluminescent! Use glow-in-the-dark paint and have the students only put it where the creature really has it. Is there a dark room you can take your creatures to? How different is it in the dark? Finally, have a discussion about what will happen to these creatures if the ocean is polluted.

Compact Disc Aquarium

You can have your own beautiful classroom aquarium without the hassle of caring for fish or cleaning a tank. Have plenty of picture books on hand to look at the beautiful colors and shapes of the fish that live in oceans and lakes. Search online for tropical fish photos and you will find many more than you can use. Can your students guess their names? Some of them sure are funny! After you've looked through and read a little about the amazing variety of fish in the world, make your own aquarium based on what you've seen. The best part is that you'll be reducing pollution and protecting the planet and all its fishy inhabitants by reusing old CDs to make your fish! Ask for scratched CDs from your school library, other staff members, or parents. You'll need:

- Construction paper
- Glue
- Two old CDs per child
- Yarn
- Tissue paper
- Googly eyes

Cut lips, top and bottom fins, and a tail out of construction paper. For very young children, you may want to have some templates to choose from or even precut pieces. Glue them into place on the writing side of one CD so they extend past the edge. Glue a long piece of yarn going up from the middle of the CD out the top. Glue the second CD directly on top of the other CD, writing-side down, so the sides with writing are both on the inside of the fish. Cut a rectangular piece of tissue paper and fold it like an accordion small enough to slip through the middle hole. Pull it through and fluff it open for the side fins. Now paste on some eyes and your fish is ready to swim! Hang your fish from the ceiling for an aquarium above your heads. When sunlight hits the CDs, it makes beautiful reflections of light!

School Projects

Can a school coordinate projects that protect aquatic ecosystems? Absolutely! There is a solution for every problem, and schools are a natural place to create solutions, experiment with them, and teach responsible behaviors to create a better world.

Favoring Fish

Almost every school serves fish in the cafeteria. What kind does your school serve? With 90 percent of big fish gone and more than 80 percent of the world's fisheries in danger from overfishing, it is imperative that people choose fish from sources that catch or raise them sustainably (meaning there will still be more of them for future generations). It's easy to find out whether your fish is ocean-friendly by using the online database at *www.fishonline.org*. When your school makes the leap, launch the learning by letting everyone know you're serving sustainable fish and you're proud of it. The kids can make signs and you should definitely organize a celebration.

Recently, some major corporations announced they would begin buying sustainably sourced seafood for their North American stores in three to five years. The grocery chain Whole Foods has also promised to shift purchases away from threatened fish species. Your school can do it, too!

Adopt a Watershed

A watershed is an area of land that collects and redirects or drains water (like rainfall) into a common body of water, like a river or lake. All living creatures depend on watersheds. You can protect the creatures and plants living in these waters by protecting the watershed. When you adopt a watershed, you commit to some of the following activities:

- Reduce pollution by not using pesticides, not pouring used oil or other chemicals in the street, disposing of household hazardous waste appropriately
- Make signs to mark storm drains.

- Clean up litter from around storm drains and along shorelines.
- Watch the watershed to monitor the conditions.
- Educate other people about the watershed.

Adopting a watershed makes a great ongoing program for your school. Different tasks can be assigned for different age groups and the project can be carried on year after year. You can get started by visiting the U.S. Environmental Protection Agency's "Adopt Your Watershed" website at *www .epa.gov/adopt*.

In a similar vein, you can adopt dolphins, seals, and other water critters by going to *www.wildlifeadoption.org*. You'll have to do some fundraising to go this route, but it's a great way to bring a personal touch to a serious issue. For most classes, it would only take about $1 per child to do the cheapest adoption package. When you choose to adopt a creature and support their protection, you also receive a stuffed animal representing your adoptee for your classroom and a package of educational materials.

There are a lot of competing expenses at schools. With tightening budgets, parents might be asked to pitch in funds more and more. Respect their budgets by not nagging them repeatedly to donate for your special classroom activities. Ask once or twice, and then keep a donation jar in your classroom for spare change. Remember to regularly ask local businesses for donations.

Field Trips

Learning about all of the amazing creatures that live underwater makes everyone want to go check them out. Get hands-on (or eyes-on) with the fishes and make friends for life by getting up close and personal with underwater wonders.

Super Scope

You can visit any nearby body of water and discover the secrets of the deep (or not-so-deep) by making your own Super Scope. Most of the activity underwater is too small or delicate to capture, so watching it up-close is the best way to get in on the action. Place your Super Scope just under the surface of the water and look through it for a magnified view of wondrous water life. You'll need a plastic food-storage tub with a snap-on lid (like a yogurt container), the larger the better. You'll also need some clear plastic wrap. Here are the directions for putting it together:

1. Cut off the bottom of the tub.
2. Cut the center out of the tub's lid so only the rim remains.
3. Stretch a piece of plastic wrap over the top of the tub and snap the rim over it to hold it in place.
4. Poke the plastic-wrapped end into the water and look through. Instant magnification of the marvelous world of underwater adventures!

The reason you get magnification from this simple contraption is that when you stick the Super Scope into the water, the plastic wrap is forced up by the water pressure, creating a concave magnifying lens. Super-science for a Super Scope made out of reused material. If you want to take it one tiny step further, gather and clean clear sandwich wrap or sandwich bags for your lens so you're not using new plastic at all!

SOURCE

Take a virtual field trip to the ocean by visiting your local computer lab. Dive into *www.oceanslive.org* and you'll find video of aquanauts, fish, and coral reefs. There are also games and other educational activities. It's the ocean online (no snorkel required)!

Aquarium Adventures

It's a given that if you want to learn about aquatic ecosystems, you should visit a local aquarium. Maybe you have a location dedicated to aquatic life or maybe you decide to visit that area of your local zoo. You can also call your local department of natural resources to see if they have holding tanks or a lab that you could visit to see the types of aquatic creatures that are natural to your regional environment. If you're really scrambling, you could also visit a local pet shop and look at the different fish they have for personal aquariums. Where did they come from? How were they captured?

Whichever type of aquarium you decide to visit, make sure you know in advance what kinds of fish or other marine life they have. Prep your students with pictures you can find online and quick facts to get them thinking and coming up with questions for your guides. If you know in advance what will be there, you can even learn a few facts and then have a fish scavenger hunt.

Human Health

Fish have been a part of the human diet for ages, but they also serve other roles for maintaining human health. Scientists are just beginning to discover some of these roles. If you protect the water, you protect the fish, the planet, and all its inhabitants.

Filthy Fish

Fish are a really healthy source of protein and special fats that help brain development and function. Due to human pollution, some fish may contain harmful chemicals, like mercury, which is primarily released from power plants that burn coal. How does mercury end up in fish? When mercury is released into the air from smokestacks, it falls to the ground and into the water. It is eaten by microscopic organisms. Then small fish eat the microorganisms, large fish eat the small fish, larger fish eat the large fish, and on up the food chain until it reaches humans. Through this process, called bioaccumulation, the levels of the pollutant get stronger and stronger. By the time it reaches humans, it's at high enough levels to be bad for health, especially for young, growing kids whose brains are still developing.

You can demonstrate this process by splitting your class up to represent various creatures in the food chain. A large chunk of the class will be microorganisms, fewer will be small fish, even fewer will be large fish, and one will be a human. Give each microorganism something to represent pollution. They only have one tiny bit of pollution—not bad—but what happens as they are eaten? The small fish need to eat many microorganisms to survive, so they should go tag the microorganisms they need to eat. How many bits of pollution do they have in their bodies now? Now the few large fish have to eat several small fish (along with the microorganisms they've eaten). How many bits of pollution do they end up with? Now the one person has to eat the large fish to survive (along with all of the bits of pollution). That one person gets a lot of pollution with her dinner.

ALERT!

Even though some fish have contaminants in them, fish in general are still a really healthy food source. They are low in fat and high in nutrition, and they are a great source of the omega-3 fatty acids that are essential to good brain development. Don't be scared of fish; just be sure to find the right ones.

Eat a Coral Reef

Coral reefs are the largest living structure on the planet, and they are one of the most threatened marine systems. The reefs are created by creatures called coral polyps. Polyps are tiny creatures that form a hard skeleton to protect their bodies. Polyps use plants to help them to make their skeleton. The skeletons of many polyps stick together and form a coral reef. Corals are living animals that eat, grow, and reproduce. This takes a long time; reefs only grow at about an inch a year. They also provide homes for many, many other species. Scientists speculate there could be another 1 to 8 million undiscovered species living in and around coral reefs! Since reefs support so many types of organisms, they may be key to finding new medicines. Many medicines are already created from creatures and plants that live in coral reefs. These new drugs may be possible cures for cancer, arthritis, bacterial infections, viruses, and more.

People have barely begun to understand how important coral reefs could be to human health, but they are being damaged in countless ways. Learn more about coral reefs by making a coral reef cake! You'll need:

- An already baked sheet cake
- Frosting in a variety of colors
- Marshmallows, sprinkles, green-tinted shredded coconut, Swedish fish, licorice whips, small cookies, gumdrops, and other edible candies
- Toothpicks, spatula, rubber gloves, plates, and utensils

ESSENTIAL

Whenever you bring food into your classroom, try to find organic alternatives. For candies and cakes, the organic varieties won't be loaded with high fructose corn syrup, synthetic preservatives, artificial colors, and other chemical additives.

Come up with ways to use your candies and other materials to represent the various features of a coral reef. With younger students, the teacher needs to be in charge of one large cake. Maybe have one child volunteer at a time help construct each inhabitant of the reef. For older students, you can have smaller cakes and divide the students into small groups to do the activity independently. Before the cake is frosted, cut it into squares so that candy creatures can hide inside the cracks. When you have completed your coral reef, ask the students to review and describe the different features you've included. Dish it up! Do they know what they're eating?

Take It Home

Almost everyone eats fish at home, many people have aquariums, and tons of people go fishing for fun (and food), but how much do they know about fish? Do they know about healthier fish and how to keep fish healthy? It's time they learned.

Healthy Fish Guide

It's very important for parents to know which fish are safest for their children. Children's brains are still developing and are very sensitive to even small amounts of neurotoxins like mercury. There are a variety of organizations that have created user-friendly, pocket shopping guides for consumers to take to the grocery store with them in order to purchase the safest fish. Check them out and print some for your student's parents:

- The Environmental Defense Fund's Seafood Selector at *www.edf .org/page.cfm?tagID=1521.*
- The Monterey Bay Seafood Watch Program at *www.mbayaq.org/cr/ SeafoodWatch.asp.*
- The Natural Resources Defense Council's Mercury in Fish wallet guide at *www.nrdc.org/health/effects/mercury/walletcard.pdf.*

Every state's health department has separate warnings concerning local fish consumption guidelines, so check with them or highlight the number for your students' parents to call. Make sure your kids' brains are healthy and can process and remember everything you teach them.

Turtle Protection Tricks

Turtle species live in fresh and salt water as well as on land. Many of the species are endangered due to loss of habitat, pollution, and the commercial pet trade. Turtles love to live in wetlands. You can canoe through a wetland area and watch the turtles sunning on water lilies. They are a part of the balance of nature, which means they are needed to keep the Earth healthy. Check out this amazing website for information about turtles of all kinds: *http://42explore.com/turtle.htm.* If you live near wetlands or water of any kind, you should work to protect turtles. Here is information you can include on a handout to send home to parents for simple things families can do to help protect turtles.

- **Stop using pesticides on lawns.** It runs off into lakes, oceans, wetlands, and all bodies of water.
- **Don't capture turtles or buy turtles as pets.** Let them live in their natural habitats.
- **Clean beaches and shorelines.** Mistaking trash for food can kill turtles.
- **Don't disturb nests and help protect them from raccoons.** Place rocks around nests and then place an old stove or refrigerator rack over the stone. (Find the racks at old appliance drop-off spots.)

Now you're a tried-and-true turtle protector! Congratulations! Give yourself a pat on your shell—um, back.

CHAPTER 15

Fuzzy Wuzzies

People are mammals. People keep mammals as pets. People melt at the sight of baby mammals. There is some deep primitive connection between people and mammals, but many people don't really know much about them. Being so closely related, understanding mammals leads to a better understanding of yourself. And, as with all areas of nature and ecology, the more you know, the more apt you are to take action to create a better future for all.

What It's All About

Kids are generally very eager to learn about mammals and may already have a favorite species that they know some interesting information about. Do they have any pets or farm animals? What's their favorite animal and why?

Mammal Makeover

What do you and a giraffe have in common? You're both mammals, so you share a lot of features. Here are some of the main characteristics of mammals.

- **Mammals are warm blooded.** No matter if they live in the desert or the Arctic, mammals' bodies maintain the same temperature, making them very adaptable to life in a wide variety of places.
- **All mammals have hair or fur.** Even mammals that live in the water, like whales, have a tiny bit of hair around their mouths. Mammals' hair is made of keratin, which is also what our fingernails are made of. An important difference of mammal hair is that it is dead. Other creatures, such as bumblebees and spiders, may look like they have hair, but it's actually a living part of the animal. If you tried to cut the hair, it would hurt and injure the creature.
- **Mammal babies drink their mother's milk.** Most mammal babies grow inside their mother's womb, although there are a few exceptions, such as the duck-billed platypus, which lays eggs.
- **Mammals are all vertebrate animals,** Which means they all have spines.

Have fun learning about mammals by giving your students mammal makeovers. Each student should choose a different mammal. You can supply a list to choose from or have books that they can look through. If you can, use a digital camera to take headshots of each of the students and print up nice, large pictures of their faces. Otherwise, you can have them bring in photos from home, or even have them draw themselves. Have them glue their face onto a large piece of paper and then draw the mammal's body and other features around their face. Depending on the grade level and time, you can have them simply write "I am a _____" or you can have them go into more depth about who they are, where they live, what they eat, what their home looks like, and other fascinating facts.

There are only about 4,000 kinds of mammals. It may sound like a lot, but compared to other species, mammals are a tiny group. For example, there are 21,000 kinds of fish and 800,000 kinds of insects. And there are more creatures yet to be discovered.

The Mammals with the Most

From the tiny mouse to the huge elephant, mammals come in all shapes and sizes, and they all have special talents that help them survive. Here are some amazing record-setting mammal facts:

- The fastest land mammal is the cheetah, which can run at speeds of over 60 miles per hour for up to 200 to 300 yards.
- The largest animal in the world is the blue whale, which can grow to more than 100 feet long and weigh more than 150 tons. The blue whale is the largest animal that's ever existed, even larger than the largest dinosaur! Its tongue alone is larger than an elephant.
- One of the best jumpers is the red kangaroo, which can leap forty feet in one bound and can jump more than ten feet high.
- The tallest animal is the giraffe, which grows over nineteen feet high.
- The loudest animal is, again, the blue whale, whose rumblings can be heard up to 500 miles away. A blue whale's call can be as loud as 188 decibels, louder than a commercial jet engine, which reaches about 120 decibels.
- The sperm whale can hold its breath the longest—over an hour. This allows it to dive to the ocean floor for food.
- Shrews evolved 54 million years ago. Today some species have such fast metabolisms that they need to eat up to 1.3 times their own weight in food every day.

How do your students stack up to the mammals? Who can run a twenty-five-yard dash the fastest? How long does it take? It would take a cheetah less than a second. Measure out forty feet on the ground and see how many hops it takes to get to the other side. A red kangaroo could do it in one leap. Make a chalk mark ten feet high on a wall. Have your students jump in place next to it. Who gets the highest? How high can the red kangaroo hop? Mark off 100 feet on the floor and have the children lie down head-to-toe to see how many of them it would take to be as long as a blue whale. Borrow or buy a decibel reader to see how loud the kids can scream. Weigh the students to see how many it would take to weigh as much as a blue whale. Using their weight, how much would they have to eat every day to keep up with a shrew? Maybe you could borrow some large bags of potatoes or industrial-sized cans of food from your cafeteria to show them how much they would need to eat each day.

Global Picture

While people can get a small taste for foreign mammal life at zoos, there's so much more to be explored. Learn about some of the stranger species that don't often make it into books and movies.

Wild, Weird, and Wonderful

Stretch your imagination far enough and you might be able to invent bizarre animals that aren't so different from real-life weird mammals. Around the world there are so many wild and strange animals. The truth really is stranger than fiction. Check out these guys with your students: star-nosed mole, elephant shrew, long-beaked echidna, pink fairy armadillo, long-eared jerboa, aye-aye, tarsier, bush dog, lowland streaked tenrec, pygmy marmoset, and Malayan tapir.

You can have your students do short research essays or poems about them. For older students, use this list and then make up some names of fake animals. Assign each student a real or fake animal (they should keep it secret if it's real or not). Their homework assignment is to draw a picture of their animal and then write a little bit about it. Encourage the students who get fake animals to make them strange but believable. Then have all the students bring their pictures and bios back to school for a show-and-tell. Have the rest of the class try to guess whether it's a real animal or not.

National Geographic for Kids has a website that's filled with high-quality information and images to teach kids about animals. There are videos, activities, games, stories, a blog, and much more to keep your students busy and learning for hours. Visit *http://kids.nationalgeographic.com*.

Going, Going, Almost Gone

Extinction means a plant or animal is gone forever. Dinosaurs are extinct. Extinction has been happening since the beginning of time from natural causes like changes in climate or volcanic eruptions. Nowadays, extinction is happening much faster because people are not being careful enough. People are destroying the natural habitats of animals, over-hunting animals, and poisoning them by using insecticides and pesticides. Luckily, more and more people are recognizing the need to better protect animals and the Earth. First, people learn about the problem, and then it's easier to find a solution.

You can learn more about the problem by making an endangered animal zoo. You can use a bulletin board or make a wall display. Create fun cage designs and have children draw pictures of endangered or even extinct animals. Then put the pictured animals in the zoo.

You can have older students research why these animals are threatened and what can be done to protect them. If you make the zoo a hallway display, you could even post a petition next to the zoo to gain support for the Endangered Species Act or some other policy or effort to protect animals. The U.S. Fish and Wildlife Service has a great kid's website that discusses the Endangered Species Act at *www.fws.gov/endangered/kids/index.html*.

For the Classroom

You probably have enough wild animals in your classroom (i.e., your students), but you can teach them about their local mammal cousins with some fun and educational projects. Exotic animals may seem more interesting, but it's fascinating and empowering to understand your local ecology.

In some school districts, parents have complained that schools' environmental curricula taught paganism. If you find yourself answering questions about your curriculum, keep an open mind. Ask what part of the curriculum the parent finds inappropriate and why. Most religions support the idea of stewardship, but some do find offense in the idea that humans are related to animals or in using the term *Mother Earth*.

Animal Tracking

Animals leave behind many signs that they've been there. From broken branches to scratched bark, the more you look, the more you'll see. One of the easiest signs to look for is footprints. Set up your own "trap" to get some good footprints to examine.

SOURCE

Tracking can be really fun and educational. The Wisconsin Department of Natural Resources has a useful environmental education site called EEK! at *www.dnr.state.wi.us/org/caer/ce/eek/index.htm*. You can search for animal tracks and find a great quiz for beginners.

First, warn your custodial staff about your experiment. Find a grassy or wooded area on your school grounds. Look for a patch of ground that is somewhat open. Moisten it with some water so it's a little muddy. Be careful that it's not too squishy; you want to capture a nice footprint. Place a log upright or a cinder block in the middle of the space and put some bait on top. You can use almost any type of food, such as leftover meat or bread. Elevating the bait will force the critter to stand on its hind legs to get the food, ensuring the best footprints possible. Leave your trap overnight and visit it the next day to see if there are prints. If not, keep checking back. Food left outside doesn't stay secret for too long! When you finally do find some prints, use a local field guide to identify what type of animal took your bait.

Healthy Habitats

An animal's home is called its habitat. Animals live in very different habitats. Have your students select an animal and then learn about its habitat. When they have a clear idea of what the habitat is, they should create a diorama showing the animal in its habitat. Remind them to do the background first. Encourage them to use natural materials like twigs and stones to make their dioramas. The second part of the assignment is to find out if the habitat is threatened at all, and if so, by what? Have them draw what may be threatening the habitat and cut around it, leaving a tab so it can be attached to the top of the diorama. It should be connected to the outside and made so that the picture of the threat can fold up on top of the box, out of the way, or be flipped down so it hangs in front of the diorama (but not blocking out the whole diorama).

School Projects

Whole schools can get in on the fun of learning about and protecting animals. It seems a natural project since most schools have mascots and many of them are mammals. Does your school have a mascot? Why was it selected? Learn all about it. Is it endangered?

Adopt an Animal

Adopting an animal is a great way to show your school supports protecting wildlife. You can either set up the adoption through a local zoo, wildlife refuge or rehabilitation center, or a national nonprofit. If your school has a central display area, you can post pictures of your adopted animal along with information about it. Since adoptions aren't free, you can have a donation box or bucket where people can toss spare change to support the effort.

Host an Animal Fair

Maybe you've heard of or even held a science fair before, but have you ever held an animal fair? You can try to coordinate the curriculum with other teachers in order to have all sorts of animal projects to display, or you can make it an extra-credit effort. You can coordinate it as its own event or have it going on at the same time as parent-teacher conferences. Be flexible, be creative, and be sure to ask your students for their ideas. Here are some ideas to get you started:

- Display animal arts and crafts made by students.
- Have a reading area with students' research reports or stories about animals.
- Invite your local pet shelter or humane society to come and set up a table with information.
- Invite local nonprofit organizations that work on animal protection and conservation issues to organize a table with information and displays. It could be focused on local wildlife or global wildlife.
- Invite local state park staff to come and have a table with information and interpretive resources about local wildlife.
- Ask a local farmer to bring some farm animals for a petting zoo in your schoolyard.
- Play endangered species chairs (like musical chairs). Place a picture of a different animal on each chair. Which animals will disappear first?

There are so many ways to adapt the animal fair; just have fun with it. Have students help plan it so they are more excited to participate.

Field Trips

Getting out to see animals in the fur is always an exciting field trip for kids. They may have already done it several times in their lives, but it never gets tiring and there is always something new to learn. Before going, ask if any children have been to similar places, what they thought of them, and what they learned.

Zoo

Almost everyone loves a trip to the zoo. Before you take your students, get a list of all the animals you will see. Ask the students what they know about these animals. You can either do it as a class or have the students write down what they know individually. With older students, have them bring a notebook to the zoo and write down two or three facts or observations about each animal they see. Test their knowledge again after you return. Are there certain animals that everyone learned a lot about? Were any animals somewhat unmemorable? Why do they think that is?

Make sure that whatever wildlife you plan on visiting, the children are aware that they should never try to touch a wild animal. Remind them that even domesticated pets and farm animals should never be approached or touched without adult supervision. Even if an animal looks calm and kind, you can never predict if it will get scared of you and bite.

Wildlife Refuge

Your students can learn all about local wildlife up-close and personal at a wildlife refuge or rehabilitation center. Make sure you research what animals will be there before you go so you know what you are looking for. Except for injured animals, which are kept in special enclosures so people can help them heal, the animals run free like in nature, not like a zoo. Since it's more difficult to actually see an animal in its natural habitat, make the field trip a scavenger hunt. Make a list (maybe with simple drawings) of the wildlife that live at the refuge. Give your students a copy and have them check off animals as they see them. When you return to the classroom, find out if there are any animals that no one saw. Why do they think no one saw it? Is it nocturnal? Does it hide during the day? Are there very few of them? What other reasons might there be?

Human Health

Mammals have always been important to people. People eat them, use their hides for shoes and clothes, drink their milk, make pets of them, and use them in scientific research. They are essential to human life, so it's important to protect them. Healthy mammals mean healthy people.

There Otter Be a Law

Animals often offer early warning signals for how humans are impacting the planet. For instance, after studying dying otters on the beaches of California, scientists found that dangerous bacteria from cat feces was flowing downstream and into the otters' watery habitat. How was it getting there? People were allowing their cats to do their business outside instead of in litter boxes. When it rained, the feces were washed into storm drains, into waterways, and eventually out to the beach, which the otters shared with children and families. The otters were much more sensitive to the bacteria, but human exposure to it can cause illness. The simple answer? People needed to keep their cats inside and clean litter boxes by sending dirty litter to the local landfill in an enclosed paper bag. If your students want to take it one step further, they can get "green" kitty litter that is made from wheat, corn, recycled paper, or reclaimed sawdust. These are much more Earth-friendly options.

Unlike other creatures, young mammals learn from experience and parents pass on life knowledge. This is a primary reason for the evolutionary success of the mammal. Learning is also how children can become successful adults, and adults need to learn from past mistakes so they can better protect the Earth.

Both dog and cat waste can be harmful to the environment and to human health. If it is left out, it can become a breeding ground for bacteria and parasites. Some cities have laws about cleaning up pet waste. Does your city? If not, write to your mayor and ask about creating one. Also, do your part to safely clean up after your family pets.

Mammals on the Menu?

Keeping mammals healthy helps keep much of the food we eat safer. There is a lot of discussion these days about eating meats. Is it healthier to be an omnivore or a vegetarian? Which is best for the Earth? There are no clear-cut answers. It is important to remember that healthy meats as well as healthy vegetables will keep everyone healthier.

Ask your students to talk with their parents about their choices in feeding their household. Are they vegetarian and if so why? Do they eat organic meat? Do they understand what that means? Will it be better for human health as well as Earth health? Here is some information to get them started.

- When mammals such as cows are fed grain or hay that have been sprayed with pesticides, the humans who eat these meats are also eating pesticides. When farm animals are given hormones, people end up eating the hormones as well.
- Cutting back on meat is a green option, but so is choosing organically grown meat. Have your students use the Center for Science in the Public Interest's Eating Green Calculator to find out how their diets impact their health and the environment. You can find it at *www.cspinet.org/EatingGreen/calculator.html*. Ask your students to write a report about how eating green can help the Earth.

Dog and cat waste can harm the environment, and so can conventional flea treatments. Flea collars and shampoos have pesticides in them. Find nontoxic alternatives for flea control at *www.alt4animals.com/flea.htm*.

Take It Home

Even though mammals are the smallest class of creatures that inhabit the Earth, they are still a cornerstone of life and have a lot of influence (especially people!). Most people don't think about how they are constantly interacting with and linked to mammals, but the following activities will shed light on the bonds.

Animal Census

After identifying and discussing what mammals live in your community—including domesticated animals like pets or farm animals—have the students go home to do a backyard animal census. A census is when the government counts how many people live somewhere, but this census will count how many animals live in your area. It's not going to be completely accurate, but it's fun to watch and try.

Give the students a couple of days to watch their backyard and encourage them to ask their parents for help. They should take time to watch the yard early in the morning, in the afternoon, and at dusk or at night. In a notebook, they should keep track of what animals they see and how many there are. They might accidentally count the same animal several times if it keeps returning to the yard, but that's okay. Another option would be to photograph all the student's backyard mammals. When the students return, tally all of the results and find out what everyone saw. Why might there be a lot of a certain animal? Why so few of another?

The Mammals in Your House

In this at-home activity, children will explore how many different ways mammals are part of their life. Younger students will need their parents' help, so you may need to write a quick letter enlisting their assistance. In essence, you want the children to survey their home for all links to mammals.

ESSENTIAL

This activity is a great one to start your mammal unit. It quickly gives students an idea of how interconnected people are to mammals. It can also provide your classroom with some great props if your students bring in toys and books that feature mammals. Make sure students' items are clearly labeled and kept in a safe spot.

Pets are an obvious mammalian presence, but what about food? Do they eat meat? What kind? What animal does it come from? Milk, cheese, yogurt, ice cream? How about leather items like shoes, belts, clothing, or even furniture? What animals did they come from? How about entertainment? Do they own any books or movies that have mammals in them? What are they called? How about animal toys? What else? Have them share their lists in class. Ask if they were surprised to find so many mammals in their lives. What mammal is the class favorite?

CHAPTER 16

Creeping Crawlies

In Greek, "crawling things" are known as *herps*. Thus, herpetology is the study of the creeping crawlies known as amphibians and reptiles. While these two classes of critters are generally studied at the same time, they are actually very different. It's just that naturalists ages ago thought they were more similar and the practice has persisted. Whether you choose to study them together or give them their separate stages, it's time to give a big hoorah for herps because they are disappearing quickly and they need your help.

What It's All About

There are more than 8,000 kinds of reptiles and more than 6,000 kinds of amphibians. Box turtles can live well over 100 years, frogs can breathe through their skin, and the European olm can go ten years without eating. Herps are extremely adaptable and have a lot to teach people about sustainability.

Radical Reptiles

All reptiles have three things in common: they are covered with dry scales (they're not slimy), most come from eggs, and they can't maintain their own body temperature like humans. Many reptiles make people cringe, but one of the most popular reptiles is the chameleon. Chameleons are long, flat lizards that live mostly in trees. They move very slowly as they hunt for insects to eat. When a chameleon spots an insect, its tongue shoots out to catch it. Two cool things about the chameleon's tongue: it moves so fast humans can't see it and it's extremely long—one and a half times the length of a chameleon's body. What if your tongue were that long?

Does anyone know what makes a chameleon extra-special? It can change colors! Many people think the chameleon changes color to blend in with its surroundings in order to hide from predators, but that's not true. Chameleons change colors according to their moods, when they are angry or scared.

Reptile eggs are not hard like chicken or bird shells. They are soft and rubbery. If you want to see and feel what they are like, soak a hard-boiled egg in vinegar overnight. The next day, the egg will be soft like a reptile's.

It is true that many herps look much like their habitat. Sometimes it is really difficult to spot them. Have your students be herps by trying to find where they can blend into the background based on the color of their clothing.

They might be able to blend in with the walls or floor of the classroom. You can also take them outside to try to match their surroundings. Another idea is to give them warning that they should dress to match their environment the next day. Ask them to try to wear clothing that helps them blend in with their surroundings.

Amphibian Alphabet

Amphibians are cold-blooded like reptiles, but that's where the similarities end. Amphibians are broken into three categories: salamanders, frogs, and caecilians (see-SIL-ee-ans). Amphibians have moist skin and they lay eggs without shells. Some amphibians give birth through their back, and some can live without lungs. These types of amphibians, and many more, are known as evolutionarily distinct because they are so strange and have developed such amazing adaptations over time. Learn about more of these creatures at *www.edgeofexistence.org/amphibians*.

SOURCE

Reptiles and amphibians have historically been the villains in old folklore. You can find illustrations of this and additional information about herps at *www.livingunderworld.org/caudata*. Why do people fear herps? What kinds of stories have created this fear?

Have each child select a letter of the alphabet and then find an amphibian whose name begins with that letter (you may need to fudge a little with the letter *X*). They should draw a picture of the amphibian, write its name in large decorative letters at the top, and then write some of the crazier facts about the animal at the bottom. Make a cover for the alphabet book and bind it. For smaller children, you can print pictures of the amphibians, write their name on the picture, and write the first letter of their name in uppercase and lowercase in the corner. Can they identify the letters? Can they put the letters in alphabetical order? Can they spell words with the letters?

Global Picture

Herps live everywhere and have exhibited an amazing ability to thrive. While they have existed since before dinosaurs, humans have definitely had an impact on their homes throughout the globe. What's going on and how can you help?

Personal Protection

Just like people, herps want to be able to protect themselves. They have come up with some pretty imaginative ways like camouflage, shells, and "costumes" (like the frill-necked lizard that appears bigger or fiercer than it actually is when it expands its neck flaps). For many, many years these techniques have helped them survive, but it doesn't help them survive among human development. You can help them survive by getting people to sign the Amphibian Ark petition for protection, which you can find at *www .amphibianark.org.*

SOURCE

The University of Michigan Zoology Department has a website that has frog calls. Learn how to recognize the frogs in your neighborhood by their calls by going to *http://animaldiversity.ummz.umich.edu/site/topics /frogcalls.html.*

You can print the petition for people to sign or encourage them to sign it online. You can even have a fundraising event to earn money to help amphibians. Go to *www.kidsforsavingearth.org,* click on "Programs," and then check out "Fundraising Opportunities." Every little bit helps and you can encourage your students to speak up for amphibians and get civically engaged. One of the best things everyone can do to protect the planet and all of its inhabitants is to learn about the issues and then teach others. Everyone can do it!

Herps, Herps, Everywhere

Herps are extremely adaptable. Since they have figured out so many mechanisms for survival, they have figured out how to live almost anywhere. Have your students explore the diverse living conditions of the herps and reinforce their geography education by having them map the habitats of herps.

Using books or the Internet, look for a wide variety of herps. Look for amphibians, reptiles, lizards, frogs—the whole gamut of herps. Where do they live? Students can draw small pictures of each herp and then tape a picture of it to its natural habitat on a world map.

Frogs in Fashion

A good way to advertise the issue of endangered herps is to make a T-shirt. You can say whatever you wish on your shirt, but by simply having the kids draw their favorite herp and the words *I Love Herps*, you can bet people will be asking them to tell them what a herp is.

You can scan the designs into the computer and order heat transfer paper (or iron-on paper) to print out the design. Iron the design onto a T-shirt of your choice. Maybe you can find used T-shirts to use for this project.

ESSENTIAL

Frogs are the most popular herp, and most major conservation efforts are centered on their survival. Still, there are other herps that need help and attention, too, such as alligators. Most of these activities can be adapted to any amphibian or reptile. You should definitely let your students help decide which species to focus on.

For the Classroom

Herp, herp, herp. It's all about herps. It's a funny little word that covers some funny little creatures. Have fun learning about them with these easy classroom projects.

Magnificent Metamorphosis

From an egg to a tadpole to a polliwog to a frog, watching the development of these amphibious creatures is quite amazing. You used to be able to walk down to your local pond and catch a bucketful of tadpoles to raise, but populations are dwindling and it has become illegal in many areas. Today, you can order frog hatchery kits that come with a small tank, instructions, educational information, and everything else you need to watch tiny frog embryos hatch into tadpoles and develop, over eight to ten weeks, into frogs.

When your tadpoles hatch, they look like tiny fish and they breathe through gills. Can you see the gills using a magnifying glass? Over the next six to eight weeks, the tadpoles will first grow fat tummies, then they'll grow back legs and feet, and finally they'll grow front legs. For the next two weeks, they'll stop eating and begin living off the energy stored in their tail. The tail slowly shrinks; when it disappears, you have a frog that will now breathe air with its lungs.

Any time you have wildlife in your classroom, it is important to address sanitation issues with your students. If anyone touches the creatures (or even the habitat), they should wash their hands well with soap and water. Use regular soap; it has been shown to be just as effective as antibacterial soap and does not contain the toxic ingredient triclosan.

Snake Tales

Most of Aesop's fables use animals to tell the story and many use snakes. Find the story "The Serpent and the Eagle" to read in class. In the fable, a snake was about to kill an eagle when a man saved the eagle's life. In retaliation, the snake left some venom in the man's drinking horn. Unaware of this, the man went to take a swig, but the eagle knocked the horn out of his hands, spilling the water and the venom onto the ground.

Have your students discuss the moral of the story. Older students can write their own short fable using a snake as one of the characters. What lesson do they want to teach their readers? For younger kids, you can help them make a snake as a craft project using old neckties. They just sew or glue the small end of the tie shut, fill it with rice or beans, sew or glue the large end shut, and decorate their snake.

School Projects

Asking your school to get involved in a herp project may provoke some raised eyebrows. Staff, parents, and other students may need a mini-education on the wonderful world of creeping crawlies to get them excited about highlighting and helping herps.

Frogwatch

You can help scientists protect frogs in twenty minutes a week. Frogwatch USA is a frog- and toad-monitoring program that gives you a real chance to make a difference. All you need to do is collect basic information about the frogs and toads that live near you and send it in to scientists to analyze. This long-term amphibian study, managed by the National Wildlife Federation in partnership with the United States Geological Survey, is helping scientists find ways to help stop the decline of frogs. The first step is registering at *www.frogwatch.org*.

Get your Frogwatch materials today, set up your frog-watching team, and help protect your local frogs and toads. Get your neighborhood involved by designing a frog-watch poster and giving one to each neighbor.

Herp Exhibition

Host an exhibition of herps by having students volunteer to bring in examples of herps like stuffed animals or other toys they have from home. They should make a placard that has information such as the common name, the Latin name, and where their herp lives. Set up a display in a prominent location or have it set up as a "zoo" during a planned event like a school carnival or parent-teacher conferences.

Field Trips

Reptiles and amphibians are very good at hiding, but they are around us every day. You can choose to take your students into a natural habitat if you know you'll find some signs of life. Even if you don't, you could look for signs like eggs, larvae, trails, or habitats. Otherwise, go where you'll be guaranteed to see critters, where they have been captured for studying.

Springtime Frog Fling

Spring is the best time to get out to see frogs. Since they are at the very beginning of their metamorphosis, it is much easier to see them (tadpoles can't jump away). Visit ponds, wetlands, woodland pools, slow-moving streams, beaches, or docks. If you can, have the children dress in rubber boots or old sneakers. Bring nets, clear plastic containers, magnifying glasses, and field guides. Have older students collect data on how many of each critter they see, what type it is, and what stage of development it's in. Younger students can draw pictures of what they see. You should also have them pay attention to the habitat of the frogs. What kinds of plants and food do they need to survive?

Since most frogs are endangered, it is very important not to disrupt their habitats. Encourage your students to observe and examine frogs and their habitats, but to try to leave everything exactly as they found it. The same advice should be given for any natural exploration. They wouldn't want someone taking them from their home or messing up their house, so they shouldn't do it to other creatures.

Humans Give Herps a Home

There are many places where herps are held in captivity for humans to study and protect. Zoos, aquariums, and local universities are just a few of the places you can look into for learning hands-on about herps. The added benefit of learning about herps in these locations is that someone very knowledgeable and passionate about the critters will encourage you and your students to get over any fears or misconceptions you may have about creeping crawlies. As an experiment in attitudes, before you go on your field trip, have students write down or discuss how they feel about herps. Are they scared of snakes? Why? What do they think about lizards, frogs, and toads? Ask the same questions after the field trip. Have anyone's opinions changed?

Human Health

There's a common myth that if you touch a warty toad, you'll get warts. It's completely untrue, but there are others ways that herp health is connected to human health.

There are stories throughout history of frogs falling from the sky, and while they may sound crazy, they're actually true! There have been news accounts of it as recently as 2005 in Serbia. What causes this kooky phenomenon? Strong winds pass over a body of water that has many frogs in it, pick them up, and drop them somewhere else.

Croaks of Caution

Do you know what a bioindicator is? It is something living, like a plant or animal, that tells you about the environment it is living in. If the plant or creature is healthy and thriving, it means the environment is healthy and good. If the plant or animal starts disappearing or getting sick, it means something is changing in the environment. Frogs are good bioindicators because they are intimately tied to both water and land. They live part of their life in each habitat. They are very sensitive to any changes in the environment and can tell us when problems are developing at the ecosystem level.

Back in 1995, a group of students in Minnesota were outside exploring surrounding swamps and ponds. These students found deformed frogs with things like extra legs and eyes, and they reported it to the local government. No one knew why the frogs were deformed in the beginning, but researchers eventually found that, among other things, there were high levels of farm pesticides and fertilizers in the water where the frogs were living. Since then, much more research has been done on the potential harm pesticides and synthetic fertilizers could be causing in the environment, as well as what it means for human health.

When people notice changes in bioindicators, they can look into the problems and start to develop solutions. In response to the deformed frogs in Minnesota, many people are now pushing for the government to regulate the use of the pesticides and reduce how much ends up in the environment. Other people have decided that since pesticides are poisons, it's bad to use them at all. What do you think should be done?

Protecting the Earth protects all species, including humans. As you create your green classroom and expand your green curriculum, always try to remember to show how everything is interconnected. When discussing ways to protect herps, ask whether these activities protect other species as well. What have your students already learned that can be applied to various issues?

Frog Pharmaceuticals

Some frogs make their own poison, kind of like how people sweat. The slime on their bodies has different types of poisons to protect them from predators. Tribes in the rainforest have used these poisons on the tips of spears and arrows for generations, and more recently, scientists have been investigating medical uses for frog slime.

According to the San Diego Zoo, one laboratory has developed a new painkiller from the substances produced by the phantasmal poison frog. It is 200 times more effective than some of the strongest human-made painkillers, but it doesn't have all of the bad side effects! Poison frog secretions also show promise for the creation of muscle relaxants, heart stimulants, and even drugs to help people with AIDS. It is important to protect frogs so that humans can learn from them and use their unique adaptabilities in ways that can benefit the whole planet.

Take It Home

Most parents don't want herps at home, but just because herps aren't cute and cuddly doesn't mean they don't deserve respect. Let's hope your students have a deep desire to help the herps after everything you taught them. Have them get their families involved, too!

Top Tips for Helping Herpy Hoppers

Frogs, toads, salamanders, newts, and other amphibians are going extinct. The Association of Zoos and Aquariums (AZA) is pushing a major conservation effort to address the amphibian extinction crisis. Here are some of the ways they have identified for everyone to be frog friends.

- **Look, listen, and learn.** Then teach others what you know so everyone can be friends to the frogs.
- **Visit an AZA-accredited institution near you.** These accredited zoos and aquariums have breeding programs and conservation efforts to try to help protect frogs and other amphibians.
- **Create healthy herp habitats.** Don't use pesticides. Build a backyard pond with logs, rocks, clean water, and leaf litter for healthy, happy herps.
- **Be a responsible pet owner.** Keep your dogs and cats away from wildlife.

Water conservation, energy conservation, and pollution prevention are also important ways to protect amphibians. Can your students come up with some ideas for steps to take at home?

Herps at Home

Have a homework assignment for kids and parents to work together on learning about native species. You can make it any sort of assignment you like. Here are some ideas:

- Draw the life cycle of the herp.
- Write a short story with illustrations about the herp.
- Make a life-size model of the herp and be able to describe the body parts.
- Write a herp song or poem.
- Learn the herp calls and teach them to other students.

What other ideas can you come up with for getting students and their parents to learn about herps?

CHAPTER 17

Bugs Don't Bug Me

People do their best to squash, smash, and generally destroy the bugs they come across in their lives, but bugs are actually very important to the ecosystem. It is curious how something so small can cause so much fear and panic, so where does all that hysteria come from? What can you do to change your attitude and your students' attitudes about bugs? As with almost anything, the more you know, the less you fear. Teach children about bugs and the important role they play in the ecosystem and you'll add another building block to their foundation for a lifetime of stewardship.

What It's All About

Arthropods are the most numerous animals on Earth, making up about 90 percent of the animal kingdom. This extremely diverse group of more than a million species includes insects, spiders, crayfish, crabs, water fleas, millipedes, butterflies, ants, and beetles.

Insects Versus Spiders

An insect's body has three parts: a head, a thorax (the middle part of the body), and an abdomen (the final third of the body). They all have six legs connected to their bodies at the thorax. You can remember which bugs are insects by remembering 3 + 3 = in6 (insects). Three pairs of legs and three body parts is an insect. Spiders have two body parts: the abdomen and the cephalothorax. They have eight legs connected to the cephalothorax.

You can catch insects and spiders in a small plastic bag that you've poked some small air holes into. Place the bugs inside, lay the bag gently on top of some white paper, and examine each bug with a magnifying glass. Release the bugs within thirty minutes so you don't harm them. For each bug, students can draw what it looks like and try to identify what type of bug it is.

SOURCE

The Amateur Entomologist Society is a great place to learn more about bugs. You can join the club and go online for educational information, including games and art projects. Go to *www.amentsoc.org/bug-club.* The organization is based in London and has been protecting bugs since 1935.

A Lot of Good a Bug Can Do

Crown the insects as kings and queens because they rule the world. Plants, fruits, vegetables, and flowers would not grow without insects to pollinate them. In addition, spiders provide people with silk, bees produce beeswax, and other bugs give us dyes from their scales. Insects also recycle natural wastes like dead plants, animal carcasses, and manure by eating and digesting these materials and turning them into beneficial fertilizers for healthy soil. Many birds, fish, and small mammals would starve to death if they did not have insects to eat.

FACT

Just as states have a state flower, most states have a state bug. What's your state bug? Where does it live? Is it endangered? If so, why? Does it have to compete with other bugs for food? Is it losing its habitat? How can you help protect it?

If all the good bugs were gone from the Earth, life would end as we know it. For example, bees pollinate more plants than any other insect, so if they disappeared from Earth we wouldn't have enough food. There would be great famines. Unfortunately, bees truly are disappearing. One way to better protect bees is to stop using pesticides. That means buying more organic food and not using pesticides on your own yard. A very good video called "Silence of the Bees" can be found at *www.pbs.org/nature*. Play it in class and then ask the kids to draw posters of bees pollinating. Write the words *Protect Bees*. Then choose from the following list of ways to protect bees.

- Plant plants that bees like.
- Don't use pesticides.
- Give them a safe, protected habitat.
- Plant vegetables and let some go to seed.
- Become a beekeeper.

Are there other ways to help protect bees? There are so many solutions to all of the problems facing the Earth, and every single one is important. Do what you can. Then celebrate your efforts!

Global Picture

Bugs are everywhere, all the time, whether you're noticing them or not. There are different types of bugs all over the world.

Insects as Ingredients

Warning: this is not for the faint of heart. People eat bugs. People in different areas of the world have been eating bugs since the beginning of time. Entomophagy—the consumption of insects—has been around for thousands of years in some cultures. Today, about half the people of the world eat bugs as a regular part of their diet. In markets in Thailand you can buy silkworms, grasshoppers, and water bugs by the pound. South American movie theaters sell roasted ants as snacks just like popcorn, and Japanese supermarkets stock their shelves with aquatic insect larvae. People in the United States may gag at the idea, but the average person eats about a pound of insects a year without even knowing it. According to the U.S. Food and Drug Administration, insects are unintentionally caught up in some of our favorite foods. Three and a half ounces of chocolate can have up to sixty insect fragments, tomato sauce can contain thirty fly eggs, and peanut butter can have thirty insect fragments.

ALERT!

The idea of eating bugs is not popular in the United States. Before you start discussing it with your students—definitely before you try a recipe—send some information home to parents. Let them know you'll be discussing the issue and why. Invite them to participate if they're brave enough!

Eating bugs is healthier than eating meat. Bugs are loaded with iron, calcium, protein, and other nutrients, and they're extremely low fat and low in simple carbohydrates. Eating bugs is more environmentally friendly, too. Raising cows, pigs, and chickens takes a lot of food, water, and energy. Bugs, not so much.

Have your students do some research and find a recipe that uses bugs. Where is the recipe from? Does it sound good? For the more adventurous, try an actual bug recipe. Don't require students to eat the bugs, but make it available for anyone to try. Check out David Gordon's *Eat-a-Bug Cookbook* and *The Compleat Cockroach*.

Dragonflies are amazing insects! They eat millions of biting flies and mosquitoes. Their eyes contain up to 30,000 individual lenses. Human eyes only have one. Dragonfly nymphs (the first stage after hatching) live in the water for about a year. One variety of dragonfly has been clocked at speeds of 36 miles per hour!

Bug Travelogue

Butterflies are perhaps one of the only bugs that almost everyone enjoys. They are beautiful creatures that inspire artists and poets alike. Butterflies are also some of the busiest global travelers. The monarch butterfly travels more than 2,500 miles every year on its annual migrations. You can visit *www.monarchwatch.org* to find a variety of educational information about monarchs, as well as guides for watching monarchs and monitoring their migration.

Whether or not you can find monarchs in your region, you can build a butterfly house to watch and examine your own native species. Here's what you'll need to build your butterfly house:

- 3 × 6 foot piece of netting
- 18-inch piece of yarn or ribbon
- 12-inch diameter circle of cardboard
- A small branch

1. Fold the netting in half the long way, then halve it again. Bunch each end and tie it closed with a piece of ribbon or yarn. Hang the butterfly house outside.

2. Carefully open the overlapped edges of netting and insert the cardboard disk flat into the bottom. It should naturally draw the sides out to open up the inside of the house.
3. Slip in the branch so that it stands up and carefully draw the edges of the netting back around to close the house. Catch a butterfly and gently place it in the house.

Butterflies are very fragile so it's best for an adult to capture and place the butterfly into the house. Be very careful with the wings. Butterfly wings are covered in delicate scales that catch the wind and help the butterfly fly. If you touch them too heavily, you can damage the scales and impair the butterfly's ability to fly. Feed it with homemade nectar made from nine parts water mixed with one part sugar. Stir until the sugar dissolves. Fill a small dish with cotton balls, moisten them with nectar, and place it in the bottom of the house. Release the butterfly after a day or two (or sooner if it doesn't seem to be eating) so it can lay eggs to have more beautiful butterflies.

For the Classroom

Insects are interesting! Make your students go buggy with fun projects that teach them all about these tiny creatures. You can keep bugs in your daily routine the whole year through by having a morning or midday wiggle where the kids get to move like bugs. How do their attitudes about bugs change over the year?

If you want students to get over fears of bugs and the perception that they are gross, you need to get over any of your own. Be aware that how you respond to bugs sets an example for your students.

Insect Hide and Seek

Bugs use camouflage to hide from predators. One example is the walking stick, which looks like the twigs and branches around it. Play insect hide-and-seek by having your students design their own bugs that could hide around your classroom. You can have them make the bugs out of paper or have them create three-dimensional bugs with clay. They can make them the color of the desk, or wall, or a poster on the wall. Take turns having small groups hide the bugs around the room and then giving another small group two or three minutes to find as many as they can.

Ant Farming

Ants are so abundant they're some of the easiest bugs to capture and observe. Here are some interesting facts about ants to get students intrigued before you begin your colony.

- **Ants' legs are very strong so they can run very quickly.** If a person could run as fast for his size as an ant can, he could run as fast as a horse.
- **Ants can lift twenty times their own body weight.** How much would you be able to lift if you could do the same?
- **An ant brain has about 250,000 brain cells;** a human brain has 100 billion. One ant has much less brain power, but an entire colony of ants put together has the same brain capacity as a human.

Learn more about the amazing ant by starting an ant farm. You can either buy an ant farm through a pet store or online or you can excavate a native ant colony. You can find ants almost everywhere. To make your own colony, simply find an active colony, dig it up with a shovel, place the ants and surrounding material in a large container or bag until you get back to the classroom, and then place them in a large, clear plastic container or glass aquarium. It's optimal if the habitat is about the same size as what you've dug up. Let the ants adjust to their new home for a few days. You can feed them food scraps like peanut butter, jelly, yogurt, fruit scraps, or even dead insects. Be sure you keep the container tightly enclosed so the ants don't escape and infest your room. If you have a safe space outdoors, it might be best to keep it there. Also, be sure to find out if any of your students are allergic to ant bites.

Ant colonies have different rooms, called chambers, that are connected by tunnels. They're just like human buildings with rooms and hallways. Can you find the nursery, food queen, eggs, and trash chambers in your ant colony? Keep an ant journal next to your farm and write down observations each day. Is the population growing? How is the farm changing?

School Projects

Whether your school is trying to get rid of bugs or promote science curriculum that teaches about bugs, there are always positive and negative perceptions about insects. Push for the positive by making even the bad bug situations better.

Insect IPM

Schools do their best to keep bugs far away. It's a basic health issue, but the pesticides many schools use to get rid of bugs can be dangerous for health as well. Recognizing the risks associated with using pesticides around children, many schools across the country are turning to safer pest control programs known as "integrated pest management" (IPM). IPM means that staff first try to prevent problems, then try natural and nontoxic approaches, and only resort to chemicals if all else fails. Usually, it doesn't come to that, which means many schools save money in addition to protecting health and the environment. Get your school on the path to IPM by sharing resources from the U.S. Environmental Protection Agency; you can find them at *www.epa .gov/pesticides/ipm*.

Grow a Garden of Butterflies

With so much habitat destruction occurring everyday, even the smallest flower garden is bound to attract a bounty of beautiful butterflies. It's educational, inspiring, and a simple way for your school to help protect the local butterfly population. You'll first need support from staff and maintenance. Then, you'll need a team of students, staff, and parents to commit to building the bed and beginning the garden. Create a butterfly awareness campaign with your students to inspire interest in creating the garden. Have your students create beautiful, large butterfly-shaped posters with quick facts about butterflies and randomly place them throughout the school. Sneak butterfly bookmarks into newsletters or take-home folders. Come up with creative ways to get the school buzzing about butterflies.

The first year of growing the garden takes the most energy, but after a few years, the garden will virtually take care of itself. It is definitely a worthwhile investment. Get all the advice you need to get started at *www .monarchwatch.org/garden/guide.htm*.

ALERT!

Adults are well aware that some bugs bite and sting, but not all children understand. Make sure your students do not try to catch or touch bugs unless they have checked with an adult to make sure it's safe. Make sure you know if any of your students have allergies to bee stings or bug bites, and have an action plan in place in case it happens.

Field Trips

Take one step out your door and you're in a bug's world. It's not difficult to come up with field trips for bug watching because you can go virtually anywhere to watch them. Here are a couple of ways to get started, but use your imagination. After you've learned about bugs, remember to keep watching for them and talking about them all through the year.

I Spy Insects

Insects are everywhere, in homes, yards, garages, basements, around building foundations, in gardens, around lights at night, near streams and lakes, under logs and rocks, at parks, in forests, and pretty much any place else you can imagine. Put together a bug-collecting kit and go to your nearest park or woodland to start exploring. What you'll need:

- Keep observation notebooks to help track the expedition. Students can draw pictures and try to identify what types of bugs they collected. They should also note where they found each bug.
- Use tweezers to pick up larger insects.
- Have plenty of containers for holding the insects if you plan on bringing any back to the classroom. Small film canisters or yogurt containers work well for this.
- Build a pitfall trap to catch bugs if you have some time. Dig a small hole and insert a yogurt container. Put some bait like a scrap of food in the container. Place four medium-size rocks in a square around the hole. Place a piece of cardboard over the rocks to provide shade to the pitfall and brace it with a smaller rock. Return a few hours later to see if you've caught anything.
- Colanders can be used for scooping bugs from water.
- Butterfly nets are best for catching flying insects. You can buy one already made or make your own from some netting, a hanger, and a dowel or broomstick. First, cut a large isosceles triangle out of the netting and then sew the long sides together into a cone shape. Form a loop from the hanger. Fold the open edge of the cone down around the loop and sew it. Attach the hanger to a dowel or broomstick. Flying insects are best caught using a downward motion as they tend to fly up.
- Beat sheets can be used to collect slow-moving or small insects from plants. Place a light-colored pan or sheet of paper under a plant. Gently shake the insects off the plant onto the beat sheet; then grab them with tweezers or dump them off the sheet into a jar or another container.

As you look for bugs, remember that dead insects in good condition for examination can often be found on windowsills, car grilles, and walking paths.

Entomology Adventures

Visit a local university's department of entomology. You can call in advance to discuss the best way for them to host your field trip. They may have a laboratory they could walk you through, or they may just open a classroom and bring in specimens. If they don't generally host elementary field trips, ask them to invite college students to share projects and reports on a certain day for extra-credit. Find out in advance what types of bugs they have or will be talking about. Learn a little about them in class and then help your students prepare questions to ask.

Human Health

Everyone knows the sting of a mosquito or bee and the itching or pain that follows, but bugs mean more to human health than these irritating moments. Insects play a role in protecting the health of the planet, which means protecting human health, as well. However, some insects do pose dangers, so it's wise to recognize risks, too.

Spiders Are Special

Have your students ever read the book or seen the movie *Charlotte's Web*? Charlotte is an amazingly helpful spider, and, overall, most spiders are. Spiders eat other bugs and mites that are much more of a nuisance to people than spiders are. Without spiders, there would be far more insects and mites bothering you every day. There are only four types of spiders in the United States that can bite and cause harm: the tarantula, the black widow, the brown recluse, and the hobo spider. Show your students pictures of these spiders so they know not to touch them. Actually, they should just let all spiders be. They are busy keeping your homes, buildings, and gardens free of nuisance pests like cockroaches, silverfish, crickets, and flying insects. If you notice a lot of spiders, it's an indication that you need to keep things cleaner. In a clean building, spiders will still thrive, but they won't become a nuisance themselves.

Illness from Insects

Some bugs really are bad because they can carry dangerous diseases like malaria (from infected mosquitoes in places like Africa) or Lyme disease (from infected deer ticks in some parts of North America). It's important for people to be aware of what bugs in their region could potentially cause illness or disease. For many of these bug bites, early detection is the key to health protection. Check the U.S. Centers for Disease Control website to get started learning about what to watch for in your area. Go to *www.cdc .gov/ncidod/diseases/insects/index.htm.*

Try not to make your students scared of bugs, but help them be aware of what to look for. For very young students, this information is better left in the hands of the parents. Often your local health department will have brochures or fact sheets you can share with them.

SOURCE

Bug-Go is a Beneficial Bug Bingo Game you can find at *www.uky.edu /ag/ipm/teachers/bug-go/bug-go.htm.* It's a fun game that teaches kids insect identification, and it also teaches how some bugs are really helpful. Print it up and laminate the pieces so you can play with students for years to come.

Take It Home

Get your students acting as educators to reinforce what they've learned in class and help their parents get a better understanding of bugs. You can also take this opportunity to teach parents how to safely deal with bug problems.

Bug-off Bugs Safely

No one wants bugs at home, and some—such as cockroaches—can pose health problems. However, the pesticides people use can be harmful to children's vulnerable, developing bodies. Have parents visit *www .beyondpesticides.org* to find safer ways to rid their home of pests. As an assignment to get parents acquainted with this resource, have students ask their parents what kinds of bugs they've had to deal with in the past and what they did to get rid of them. Then have them visit "Beyond Pesticides" to find a safe way to get rid of that pest. The student can write it all down and share with the class. Even better, have them all write it down and illustrate it on a piece of paper. Make copies for everyone, bind them, and send them home as nontoxic bug-banishing guides.

FACT

Vinegar applied to a mosquito bite helps reduce the itch, and a paste made with baking soda and water applied to a bee or wasp sting helps reduce pain and swelling. Keep these simple kitchen ingredients in mind during the buggy season.

Lice Are Lousy

Head lice are no strangers to small schoolchildren, and every parent is bound to have to deal with lice at some point. While lice are an irritating nuisance, you don't need to resort to a chemical arsenal to treat them.

1. Kill the lice using plain mayonnaise at room temperature. Cover all of your child's hair, behind the ears and down the neck a little. Leave it on for two hours to smother the lice and developed eggs. Remove and shampoo.
2. After shampooing, rinse with vinegar to loosen the glue that holds nits onto the hair shafts. Rinse with hot (not too hot!) water.
3. Comb the hair with a regular comb, and then use a nit comb, which you can find at local drugstores.
4. Under bright light, check through the hair in tiny sections once it is dry. If you find any nits, pull them off with your fingernails, comb them off with the nit comb, or cut the strand of hair off. Put each nit or hair into a bowl of vinegar.

5. If you see more than a few nits, thoroughly wet a towel with a mixture of half vinegar and half water, wrap your child's head with the towel, and leave it on for one hour. Let the hair dry, and then check for nits again.
6. Check hair daily for any missed nits.
7. Check everyone else in the house and warn parents of children your child has been around.
8. If you continue to find nits, start the mayonnaise process again seven to ten days after the first application.
9. All bedding and clothing will need to be washed in hot water or placed in the dryer on high heat for a half an hour. Anything that can't be washed can be placed in an airtight plastic bag for a week (lice can't live off their human home for more than a day or so).
10. Vacuum your house and car thoroughly; dispose of the vacuum bag.

You can also look for nontoxic lice shampoos. Just go online and do a search for "nontoxic lice control."

CHAPTER 18

What's up with Weeds?

There are roughly 18,000 plant species native to North America. These plants are the basis of all the ecosystems that ultimately build a healthy environment and make the landscapes unique and beautiful. Weeds are plants that grow where they shouldn't, but all weeds aren't bad. Sometimes a weed is a plant growing where nature intended, but not where a human wants it. Other times, weeds truly are unwelcome guests that can cause a lot of trouble to the environment. These types of weeds are known as biological pollutants.

What It's All About

Since weeds aren't all bad, it's good to be able to distinguish the good and the bad from the just plain ugly. Understanding weeds can help children build a new relationship with plants in general and gain respect and knowledge of biodiversity.

Wildflower or Weed?

There are many ways to teach students about plant identification. Begin the discussion by asking the children if they know the names of any weeds. Why do they think they are weeds? Many people believe dandelions are weeds, but many children think they are beautiful wildflowers. Using books, homemade flash cards, or the Internet, begin looking for local examples of wildflowers and weeds. When learning how to identify plants, pay attention to the following characteristics:

- Size
- Shape
- Color
- Number of petals on flowers and how the flowers are arranged on the plant
- Shape and distribution of leaves
- Stem: is it a vine, does it grow upright, or does it cover the ground?
- Reproduction: does it grow from seeds, bulbs, or tubers?
- Habitat: is it sunny or shady, is the soil sandy or more claylike, what are the surroundings like (prairie, swamp, woodlands, ditches, etc.)?

These characteristics can help you identify plants because many similar plants share features. It also helps to know as much information as possible to make it easier to look for the plant in a field guide or explain it to a botanist.

Have each student choose two local flowers to research. They should define as many of these characteristics as they can. They should also identify whether it is native or non-native and if it's helpful or a nuisance. Is it a wildflower or a weed? Why? Each child should do a quick presentation about their two plants. Then have each child draw or paint a picture of the flowers that you can cut out and "plant" along the bottom of the wall in your school hallways for a beautiful wildflower garden!

FACT

According to the National Park Service, about 5,000 plant species in the United States alone are considered to be at risk of extinction. Invasive species are the second greatest threat to native species after direct habitat destruction from development.

Wanted: Dead, Not Alive

According to the Bureau of Land Management, "Legally, a noxious weed is any plant designated by a federal, state, or county government as injurious to public health, agriculture, recreation, wildlife, or property." Noxious weeds are the worst form of non-native, invasive weeds as they cause such a serious threat. Here are some interesting and Earth-friendly ways that people have found to get rid of the worst noxious weeds. They are known as biological control methods because they use natural ways to get rid of weeds.

- **Bugs kill weeds.** For some types of weeds, researchers study what their native habitat is like and what types of organisms, like bugs, keep them under control. After years of careful research, to make sure the newly introduced bug will not harm anything but the target weed, scientists release the bug into the environment so it will naturally reduce the invasive species.
- **Goats eat weeds.** Goats can eat plants that are poisonous to humans and other animals. Their hooves aerate and till the soil and trample in their own fertilizer. Even the city of Los Angeles recently rented goats to eat weeds in downtown green spaces. Visit *http://goatseat weeds.com* to learn about this innovative form of weed control.
- **Fish eat weeds.** Many weeds are aquatic, meaning they live in water and disrupt the ecosystem. Fish have been used to eat invasive species, in much the same way bugs have been used. Scientists research what type of fish ate the weed in its natural habitat. Then they release sterilized fish into the water to eat the invasive weeds.

All of these methods help control noxious weeds without having to use toxic chemicals.

Which plants are noxious weeds in your area? Have the students make "Wanted" posters of them. The posters should include a picture of the plant, its Latin name, any "aliases" it may have, where it's commonly found, and the threats it poses to the environment or human health. You can search online to learn about noxious weeds in your community.

For nonpoisonous, nonprickly noxious weeds, get your students, staff, and parents in the habit of picking them and throwing them away when they see them. Choose even just one weed that your school can commit to picking. Post signs about it around the school with a picture so everyone has a regular reminder of what to look for.

Global Picture

Wherever plants go, there's the potential for weeds. Plants grow on land, in water, and even in tiny crevices in rocks. Likewise, weeds grow almost everywhere you give them a chance. There are probably even more plants that are considered weeds today than in the past because so much land has been developed for specific uses. Once people decide to use the land for something, they don't want anything there that doesn't belong—including weeds.

Alien Invasion

Invasive plants are those that come from somewhere else in the world. These weeds are called invasive, alien, or exotic. People may have planted them originally thinking they were pretty or they may have sneaked to their new home through no conscious effort by humans. Either way, they can quickly out-compete native plants.

The reason many people do not like invasive species is that they can quickly reproduce and multiply, since they have no natural enemies. They end up using resources like water and nutrients from the soil before the native plants can. This means they may eventually wipe out the natural bio-diversity of an area, which ends up harming the insects, birds, and animals that live there as they lose their food sources and natural habitat.

Most plants end up where they aren't supposed to because humans moved them, either knowingly or unknowingly. This started as long ago as ancient Roman times. Explorers found exotic and beautiful plants and decided to bring them home. Today, there is much more global travel and thus, many more opportunities for plants to find their ways to new homes.

- Sometimes seeds or spores are accidentally carried in the cargo of ships and airplanes.
- When ships have no cargo or a light load, they fill the ballasts with water or soil to help weigh the ship down and keep it steady in the water. When the ship arrives at its destination, the ballasts are emptied and stray plants can be inadvertently dumped in strange places.
- Many exotic species are introduced because people use them as ornamental or decorative plants. Most of the plants on the World's Worst Invasive Alien Species list were introduced intentionally for decorative reasons.
- More people are traveling the world and bringing plants, seeds, fruits, and flowers across borders.

It's never easy to find out exactly how a new species gets introduced, but you can find out where it originated. Choose a list of invasive species that grow in your state. The U.S. Department of Agriculture site *www.invasivespeciesinfo.gov* will take you to lists for your state. Assign one to each child to find out where it is from. Use a world map and chart how far the plant traveled.

Seed Banking

Climate change, droughts, floods, and human development are all placing pressures on the natural environment. One way that people are trying to protect the world's plants is by collecting and preserving seeds. People cannot always protect every natural habitat, and trying to keep and grow plants in greenhouses can become very difficult over time.

Preserving seeds is much easier because they take up such a small amount of space, they don't need much attention, and they can be kept for hundreds of years.

According to the National Strategy for Invasive Plant Management, it is estimated that invasive plants have infested more than 100 million acres of land in the United States. An addition 3 million acres are lost every year, which means invasive plants are taking over 4,600 acres every day.

The U.K.–based Millennium Seed Bank project has already gathered millions of seeds from all over the world. Norway recently built the world's largest vault for storing seeds. It already has more than 100 million seeds and keeps them safe inside the vault built deep into a glacial mountain between Norway and the North Pole.

Let your students explore the beauty of seeds by making seed art. Use a variety of seeds and dried beans that are all different colors. Have students draw a picture using a pencil on a small piece of sturdy cardboard. They should glue the seeds on to fill in the picture, almost like creating mosaic. Use seeds that are common.

For the Classroom

Weeds and wildflowers are a wonderful addition to your classroom. Do you have any plants in your classroom already? Where are their native habitats? What would happen if any of your plants ended up in a community garden or natural space? Would it survive? Could it become invasive?

What's in a Name?

Plants have some very interesting and funny names, like hound's tongue, Dalmatian toadflax, and medusa head. Find the funniest names you can or have your students look through books or online to find them. Why did each plant end up with that name? Many times it is based upon what the plant looks like. Does the plant have more than one common name? The silly names are usually common names and not the formal, scientific Latin name.

Can your class come up with a poem or song that includes some plants with silly names and short descriptions of what they look like? Choose local species and you'll give them an easy and memorable way to identify plants.

FACT

Weeds can be used as clues to soil conditions. The presence of weeds such as dandelions, brambles, nettles, and docks are an indication of highly fertile soil. Others, like daisies and plantains, are often seen in heavier, less fertile soils.

Seaweed

Ask your students if they know what seaweed is. Seaweed isn't really a weed at all. It's not even a formal term, but it generally means marine algae. Seaweed is an amazing plant found throughout the world's oceans, and it has many different uses. Different varieties are used in medicines, cosmetics, and fertilizers. One of their main uses is as food. People in Fiji eat crunchy seaweed. Some Canadians eat seaweed snacks instead of potato chips. Japanese cuisine uses seaweed in a huge variety of dishes, and seaweed agriculture is a major industry. Have you ever eaten seaweed?

You almost certainly have had some type of seaweed extract, and you probably eat it almost daily. Agars, carrageenans, and alginates are used in everything from chocolate milk and ice cream to cakes and salad dressing. Have the students go home and find as many products in their kitchen that list agar, carrageenan, or alginate. They should write down the names of the products so they can share them with the class. Were they surprised?

School Projects

Weeds and wildflowers are all likely given the same treatment at your school: mow it or spray it. Help your school be a bit more discerning and help protect the planet with a few easy projects.

Pupils Get Picking

With a growing knowledge that pesticides are harmful to human health and the environment, schools have begun to identify safer ways to control weeds on school grounds. One way to combine weed control with beneficial exercise is by having the students work in teams to manually remove weeds from the school grounds.

You can rotate the teams so the labor is broken up evenly between students. Don't forget to weed after a rainy day and to have gloves available. The best thing about manually picking weeds is that over time, particularly in turf, there will be fewer and fewer weeds to pick. Using chemicals weakens the turf, which in turn makes it more susceptible to more weeds in the future. Without the chemicals, the turf is allowed to develop strong roots and plants and it becomes better able to fend off weeds. The average amount of time it takes to develop a strong organic lawn is about three years. After manually picking the weeds for this long, there will be much less to do the following years. It's certainly a time investment in the beginning, but the benefits of not using pesticides, teaching kids about weeds and nontoxic control, and getting some plain old exercise is an unbeatable combination.

SOURCE

There are many ways for your school to address weeds without resorting to pesticides. The U.S. Environmental Protection Agency has a comprehensive website to help schools get started using Integrated Pest Management. It focuses on natural, biological, and physical approaches to weed management. Visit *www.epa.gov/pesticides/ipm*.

Plant a Native Wildflower Garden

Wildflower gardens are a great way to beautify your school grounds, and they also provide an educational resource for your students and protect the environment. Wildflower gardens with native plants are terrific because they require little care once they are established, they provide food and shelter to local wildlife, and they don't require pesticides or herbicides for protection since they are acclimated to the environment. The National

Park Service is just one of many resources you can use to help you plan, develop, grow, and care for your garden. Visit *www.nps.gov/piro/forteachers /startgarden.htm*. Here are some ideas to keep in mind:

- Start out easy, but understand that native species are hardy and easy to grow. They will quickly be able to be split and propagated to expand your garden every few years. Take advantage of perennials that go to seed and plantings that crowd the garden by having plant and seed sales.
- Get as many people on board for planning and tending to the garden as you can. Many hands make for light work!
- Get resourceful when you look for plants. Get permission and salvage seeds or seedlings by hand from other gardeners' beds or native habitats. Ask a local nursery to donate native plants. You could ask them to have a specified shopping day or week where a percentage of the profits are used to provide your school with plants. Then spread the word and get the parents, staff, and people in your community to do their gardening shopping during that time.

Planting a native garden is a lifelong gift to your school and all of its students. Take this opportunity to make one on your school grounds. If you already have one, develop another one in a different location, expand the existing one, or even develop another kind (like a native water garden or succulent garden).

Field Trips

Set one foot outside and you'll likely have weeds or wildflowers in view. Even deep in the big city, weeds find their way into cracks in the sidewalks and roads. They are tenacious little plants, so it shouldn't be hard to find some when you get outside.

Schoolyard Scavenge

You may be surprised how many types of weeds and wildflowers are trying to thrive on your school grounds. Take your students outside for an afternoon of scavenging to take a closer look at the mini-ecosystem you walk through every day. A great way to collect and organize your specimens is by creating an herbarium. An herbarium is simply a collection of plants. You'll need the following supplies:

- Garden tools
- Gardening gloves
- A field guide
- A notebook
- A pencil
- Wax paper bags

Have your students scout out the weeds by looking for plants that seem out of place. Look for ones that are climbing trees, sprouting up through cracks in cement, or growing in large patches in the grass. When students find one, they should sit down by it and start writing down information about the plant as they wait for you to arrive to snip the sample. They should note the soil conditions, surroundings, plant size, shape, and color. They can even draw a picture if they'd like. Place the sample in a wax paper bag, and be sure to include any leaves, flowers, fruit, and roots if possible.

Return inside to create formal identification cards for your herbarium. They should include the plant's Latin and common names, where it was found and when, a description of the weed, and its typical habitat. You can also include any other information you deem relevant or interesting. As your students make the identification cards, you can use an iron to press the specimens into the wax paper bag, which should help preserve them for studying for at least a few months. Remember to keep a thin linen cloth between the iron and the bag so the bag doesn't stick to the iron.

ALERT!

Be sure to scout the area you will be exploring for poison ivy or plants that could potentially harm a child or trigger an allergic reaction. Remove these in advance or mark the area with lawn flags or posts and string so children know they should stay away.

Go Native

Visit a local nature reserve to explore your region's natural landscape. Call in advance to get a list of native plants and a list of invasive species. Study these plants before you take your trip so your students know what to look for when you arrive. By just looking at a picture of each plant, can they tell which is a weed and which is a native wildflower? How does the park control weeds? How have they observed differences in the landscape with the presence of the weeds? Do they push out other plants? How do the local wildlife and birds respond to the weeds? Is there anything that students and other citizens can do to help stop the spread of invasive species?

Human Health

Just as some plants are considered desirable and some plants are considered weeds, some plants are good for people and some plants are bad. Simply because people live near and walk past or even pick different weeds all the time doesn't mean they are perfectly safe. Likewise, people may be picking "weeds" that have beneficial qualities.

Never eat a weed unless you are absolutely positive it is an edible plant. Also, weeds that are growing on road shoulders may have been sprayed with pesticides or may be covered with litter, so they are not safe to eat. And just because a plant is an edible weed doesn't mean that every piece of it can be eaten. Some edible weeds must be cooked first! Know your weeds.

Don't Eat Me

It's hard enough getting most kids to eat vegetables, so it's unlikely that you'd have to worry about elementary-school kids eating plants. Still, there are many weeds and plants that are poisonous to people, and children should be aware of the dangers. Most of these types of weeds are listed in each state's noxious weed list; they must be by law. You can find your state's list through the USDA at *http://plants.usda.gov/java/noxiousdriver*.

Perhaps the best way to impress how plants can be dangerous to health is by starting the discussion with common plants that can be harmful. We eat fruits like rhubarb and tomato, but the leaves of the plants are poisonous. We are surrounded by many beautiful plants, many of them cultivated intentionally by gardeners, which can be harmful as well. The stems of a daffodil or the flowers on a foxglove are just two examples. People need to be very careful about ever putting any part of a plant into their mouth. Children have gotten sick simply by using hollow stems like straws.

If you can, invite someone from your state university extension service to talk to your class about poisonous plants. If at all possible, have them bring specimens so everyone is very clear what they look like and what they need to look out for.

Pick invasive weeds before they go to seed. This prevents them from reproducing. In addition, make sure you throw them away in the garbage. If you put them in your compost pile or just throw them in with other brush, they still have a chance to reproduce.

Nature's Medicine Cabinet

Plants can be poisonous, but they can also have medicinal properties. For thousands of years, indigenous peoples have used native plants for their healing qualities.

- The common dandelion has amazing healing qualities. Fresh dandelion juice is useful on wounds because it has antibacterial qualities. The latex in the dandelion sap can be used to remove warts and corns. Dandelion is also used for digestive disorders and skin problems.
- Red clover is used as a sedative and a cough suppressant. It can also be used to treat skin problems and even cancer.
- Mullein has been shown to have antihistamine and antiviral qualities.

Are there any common weeds in your region that have medicinal qualities? Maybe they are simply edible. Dandelions are used for salads. Can you find a local wildflower recipe to try in class?

Take It Home

Where many adults see a weed, children see a wildflower. Generally, if a plant has a flower, a child will see it as a flower. It's fun getting children to start the discussion with parents about what makes a weed.

Weed Wizardry

Every homeowner has battled weeds. Many people are accustomed to grabbing pesticides as a quick fix. Many people believe the government wouldn't let them be sold if they weren't safe, but pesticides are poisons. There are many other ways to get rid of weeds.

- Use mulch in gardens. Anything like old leaves or woodchips can be placed on any open soil around plantings to keep weeds down and hold moisture in the soil. It will also add nutrients to the soil as it degrades.
- Spray vinegar on weeds. Vinegar is very acidic and kills weeds very quickly, especially on hot, sunny days. Be careful not to get the vinegar on surrounding plants; it will kill any plant it touches. That said, it's best used for weeds that emerge in cracks in sidewalks and driveways.
- Hoe weeds or pull them by hand. It's good exercise, and you'll be sure you've gotten rid of weeds. You'll also create a space that is healthier for the plants or grass you want to thrive. Once they get stronger, the good plants will fight back more of the weeds on their own.
- Perennial weeds store energy in their roots. Cut down the tops of the weeds, allow them to grow back until they begin to sprout, then cut them back again. Repeat this until all of the energy is drawn out of the roots and they die.

Have students and their parents select one technique from the list, or have them research other nontoxic methods. Have them try out their chosen method and report back after one week, two weeks, and one month on how effective the technique has proven to be (or not to be). If they live in an apartment, maybe they can experiment with weeds in the front sidewalk or parking lot. Which methods are working best? For ones that aren't working so well, is there a better technique that may work for that specific application? Go to *www.beyondpesticides.org/lawn* to find out about lawn care pesticide dangers and alternatives.

Weed Watchers

In many areas of the country, there is a growing need for volunteer weed watchers to help control invasive species. Weed watching is fun, and it's a great reason to get outside and explore. Learn about the invasive species of your region that harm the local ecology. Generally, you can get information from your local university extension services. The Nature Conservancy also has an invasive species program that takes on invaders in all fifty states and thirty countries around the world. Visit *www.nature.org/initiatives/invasivespecies* to learn more about your region and how you can get involved. Make "Weed Watcher Guides" that your students can take home and use with their families. As an assignment, have the students keep track of how many invasive weeds they find and eliminate in one week. Which weed appeared the most? If they have a digital camera, have them take a photo of the weed and print it out for your classroom bulletin board.

CHAPTER 19

A Lot of Good the Woods Can Do

From tiny little seeds come enormous, beautiful trees. Trees provide homes for birds and animals. People's homes are built using wood from trees. Trees grow food for birds, animals, and people. They absorb carbon dioxide and release oxygen, acting as natural, giant air filters. Trees are essential to a healthy planet. They are beautiful to look at and fun to play in. Unfortunately, 8,000 tree species, about 10 percent of the total number, are at risk for extinction. Learning about trees will enable you and your students to protect them.

What It's All About

Children are almost naturally drawn to trees like little monkeys, so it isn't hard to teach your students to love the trees around them. More important, your task is to teach them that trees are much more than jungle gyms. Tell them about how many different types of trees there are and how many amazing things they do.

From the Forest to the Woodland

Forests and woodlands are environments that are mostly trees. Forests cover about one-third of the world's land and are found in many regions throughout the globe. Depending on where they are found, forests come in many forms with different climates, wildlife, insects, and plants. Some of the world's forests include temperate forests, tropical rainforests, cloud forests, coniferous forests, and boreal forests. Split the class into five groups to research each type of forest. Where are they found? What types of trees are in them? What types of animals, birds, and plants live in them?

Make your own classroom forest using your students' hand and arm imprints. Paint each child's palm and forearm brown using finger paints and print it on a large piece of paper. The arm is the tree trunk and the hand is the branches. After washing off their arms, the students can make fingerprints in different colors to represent the leaves of the tree. Hang the trees together on the wall to make a classroom forest.

Designate one large wall of your classroom to be a year-round mural. Every time you make a craft that represents a specific part of nature, you can add it to the wall in its respective place. As the year goes on, you'll show the planet's biodiversity!

Lean on Trees

People have relied on trees for thousands of years. They are a source of fruit and nuts. They provide paper and wood. They are an extremely valuable resource. Have your students do a survey of your classroom. You can do it as a group, so everyone gets a feel for what to look for. Are your books made of paper? How much paper is around your classroom? Are your desks or tables made of wood? How many pieces of furniture are made of wood? Even though you can't see it, there is a wood frame inside upholstered furniture. Look around your windows and doors. Are there wooden trim pieces? Is the floor wood? Do you have tissues? How about wooden pencils?

After you've done the survey as a class, send your students home to measure how much they rely on trees. At home, they should also explore their pantry and refrigerator and try to find all of the foods that come from trees.

Global Picture

Trees are a vital part of biodiversity and culture throughout the world. With the population increasing, more trees are being harvested for wood and cut down to make way for cities and farms. The trees cannot grow back as quickly as people are cutting them down. Understanding trees and forests the world over can help people create innovative solutions to protect them at home.

A World of Wild and Wonderful Trees

Trees have inspired art and poetry throughout the world and throughout the ages. Some trees are so amazingly huge or odd or beautiful that a person's jaw can't help but drop when they see one of them. Here are some of the most amazing examples:

- **Baobab trees** stand very tall with no branches until the very top, making it look as though it was planted upside-down. The trunks are very, very thick to store water inside because they live in harsh, dry climates.
- **L'Arbre du Ténéré** (the Tree of Ténéré) is just one tree that was, until the 1970s, the most isolated tree in the world. This tree had no neighboring trees for 250 miles. The Tree of Ténéré was about 300 years old and had stood alone for decades.

- **Giant sequoias,** which only grow on the West Coast of North America, are the world's largest trees. The biggest has been named General Sherman, and it stands more than 270 feet high and weighs more than 6,000 tons. This tree is about 2,200 years old.
- **The banyan tree** shoots roots down through the air from its branches, making it look as if it has roots draped all over it.

There are many other species of trees and even single trees that spark awe and amazement from people. Maybe your students even have a favorite tree in their yard or at the park that they love playing in or looking at. Either by researching interesting trees or by choosing a personal favorite, have your students write a bit of "poetree." It can be a rhyme or a limerick or a haiku, whatever you'd like to require. Have them write about the tree of their choice and draw a picture of that tree to accompany the poem.

Fading Forests

Intact, healthy forests play a large role in supporting all forms of life on Earth. Still, many forests are being clear-cut. Clear-cutting means the cutting down and removal of all trees from a given tract of forest. The environmental problems that this causes include:

- The sudden removal of forest canopy, which destroys the habitat for many forest-dependent insects and bacteria
- An increase in global warming
- The elimination of fish and wildlife species due to soil erosion and habitat loss
- The removal of underground worms, fungi, and bacteria that condition soil and protect plants growing in it
- The loss of small-scale economic opportunities, such as fruit picking, sap extraction, and rubber tapping
- The destruction of recreational opportunities

Read *The Lorax* by Dr. Seuss. It's entertaining and educational for all age groups. The Lorax is a fuzzy little fellow that speaks for the trees. As the forest is being cut down, he repeatedly pops up trying to show how much the logging is hurting the creatures of the forest. In the end, there is just the word *Unless*, and the little boy in the story wonders what it means. The moral is "UNLESS someone like you cares a whole awful lot, nothing is going to get better. It's not." Everyone needs to do their part.

Have your students design their own "*UNLESS*" reminder. They could paint the word on a rock, use lettered beads to spell it on a bracelet or necklace, or anything else they can come up with.

For the Classroom

You've already been examining how trees are intricately tied to human life, but there's so much more to know. Take plenty of time to appreciate trees, but make sure you study different types so you aren't missing the forest for the trees!

The Secrets of the Rainforest

What makes a forest a rainforest? Tropical rainforests receive between 160 and 400 inches of rain each year. How much rain does your locale get each year? All of that rain makes rainforests chock-full of life and nutrients. Rainforests are so full of plants and trees that they play a very large part in controlling the climate of the Earth. People also rely on the rainforests for certain foods and medicines. Unfortunately, rainforests are being cut down at an alarming rate to make room for farms or to get at oil underneath them.

Unlike other types of forests, rainforests cannot be replanted or replaced. This is because the relationship between the plants, animals, and insects that rely on one another is diverse and complicated. It is an interconnected system that has been evolving for almost 100 million years. Once it has been cut down, it is gone forever.

Almost every minute of every day another acre of rainforest is cut down. Help protect the rainforests by joining the Kids for Saving Earth Forest Protection Plan. This plan is protecting and adding to an existing national park in Costa Rica. Visit *www.kidsforsavingearth.org/programs*

/rainforest.htm to start learning about this amazing forest and how you can help protect it.

Kirigami Tree

Trees come in all sorts of beautiful shapes and sizes. Look through books with pictures of trees and discuss the basic shapes of trees. Some are triangular, like evergreens, and some are more like lollipops, with trunks and circular tops. What other shapes are there?

Kirigami is like origami, but you can cut the paper instead of only folding it. Give each student two pieces of construction paper and have them lay one on top of the other. They should sketch a basic shape—just the outline, no details—onto the paper. Then, they fold them down the middle the long way (still, one on top of the other). Cut along the outline on one side of the fold. Like cutting snowflakes, it will cut through all four layers of paper. Open the pieces and use tape or glue to connect the two pieces of paper along the folds. When they are connected, you should be able to open them up and square them so that the four halves are perpendicular and each tree is able to stand on its own. From here, have the students cut more detailed branches into the basic shape to make the trees really come to life.

Did you know one of the oldest living trees is a 4,700-year-old pine tree in California named Methuselah? Or that in Arizona there's a forest of petrified trees that are actually 200-million-year-old fossils? Are there any trees or forests that make the record books in your area?

Adopt a Tree

Have you ever really watched a tree? In many climates it's obvious when buds form in the spring or when leaves change color and drop from the limbs in the fall, but what about all of the other subtle changes? In this activity, your class will adopt a tree to study and report on for the whole school year. They'll see how trees grow and change, just like people. Here are the basic steps:

1. Have the class select a tree, preferably a nice specimen in your school-yard so it's easy to watch.
2. Keep a camera handy to take a photograph each week and make a poster that has the name of the species and any other pertinent information (location, approximate age, size, etc.). You can even have the class vote on a pet name for the tree if you'd like to personalize it.
3. Attach a few sheets of paper to the poster where students can write down weekly observations about how the tree changes.

What happens to the tree? Can you see signs of growth? Do the leaves change? Does it grow any flowers, fruits, berries, seed pods, or nuts? What kinds of animals or birds frequent it? Does it ever look affected by climate (like when it's very dry or very cold)?

After many months, your students should have a much better understanding of and respect for trees. As an end-of-the-year celebration, have a picnic in the shade of your tree and say goodbye to it for the summer.

School Projects

Everyone's heard the cliché "it's a jungle out there," and it certainly applies to schools. Even though a school can sometimes seem like a jungle of activity, you can still coordinate activities that help protect forests and trees.

Tree Planting

Planting a tree is a wonderful experience for anyone. It's a magical moment where you get a chance to plant something that will be around for decades or perhaps even centuries. It's making a mark on the landscape and investing in the environment in a simple and beautiful way. There are a wide variety of ways to engage in the celebration of planting a tree. You can plant one tree on your school grounds or maybe you have room for several. You can participate in community tree planting at parks or at nature preserves to help re-establish a local native habitat. Whichever route you go, make sure to consult with a professional to ensure that you choose the right species and the right location for your tree. You'll also need to know exactly how to care for your seedling for the first few years until it establishes itself.

Good Wood Works

Sustainable living is a difficult concept for kids to understand, but it's worthy of serious discussion with your students. Sustainable living means finding a way to live without harming the Earth and making survival difficult for future generations.

SOURCE

The Arbor Day Foundation is one of the premier national organizations working to educate and inspire people to protect trees. Visit their website at *www.arborday.org* to find a wealth of information about trees and tons of activities for kids and communities. And don't forget to celebrate Arbor Day in April!

Obviously, people need trees, not simply for a healthy environment, but for all of the resources they provide. To make sure that people can continue to rely upon trees as a resource, people need to implement sustainable forestry. Sustainable forests are planted and grown in an environmentally responsible way, are socially beneficial, do not compromise the local culture, and are economically, viably managed. Instead of clear-cutting forests, trees for lumber are grown in a way that is good for the planet. Encourage your school to buy sustainably forested woods, which are certified by the Forest Stewardship Council (FSC), and encourage your students to teach their parents about buying wood products from stores that sell FSC-certified lumber. That means the wood is grown and harvested in a way that is good for the Earth. Schools, students, and parents can all visit *www.fscus.org* to learn more.

Field Trips

Like almost every subject in this book, trees are just outside your front door, so it shouldn't be hard to plan a field trip to explore. Field trips don't always have to mean having to board a bus or shelling out money to visit a special exhibit. Getting outside and exploring nature is just as enriching.

Go Local

You can choose any local woodland or forest for a field trip to study trees. It can be a vast expanse of trees or a small urban grouping. Either way, just get outside and take some time to get to know your wooded neighbors. You can scout the area in advance in order to teach the children about the trees in advance so they'll know what to look for. You can also bring a few field guides and have the children try to figure out what species of tree each one is. The educational experience is yours to adapt based upon what your classroom and learning needs are.

ESSENTIAL

It's important to get rid of wood in a responsible way. If your school is getting rid of old tables or shelves or even doing a construction project that requires ripping up a wood floor, try to do it carefully. Post a notice on Craigslist or Freecycle to see if anyone in your community would like to reuse the wood!

A fun craft to do while you are studying your local trees is to do leaf prints on fabric for the students to take home. Any leaf will work, other than dried, dead leaves from the ground. You'll need:

- Thumbtacks
- Pieces of white cotton or linen (perhaps cut from an old sheet or T-shirts) that are just slightly smaller than the wood
- A small piece of wood
- A hammer
- A spray bottle with some vinegar in it
- An iron

Have each student pick their favorite leaf. Using the thumbtacks, affix a piece of cloth onto the board. Use the hammer to gently tap around the edges of the leaf. The chlorophyll from the leaf should bleed out onto the fabric. Remove the leaf and any leaf bits. Remove the fabric from the wood. Back at the classroom, spray the fabric with vinegar and iron it to make the image permanent. You can use a permanent marker, fabric paint, or even embroidery to have the students write what type of leaf it is.

Look Down to the Floor of the Forest

It's hard to believe, but the floor of a forest is like a miniature zoo, and it's such an important part of the balance of nature. All of the debris that falls to the ground decomposes and returns to the soil to feed the trees. It's an amazing cycle of life. There are many small creatures and organisms that live on the forest floor to help with the decomposition process. Look under logs and rocks to find where they hide.

It probably goes without saying, but when children use a hammer, they should be closely supervised. If you can, find a smaller size hammer that's easier for them to use than the regular size, which is rather unwieldy.

Either go to an actual forest or find a cluster of trees with a natural habitat below them (no grass). Use magnifying glasses and notebooks to explore and record what you find. Look at the plant and tree debris on the ground. Can you tell which plants or trees it came from? What is happening to it? Is there anything under large rocks? What's under fallen logs?

Human Health

You may not know it, but trees help keep you healthy every day. From cleaning up human messes to growing food and providing ecosystems that support the growth of plants people use as medicines, trees are multitasking for public health all the time.

Trees are True Planet Protectors

Trees do so much to keep the planet healthy. They clean up so many messes that people make, ensuring that our air, land, and water are healthy. Here are two of the amazing jobs they take care of:

- Trees are giant natural air filters. They breathe in the air people create and breathe out fresh, clean air.
- Trees also suck up nasty pollution like farm chemicals and sewage from the soil using their roots. This is called phytoremediation. Sometimes they store the pollutants and sometimes they can actually change the pollutant to make it less harmful.

Have a tree appreciation day by discussing all the ways that trees keep the planet healthy. You can also find out if your community has a local nonprofit that focuses on tree conservation or if your city has a tree protection program. Write letters (on recycled or reused paper) to support their efforts.

Smokey the Bear

Forest fires are an important part of the natural life cycle of wooded areas, but human development has increased the amount of forest fires to the point that they're not always helpful and can be very devastating to both natural and human communities. Visit *www.smokeybear.com* to learn more about wildfires and how you and your students can prevent them. By preventing forest fires, people protect wooded natural habitats. They also prevent the harm that can come from fires that encroach on residential areas and the massive amounts of air pollution forest fires create. It's a win, win, win situation.

Take It Home

Make sure your students know the importance of trees before you send your classroom knowledge of trees back home. Do your students have any trees in their yards? Do they have a favorite one they climb at the park or at a friend's or family member's house? What are some of their favorite memories of playing in trees?

Trees may look strong, but some species have weak branches. Kids should be warned that not every branch can hold their weight. They should be careful about grabbing branches and swinging on them by first testing the sturdiness or having an adult test for strength.

Tree-mendous Trees

Have students try to find the most exceptional trees in their community by giving them basic guidelines to gauge the trees, such as:

- Height
- Trunk circumference
- Leaf size
- Crown spread

Students should use the same set of measurements and go out into the community with their parents to find the best of the best. They should write down their measurements and where the tree can be found. When they return to class, they can compare with the other students to find who has found the most truly tree-mendous trees!

Meet the Neighbors

Your students walk by trees in their neighborhood every day. Have them create a guidebook about their local trees in order to take a closer look and stop to check out their neighbors! Working with their parents, they should:

- Take a stroll through their neighborhood with a field guide to try to identify all of the trees in their neighborhood.
- Write down the name and present characteristics of each tree.
- Take a photo or draw a picture of each specimen.
- Take a picture or a sample of each tree's leaf, fruit, seed, and/or berries.

Share each student's guidebook in class. Which trees are common to all or most books? Do any of the students have unique trees in their books? Why might that be? Maybe people planted ornamental trees that aren't native to the area. Where do they originally come from?

CHAPTER 20

Beyond the Elementary School Classroom

Obviously, there's a lot of life beyond elementary school. Maybe you'll find yourself one day in a different environment like a church or scout group wanting to teach environmental education with kids either younger or older. Maybe you have your own children and want to offer ideas to their caregivers and teachers. Either way, here are a wide variety of ways to expand the ideas and activities within this book to different age groups and different environments.

Upgrade for Older Kids

If you teach older kids and want to get them inspired to help protect the Earth, there are many ways you can go. You can simply teach them some background information about environmental issues and encourage them to develop their own projects for further learning. If you're not ready to hand off that much control, here are some ideas to get started.

Get a Grip on Government

Learning how to create positive change in your community through hands-on experience is an invaluable lesson for life. Your students will never forget their experience, and perhaps it will inspire them to become engaged in community service.

Have your students decide on an Earth-saving project they want to take on—energy conservation at city hall, pesticide-free park management through the parks and recreation department, wildflower and native habitat plantings throughout the community, or a recycling curbside pickup for your community. Pick one and go for it. Here's a general outline of how to get started:

1. Describe your project and list the outcomes you want from it. Define the problem and potential solutions. What will it cost? Are there any similar programs in the area that you can model? What benefits are the communities seeing?
2. Begin with a letter-writing campaign to the mayor and council members. Be sure to research the topic thoroughly before you begin writing.
3. Make phone calls to set up appointments to visit with the mayor and other members of the administrative offices that most often handle the topic you want to discuss. Invite them to the city council meeting when you present your proposal.
4. Prepare for your appointments by writing a proposal. Be sure to include what you want, why it is important, when you want it to happen, and how you will help support the outcome.

5. Work with one of the elected officials or staff members to formally write out your proposal to give to your city council.
6. Contact major local media to set up interviews with your students to talk about your proposal.
7. Go as a large group to a city council meeting and have a representative or two speak to the city council to support the proposal.

Whichever governing body you decide to deal with, try to find champions from within the system to help move your effort forward. Always keep an open mind to opposing arguments and try to work with critics to find mutually beneficial solutions.

You don't have to be an expert on the environment to start teaching it to your kids. Keep it simple and let your students do the research. Let them know you're learning, too. Just take it one step at a time. Before you know it, other teachers will be referring to you as the school expert. In the meantime, refer to the real experts whenever you'd like to get more details about an issue. Call local environmental organizations, the department of natural resources, or a local college or university. Ask if someone could come and talk to your class. You can also put up a wish list of topics for volunteer speakers and ask parents to look it over. One of them may be a professional expert willing to come and talk to your class, or maybe one is simply passionate about an issue and would relish the opportunity to spread some inspiration.

SOURCE

Service learning is a method of teaching and learning experience through community service. Get your students involved in their communities and make it clear to them that their involvement is the fundamental basis of democracy. Visit *http://servicelearning.org* or check out the nonprofit environmental organizations in your community.

Teens Teaching Tots

Lower-level teachers always need additional help, and giving older students the opportunity to teach younger ones is empowering and beneficial to both age groups. Work with an elementary school teacher to design a project for your junior high and high school students. It could be putting on a play about a topic they are learning about in class. It could be creating curriculum addressing an environmental issue they are learning about. Get creative and let the students get creative, too! Decide what days and what hours you will send your students to help with the project. Require a written report from your students after it is completed. It should describe the project, why it was important, what they did, what the outcome was, and how they felt about it. Perhaps providing a project survey would be helpful to them. Always ask them to explain the positive outcome of the project.

Growing Up, Getting Deeper, and Growing Stronger

Every project in this book can be researched in a more thorough manner for upper grade levels. Empowering teens is all about providing them with knowledge and actions they can really care about. It's about making them proud of what they do. It's also about having fun, so be sure to add that to your projects. Here are a few suggestions for helping your students grow into enthusiastic community leaders.

- Add music and food to the project.
- Provide students with a list of media contacts in the community and encourage them to write press releases about their projects.
- Invite speakers to your school. Mayors, council members, and state representatives are all good role models who are involved in community action. Ask them to tell the students how they became civic leaders. Have students do some research and prepare questions in advance.
- When you finish a project, put together a book about it. Have each student write a page. Make it a permanent part of the school media center.
- A video about the project can also make it a permanent learning experience for future students.
- Get online and have students play with designing websites, wikis, blogs, or any other type of virtual engagement you feel is appropriate.

New technologies are making new forms of civic engagement possible every day.

The great thing about working with older students is that (usually) they don't need so much structure and supervision. You have much more flexibility in what types of projects to do, and, generally, if you give students freedom, they will fly.

Preschool Is for Playing

No child is too young to learn to love the environment. Without teaching young children about the fearful aspects of pollution and animal extinction, you can teach a general love and respect for nature. Instilling an appreciation for the natural world in a child gives them the foundation to want to care for it.

KISS (Keep It Simple and Silly)

It probably goes without saying, but young children need everything in the simplest form. Instead of talking about the environment, talk about specific pieces of nature. Highlight the colors and shapes of birds, plants, and insects so children begin to notice them and their beauty. Art and crafting are fundamental desires of young children, so draw and paint pictures of the natural world around you. They also love to sing and dance and hear stories, so you can find songs and books about different aspects of nature that capture their desire for creativity while teaching them the basics of nature.

Young children also love being silly. Find bizarre species to teach them about and talk about what makes them different. Kids have an amazing capacity to remember exotic plants and creatures. Make their education full of a love for life and an appreciation for diversity.

Explore and Experience

Small children learn through their senses. Find as many ways as you can to let them touch, hear, and smell nature. Here are some simple ideas for getting out into nature to explore and appreciate all there is to offer.

- Explore textures by touching bark, shells, feathers, rocks, leaves, and anything else you can find.
- Experience sound by closing your eyes and listening for birds, insects, the wind in the trees, or whatever other natural sounds you may have around you.
- Pursue smells by sniffing pine branches, leaves, rocks, flowers, fruits, or anything else that's natural around you.

As much as you can, take them outside. Encourage them to notice all of these tiny, beautiful pieces of nature. Compare and contrast colors and textures. Try to describe smells and sounds. Having a recognition of these small moments of life builds a foundation for seeing the bigger picture and appreciating nature as they grow older.

After Hours

Most schools have after-hours programs for children who cannot return home if their parents work late or who want to expand on their daily education. Your school can easily incorporate lessons of environmental protection into these quick, less-structured opportunities.

Green Kids' Clubs

Start an after-school club for kids that is focused on protecting the planet. Younger kids will need more structure and guidance. Older students will simply need a little supervision and maybe some help finding the resources they need to bring their ideas into action. Many after-school programs have Kids for Saving Earth clubs. The action-oriented curriculum provided can be mailed or you can find hundreds of simple and empowering activities online at *www.kidsforsavingearth.org*. Download the "KSE Promise" song for your first club meeting. Check out the "Defenders of the Planet" link to find out what other clubs are doing.

You can also refer to the Green Flag Program created by the Center for Health, Environment and Justice, which is a flexible three-step program helping schools across the country become more Earth-friendly. You can use their program materials by visiting *www.greenflagschools .org*. They have programs and materials for K–8, 9–12, and faith-based schools.

Child Care Centers

Most children spend a few years in child care before they progress on to school. The younger they are, the more vulnerable their developing bodies are to pollution and chemicals in the environment. Also, the younger you begin teaching children about appreciating the Earth, the firmer their desire to protect it becomes as they grow.

Eco-Healthy Child Care

Schools across the country are going green to protect the planet and to protect children's health. Child care centers are slowly following suit. Using many of the same criteria and steps that schools are implementing, your child care center can go green, too. A good way to begin is to go to *www .healthychild.org*. In addition to information on toxic health risks in children's environments, you can order the *Creating Healthy Environments for Children* DVD. This DVD details five easy ways you can clean up your day care environment and includes printable resource materials for more in-depth details and assistance.

The nonprofit organization Oregon Environmental Council (OEC) has also developed the Eco-Healthy Childcare program. It has developed a checklist of twenty-five environmental-health criteria. If participating centers meet at least twenty, they are certified and listed on the OEC website. Some of the criteria include not smoking anywhere in the vicinity of children, using least-toxic pest control methods both inside and out, and using PVC-free toys, low-VOC paints, and mercury-free thermometers. Visit *http://oeconline.org/our-work/kidshealth/ehcc* to get started.

Go Au Naturel

Young children benefit from open-ended play like stacking blocks and simple crafts. Make yours as Earth-based as possible by using natural materials such as twigs, pinecones, feathers, stones, pieces of natural textiles, and shells. Of course, you'll have to make sure the items are age-appropriate and have no sharp edges or other hazardous attributes. You can easily and inexpensively make beautiful building blocks from the branches of fallen trees. Simply saw varying lengths from a good-size branch or small log and then sand the flat ends so they are stackable. They are beautiful and textured, and their random sizes encourage more complicated buildings.

Faith-Based Earth-Friends

Churches, temples, and other faith-based institutions can incorporate green practices into their buildings and programs just like any other place of learning and life. A fundamental pillar of almost every religion is caring for one another and stewardship for creation. Emphasizing these values gives you the reasons to make sure you are taking care of the planet that supports all life. Use the same tips and projects that have been outlined throughout this book, but discuss instead why it's important to do these things based on your religious beliefs. For many religions, you can find models of how environmental protection is being discussed in relation to your value system and spiritual teachings. Try going online and searching for your religious community's name along with the words *environmental protection, environment,* or even *care for creation.* You may be surprised at what you find.

CHAPTER 21

Make a Bigger Difference

No child is too young to make a big difference in the community and the world. Indeed, it's vital that everyone take all the opportunities they can to speak up for the Earth and all its creatures. Everything people do impacts the planet. There are many good things children can do to protect it. It's vital to understand how important it is to empower students to learn how they can create a better world and a healthier future for themselves.

Social Change for Sustainability

Social change means changing the way people behave. The environmental problems the world is facing today are caused by human behavior. By educating others and pushing for better policies, a person can create behavior changes in the larger population that protect the planet.

Democracy Means Your Voice Counts

Democracy is the rule of the people. Democracy means your voice counts. Americans often take it for granted. People don't think about what it means to have it or to lose it. Children should understand that if they are worried about the environment and want to help protect the Earth, they should talk to the people who make the laws and policies. Living in a democracy means you have the right to voice your opinion and you have the right to be a part of governing and making policies.

Learn the basics about government and how to get involved by using the following resources:

- Be president for a day, learn how government affects you, and step inside a voting booth on this colorful, interactive website created by PBS (*http://pbskids.org/democracy*).
- Congress for Kids (*www.congressforkids.net*) has interactive, fun, and engaging experiences that are meant to help kids learn about the foundation of our federal government and how it affects .them.
- Kids Voting USA (*www.kidsvotingusa.org*) has high-quality instructional materials for K–12 teachers that teach valuable civic lessons throughout the school year. Some of the issues addressed include voting, elections, rights, democracy, and active citizenship.
- *D Is for Democracy: A Citizen's Alphabet* by Elissa Grodin and Victor Juhasz.
- *Graphic Library: Cartoon Nation* series by Liam O'Donnell, which includes titles such as "Democracy," "Citizenship," "Political Parties," "The U.S. Congress," and "Political Elections."

It's especially important to understand the government when you live in a society that is supposed to be ruled by the people!

It's Up to You

You hear a lot of people saying bad things about the government. Help your students understand that they can change the government by voting for the candidates they feel are best able to run the country. It's up to regular people to change what they think is wrong. You can't just complain. It's up to you.

Have your students talk with their parents about their involvement in politics, government, or the community. Do they vote? Have they ever contacted an elected official? Work together with your class to put together a survey for each of them to give to their parents.

SOURCE

The Kids' Guide to Social Action: How to Solve the Social Problems You Choose—and Turn Creative Thinking into Positive Action by Barbara A. Lewis profiles children who have taken action and accomplished amazing things. The book is a must-have how-to manual to assist children in finding a cause, creating a project, and seeing it to the end.

Who Needs to Hear You

It's important to raise awareness about environmental issues with everyone who will give you the opportunity to talk to them, but there are specific people who hold the power to actually change the laws or change the way things work.

Finding Your Reps

Our democracy is a representative democracy, meaning people vote for others to represent them in government decision-making. Everyone has a wide variety of people representing them every day, from the school board and city council to the state legislature and the U.S. Congress.

- To find your national and state representatives, visit *www.usa.gov /Contact/Elected.shtml.*
- To find your local government representatives, visit *www.usa.gov /Agencies/Local.shtml.*
- To find your school board, park board, library board, or any other very localized government representative, simply call the office or visit the website of the institution.

For state and national officials, you can give your students a prequiz by printing pictures of each one of them and mounting them on a poster along with pictures of celebrities and other random people. Can they pick out any representatives? Can they at least pick out the president and vice president? If you want to look up voting records to see how your reps have voted on environmental issues, visit *www.votesmart.org.*

Finding Business Bigwigs

Chief executive officers (CEOs) of large businesses also hold a lot of power, and their business practices have an impact on the community and the environment. You can visit *www.scorecard.org* to find your community's biggest polluters and the names of the CEOs to contact. Likewise, most major corporations have websites where you can find names and contact information. If you want to go smaller and work with a local business on something like adopting energy conservation practices or eliminating plastic bags, just call or visit the business to set up an appointment to talk to the appropriate person.

How to Talk the Talk

There are a growing number of ways to communicate with elected representatives and business leaders. Try one or try them all, just make sure to try.

Take Pen to Paper

The art of writing a good letter is almost extinct in today's modern age of technology. It's still a valuable skill and you should encourage your students to try to write one to a community leader. For very young children, you could just have them draw a picture of some environmental issue the class decides on. Then you can work together to write a letter. The students can tell you what they want to say and you can write it down.

It's Easy with E-mail

All elected officials and large business owners have e-mail addresses these days. E-mail is easy because the message gets to the recipient immediately and you can get a response very quickly as well. You also save paper and the gas it takes to deliver regular mail, so it's an environmentally friendly form of communication. Your e-mail should still have all the same parts as a formal letter. If you'd like, you can have the students write letters as electronic documents and then you can attach them all to one e-mail sent through your work address.

Make the Call

Most elected officials are very busy and difficult to catch on the phone. You generally end up leaving a message with an assistant, but you can ask to be called back. Most of the time, you can either set up an appointment for a visit or voice your opinion on a pending voting decision. Calling right before a pending vote is one of the easiest ways to be directly involved with how your representative represents you. You simply call, state your name and address so they know you are a constituent, and then you say whether you want them to vote for or against the policy. It's as easy as it gets and helps your representative know what you want.

Meet and Greet

The good old-fashioned way of getting involved is by meeting with the people you are trying to persuade. If you aren't ready to try to persuade anyone about an issue, you can meet leaders simply to ask them how they feel about different issues and what their plans are. Make a list of questions about issues your students feel are most important. Set up an appointment to meet your mayor or even governor and put them on the hot seat as your students interview them on their environmental awareness and efforts. Don't forget to send a thank-you letter after the meeting!

Spread the Word

There are so many ways you can share what you've learned with your community. Just like there are many ways to get involved in government and policymaking. Both actions are important and you should introduce both experiences to your students.

News Flash

Investigate your local media outlets, such as your local television stations, your town's major newspapers, local radio stations, and even your school. Make a list of all of them and write down their phone numbers, e-mail addresses, and street addresses. Then go to *www.kidsforsavingearth.org* and click on the "Forms" link. You will find a "News Flash" form that you can fill out and send to all your media outlets. Before you write it, be sure you fully understand the issue you are writing about. Just like a journalist, you should know who, what, when, where, and why. Maybe it's just an announcement about an eco-carnival you are having at your school. Maybe you have been studying a topic like water pollution and you want to make your community aware of a local river pollution problem. This will be an excellent writing experience for your students. You will need to go through the editing process with them.

Likewise, for local television stations, you could make a quick video public service announcement to send in. For radio, you could make an audio recording of the same public service announcement.

Make It Fly

Why don't you make your ideas fly? Making a flier about an issue your students care about couldn't be any easier. All they need to do is select what they want to write about, pick a catchy headline to put in large print, and choose a compelling image or draw a picture. Then put some information about what the reader can do or where to learn more. Voilà! It's a quick and easy way to make an impact in your community. Ask to hang them in grocery stores, libraries, community centers, and anywhere else you can come up with. Save paper by printing them on the backs of used office paper!

Radical Radio

Make your voice heard across the Internet. Kids can send in audio statements about their environmental concerns to Common Good Radio (CGR), the only Internet radio program that lifts the voices of children. Visit *www .commongoodradio.org.*

Play with Petitions

A petition is a document that is signed by many people and sent to an authority figure in order to promote a specific change. Petitions have been around in different forms for hundreds of years and were heavily used in protest in Britain back in the eighteenth and nineteenth centuries. Teach your students this simple form of finding strength in numbers.

What's Your Gripe?

The first thing you need to know is what your complaint or request is. Keep it fairly simple so when you ask for signatures, it doesn't take too much time for someone to understand the issue and decide if they want to support it or not. It should also be very specific so that whomever you are sending it to knows exactly what they are being asked to do. Saying, "protect the environment" is far too broad, as is "stop global warming." You want to create a catchy headline like "I have to clean up my messes; polluters should clean up theirs!" Then describe the problem and identify a solution. Make room for many lines where people can sign their names and write their addresses. Staple extra sheets to the cover as you gather more names. Always know in advance who you need to send it to and who has the power to answer your request.

Nabbing Names

Now that you have your petition all ready, how do your students gather names for it? Depending on their age, you can simply have them get family and friends to sign it, or if they are older, they can go around the neighborhood with a parent or with a friend to gather names. They can ask to stand in front of a local grocery store to solicit customer signatures or in front of another heavily trafficked local business. You can also ask to leave them on the checkout counters at local businesses or the library. Explain to your students to make sure to respect people's space and opinion. You should never make a person feel bad for not signing or approach them if they don't want to be approached. After a predetermined amount of time, gather everyone's signatures and mail them to the person you want to persuade, or visit the office and hand the signatures over personally.

Volunteering

Beyond being involved in policymaking and government in general, it is also very important for people to take the opportunity to volunteer in their communities. It is always beneficial for a citizen to give something back to the community, and generally people find it very fulfilling and educational. Get your students started young by finding simple ways to get connected.

Where to Offer a Helping Hand

Where do you go to find an organization that can use your help? Who will take on young kids? It's different in every community, but there is always a way to help out. Here are some resources to help you find ways to get involved in volunteering:

- Kids Care Clubs (*www.kidscare.org*)
- VolunteerMatch (*www.volunteermatch.org*)
- United Way (*www.liveunited.org*)

Check out your Yellow Pages or the Internet and look for local environmental organizations, conservation or wildlife refuges, parks, or anything else you want to get involved in. Even if the organization doesn't have something set up already, maybe you can work with them to create an opportunity for your students.

There is always someone looking for free help, even if they don't know that they could use students. You may find an organization suited for working with your students or you may need to get creative. You may want to volunteer as a class at one location or you may want to have it be a homework assignment. No matter how you do it, just do it!

What to Do, What to Do

Many organizations might wonder what a bunch of kids can do. Well, they can do a lot. Here are some ideas of kid skills that you can offer to an organization:

- . Write letters
- Fold brochures or stuff envelopes
- Clean (indoors or out)
- Fundraise
- Draw or paint pictures for publications or a fundraising art sale

Getting creative is one of the themes of this book! Kids have a lot of potential. Give them the knowledge. Give them the courage. Give them the opportunity. They will knock your socks off and create a better future for everyone!

Additional Resources

Books and Videos

Asch, Frank. *The Earth and I.* Voyager Books, 2008. New York: NY: Harper Collins.

Bash, Barbara. *Ancient Ones: The World of Old-Growth Douglas Fir.* Sierra Club Books for Children, 1994. Layton, UT: Gibbs Smith.

Cherry, Lynne. *The Great Kapok Tree: A Tale of the Amazon Rain Forest.* Voyager Books, 2000. New York, NY: Harper Collins.

Child, Lauren. *What Planet Are You from, Clarice Bean?* Orchard Books, London, UK: 2002.

Cole, Henry. *On Meadowview Street.* Greenwillow, 2007. New York, NY: Harper Collins.

Cooper, Susan. *Green Boy.* Aladdin, 2003. New York, NY: Simon & Schuster.

Fassa, Lynda. *Green Kids, Sage Families: The Ultimate Guide to Raising Organic Kids.* New American Library, 2009. New York, NY: Penguin.

Fleming, Denise. *Where Once There Was a Wood.* New York, NY: Henry Holt, 2000.

Green, Jen. *Why Should I Protect Nature?* Hauppauge, NY: Barron's Educational Series, 2005.

Green, Jen. *Why Should I Recycle?* Hauppage, NY: Barron's Educational Series, 2005.

Green, Jen. *Why Should I Save Energy?* Hauppage, NY: Barron's Educational Series, 2005.

Green, Jen. *Why Should I Save Water?* Hauppage, NY: Barron's Educational Series, 2005.

Hiaasen, Carl. *Flush.* New York, NY: Knopf Books for Young Readers, 2007.

Hiaasen, Carl. *Hoot.* New York, NY: Yearling, 2006.

Hope, Ives Mauran. *Where the Wisdom Lies: A Message from Nature's Small Creatures.* Bloomington, IN: AuthorHouse, 2006.

Jackson, Ellen. *Earth Mother.* New York, NY: Walker Books for Young Readers, 2005.

Jenkins, Steve. *Almost Gone: The World's Rarest Animals.* New York, NY: HarperTrophy, 2006.

Kids for Saving Earth. *A Trip to the Forest.* Minneapolis, MN: Kids for Saving Earth, 2003.

Kids for Saving Earth. *Just a Healthy Home and Earth.* Minneapolis, MN: Kids for Saving Earth, 2002.

Lee, Kaiulani. *A Sense of Wonder.* DVD, 54 mins. Arlington, VA: Sense of Wonder Publications, LLC., 2008. Order through *beyondpesticides.org*.

Lorbiecki, Marybeth. *Planet Patrol: A Kids' Action Guide to Earth Care.* Minnetonka, MN; Two-Can Publishing, 2005.

Lyons, Dana, and David Lane Danioth. *The Tree.* Bellevue, WA: Illumination Arts Publishing, 2002.

MacDonald, Megan. *Judy Moody Saves the World!* New York, NY: Walker Books, 2006.

Martin, Laura. *Recycled Crafts Box: Sock Puppets, Cardboard Castles, Bottle Bugs and 37 More Earth-Friendly Projects and Activities You Can Create.* North Adams, MA: Storey Publishing, 2004.

McLimans, David. *Gone Wild: An Endangered Animal Alphabet.* New York, NY: Walker Books for Young Readers, 2006.

Olien, Rebecca, and Michael Kline. *Kids Care! 75 Ways to Make a Difference for People, Animals and the Environment*. Nashville, TN: Williamson Books, 2007.

Payne, Benet. *The Worm Café: Mid-Scale Vermicomposting of Lunchroom Wastes*. Kalamazoo, MI: Flower Press, 1999.

Pringle, Laurence. *Global Warming: The Threat of Earth's Changing Climate*. San Francisco, CA: Chronicle Books, 2001.

Rockwell, Anne. *Why Are the Ice Caps Melting? The Dangers of Global Warming*. New York, NY: Collins, 2006.

Seuss, Dr. (Geisel, Ted). *The Lorax*. New York, NY: Random House, 1971.

Strauss, Rochelle. *Tree of Life: The Incredible Biodiversity of Life on Earth*. Tonawanda, NY: Kids Can Press, 2004.

Suzuki, David, and Kathy Vanderlinden. *Eco-Fun: Great Projects, Experiments, and Games for a Greener Earth*. Topeka, KS: Topeka Bindery, 2001.

Thomas, Rob. *Green Thumb*. Aladdin, 2000. New York, NY: Simon & Schuster.

Thornhill, Jan. *This Is My Planet: The Kids' Guide to Global Warming*. Toronto, Ontario, Canada: Maple Tree Press, 2007.

Tierney, Jenni. *Once upon a Rainbow*. Boulder, CO: Honeysuckle Press, 2006.

Van Allsburg, Chris. *Just a Dream*. Boston, MA: Houghton Mifflin, 1990.

Wallace, Nancy Elizabeth. *Recycle Every Day!* Tarrytown, NY: Marshall Cavendish Children's Books, 2006.

Welles, Lee. *Gaia Girls: Enter the Earth*. Daisyworld Press, 2006.

Welles, Lee. *Gaia Girls: Way of Water*. Daisyworld Press, 2007.

For more than 380 children's books about nature and the environment, go to the Childsake website (*www.childsake.com*).

Websites

Build Green Schools • *www.buildgreenschools.org*
The U.S. Green Building Council developed this website to help educate people about why green schools are important and how they can make them a reality.

Green Schools Alliance • *www.greenschoolsalliance.org*
The Green Schools Alliance is a national network of schools (pre-K through 12) that is committed to taking action to prevent global warming.

The Green Squad • *www.nrdc.org/greensquad*
The Green Squad is a project of the Natural Resources Defense Council that teaches kids about school environments and how they impact the Earth and human health.

My Healthy School • *http://myhealthyschool.com*
My Healthy School provides resources and action plans for creating more environmentally friendly, healthier, more socially responsible schools and children.

National Environmental Education Foundation • *www.neefusa.org*
The NEEF site provides a variety of resources and links to helpful organizations, publications, and national events.

North American Association for Environmental Education • *www.naaee.org*
NAAEE is a national network of people trying to teach students how to address environmental issues in a positive and empowering way.

U.S. Environmental Protection Agency Teaching Center • *www.epa .gov/teachers*
The U.S. Environmental Protection Agency hosts this site for teachers that includes a variety of classroom resources, different awards and recognition programs.

U.S. Green Schools • *www.usgreenschools.org*
The U.S. Green Schools Foundation is developing comprehensive curricula for schools to use year-round to teach children the concepts of sustainability while meeting other academic requirements.

Glossary

arthropod

an invertebrate with a segmented body and jointed legs

atmosphere

the layers of gases that surround the Earth

bioaccumulation

the tendency for pollutants to increase in concentration in living organisms

biodegrade

to decompose through nature (usually microorganisms)

biodiversity

the variety of different species and the ecosystems they form

bioindicator

a species whose health reflects the quality of the environment

bioluminescent

organisms capable of creating their own light

carbon footprint

the measure of an entity's impact on the environment based on the release of carbon dioxide

conventionally grown

conventionally grown produce, sometimes genetically modified, is the opposite of organically grown and often relies on synthetic pesticides and fertilizers

ecosystem

the interaction of all living organisms in a given environment

endangered

a species at risk for extinction

entomology
the study of insects

entomophagy
the practice of eating insects

groundwater
water below the Earth's surface

herbarium
a collection of plant specimens

herpetology
the study of amphibians and reptiles

interdisciplinary
draws from a variety of academic disciplines

organic food
food grown without the use of pesticides, synthetic fertilizers, sewage sludge, genetically modified organisms, or antibiotics

organic material / waste
natural substances

ornithology
the study of birds

pesticide
a substance created to repel or kill any species, including insects, weeds, rodents, fungus, and bacteria

sustainable
meeting present needs without preventing future generations from being able to meet theirs; includes respect for environment, economics, and equity

vermiculture
using worms to break down organic waste

VOCs
volatile organic chemicals, or compounds containing carbon that easily evaporate

Index

U

Underwater world, 183–98
Upcycling, 56–57

V

VendingMiser, 151
Vinegar, 235, 249
Volatile organic compounds
   (VOCs), 105
Volunteering, 278–79

W

Walking, 139–40
Waste audits, 35–36
Waste/garbage
   amount of, 30
   animal, 208, 209
   burning, 113–14
   hazardous, 124
   household hazardous, 66–67,
      98
   types of, 31
Waste-to-energy facilities, 145
Water, 83–98. *See also* Underwater
   world
   bottled, 42, 51, 92–93, 131
   ground-, 16, 86, 94
   from landfills, 37–38
   leaks, 88–90
   testing of, 92–93
   total amount, 84
Water cycle, 85
Water pollution, 85–87, 94–96, 185,
   189
Watersheds, 191–92
"Water Travels in a Cycle"
   (Phelan), 85
Watt Watchers, 152
Weeds, 237–50
   controlling, 239–40, 244, 249–50
   invasive, 240–41, 242, 250
   noxious, 239–40, 247
We're Not Asking for the Moon...

Just a Healthy Home and Earth
   (KSE), 101
"Who Has Seen the Wind"
   (Rossetti), 102
Why Should I Save Energy? (Green
   and Gordon), 146
Wildflowers, 238–39, 244–45
Wildlife refuges, 207
Wind, 102–3
Wind farms, 110–11, 152
Wind power, 104, 144
Wood, 144, 259
World Water Day, 87–88
The Worm Café (Payne), 77
Worms, 17–18, 71–72, 76–77
Worms Eat Our Garbage
   (Appelhof, Fenton, and Harris),
   17, 71

Z

Zoos, 164–65, 206–7

THE EVERYTHING SERIES!

BUSINESS & PERSONAL FINANCE

Everything® Accounting Book
Everything® Budgeting Book, 2nd Ed.
Everything® Business Planning Book
Everything® Coaching and Mentoring Book, 2nd Ed.
Everything® Fundraising Book
Everything® Get Out of Debt Book
Everything® Grant Writing Book, 2nd Ed.
Everything® Guide to Buying Foreclosures
Everything® Guide to Fundraising, $15.95
Everything® Guide to Mortgages
Everything® Guide to Personal Finance for Single Mothers
Everything® Home-Based Business Book, 2nd Ed.
Everything® Homebuying Book, 3rd Ed., $15.95
Everything® Homeselling Book, 2nd Ed.
Everything® Human Resource Management Book
Everything® Improve Your Credit Book
Everything® Investing Book, 2nd Ed.
Everything® Landlording Book
Everything® Leadership Book, 2nd Ed.
Everything® Managing People Book, 2nd Ed.
Everything® Negotiating Book
Everything® Online Auctions Book
Everything® Online Business Book
Everything® Personal Finance Book
Everything® Personal Finance in Your 20s & 30s Book, 2nd Ed.
Everything® Personal Finance in Your 40s & 50s Book, $15.95
Everything® Project Management Book, 2nd Ed.
Everything® Real Estate Investing Book
Everything® Retirement Planning Book
Everything® Robert's Rules Book, $7.95
Everything® Selling Book
Everything® Start Your Own Business Book, 2nd Ed.
Everything® Wills & Estate Planning Book

COOKING

Everything® Barbecue Cookbook
Everything® Bartender's Book, 2nd Ed., $9.95
Everything® Calorie Counting Cookbook
Everything® Cheese Book
Everything® Chinese Cookbook
Everything® Classic Recipes Book
Everything® Cocktail Parties & Drinks Book
Everything® College Cookbook
Everything® Cooking for Baby and Toddler Book
Everything® Diabetes Cookbook
Everything® Easy Gourmet Cookbook
Everything® Fondue Cookbook
Everything® Food Allergy Cookbook, $15.95
Everything® Fondue Party Book
Everything® Gluten-Free Cookbook
Everything® Glycemic Index Cookbook
Everything® Grilling Cookbook
Everything® Healthy Cooking for Parties Book, $15.95
Everything® Holiday Cookbook
Everything® Indian Cookbook
Everything® Lactose-Free Cookbook
Everything® Low-Cholesterol Cookbook

Everything® Low-Fat High-Flavor Cookbook, 2nd Ed., $15.95
Everything® Low-Salt Cookbook
Everything® Meals for a Month Cookbook
Everything® Meals on a Budget Cookbook
Everything® Mediterranean Cookbook
Everything® Mexican Cookbook
Everything® No Trans Fat Cookbook
Everything® One-Pot Cookbook, 2nd Ed., $15.95
Everything® Organic Cooking for Baby & Toddler Book, $15.95
Everything® Pizza Cookbook
Everything® Quick Meals Cookbook, 2nd Ed., $15.95
Everything® Slow Cooker Cookbook
Everything® Slow Cooking for a Crowd Cookbook
Everything® Soup Cookbook
Everything® Stir-Fry Cookbook
Everything® Sugar-Free Cookbook
Everything® Tapas and Small Plates Cookbook
Everything® Tex-Mex Cookbook
Everything® Thai Cookbook
Everything® Vegetarian Cookbook
Everything® Whole-Grain, High-Fiber Cookbook
Everything® Wild Game Cookbook
Everything® Wine Book, 2nd Ed.

GAMES

Everything® 15-Minute Sudoku Book, $9.95
Everything® 30-Minute Sudoku Book, $9.95
Everything® Bible Crosswords Book, $9.95
Everything® Blackjack Strategy Book
Everything® Brain Strain Book, $9.95
Everything® Bridge Book
Everything® Card Games Book
Everything® Card Tricks Book, $9.95
Everything® Casino Gambling Book, 2nd Ed.
Everything® Chess Basics Book
Everything® Christmas Crosswords Book, $9.95
Everything® Craps Strategy Book
Everything® Crossword and Puzzle Book
Everything® Crosswords and Puzzles for Quote Lovers Book, $9.95
Everything® Crossword Challenge Book
Everything® Crosswords for the Beach Book, $9.95
Everything® Cryptic Crosswords Book, $9.95
Everything® Cryptograms Book, $9.95
Everything® Easy Crosswords Book
Everything® Easy Kakuro Book, $9.95
Everything® Easy Large-Print Crosswords Book
Everything® Games Book, 2nd Ed.
Everything® Giant Book of Crosswords
Everything® Giant Sudoku Book, $9.95
Everything® Giant Word Search Book
Everything® Kakuro Challenge Book, $9.95
Everything® Large-Print Crossword Challenge Book
Everything® Large-Print Crosswords Book
Everything® Large-Print Travel Crosswords Book
Everything® Lateral Thinking Puzzles Book, $9.95
Everything® Literary Crosswords Book, $9.95
Everything® Mazes Book
Everything® Memory Booster Puzzles Book, $9.95

Everything® Movie Crosswords Book, $9.95
Everything® Music Crosswords Book, $9.95
Everything® Online Poker Book
Everything® Pencil Puzzles Book, $9.95
Everything® Poker Strategy Book
Everything® Pool & Billiards Book
Everything® Puzzles for Commuters Book, $9.95
Everything® Puzzles for Dog Lovers Book, $9.95
Everything® Sports Crosswords Book, $9.95
Everything® Test Your IQ Book, $9.95
Everything® Texas Hold 'Em Book, $9.95
Everything® Travel Crosswords Book, $9.95
Everything® Travel Mazes Book, $9.95
Everything® Travel Word Search Book, $9.95
Everything® TV Crosswords Book, $9.95
Everything® Word Games Challenge Book
Everything® Word Scramble Book
Everything® Word Search Book

HEALTH

Everything® Alzheimer's Book
Everything® Diabetes Book
Everything® First Aid Book, $9.95
Everything® Green Living Book
Everything® Health Guide to Addiction and Recovery
Everything® Health Guide to Adult Bipolar Disorder
Everything® Health Guide to Arthritis
Everything® Health Guide to Controlling Anxiety
Everything® Health Guide to Depression
Everything® Health Guide to Diabetes, 2nd Ed.
Everything® Health Guide to Fibromyalgia
Everything® Health Guide to Menopause, 2nd Ed.
Everything® Health Guide to Migraines
Everything® Health Guide to Multiple Sclerosis
Everything® Health Guide to OCD
Everything® Health Guide to PMS
Everything® Health Guide to Postpartum Care
Everything® Health Guide to Thyroid Disease
Everything® Hypnosis Book
Everything® Low Cholesterol Book
Everything® Menopause Book
Everything® Nutrition Book
Everything® Reflexology Book
Everything® Stress Management Book
Everything® Superfoods Book, $15.95

HISTORY

Everything® American Government Book
Everything® American History Book, 2nd Ed.
Everything® American Revolution Book, $15.95
Everything® Civil War Book
Everything® Freemasons Book
Everything® Irish History & Heritage Book
Everything® World War II Book, 2nd Ed.

HOBBIES

Everything® Candlemaking Book
Everything® Cartooning Book
Everything® Coin Collecting Book
Everything® Digital Photography Book, 2nd Ed.

Everything® Drawing Book
Everything® Family Tree Book, 2nd Ed.
Everything® Guide to Online Genealogy, $15.95
Everything® Knitting Book
Everything® Knots Book
Everything® Photography Book
Everything® Quilting Book
Everything® Sewing Book
Everything® Soapmaking Book, 2nd Ed.
Everything® Woodworking Book

HOME IMPROVEMENT

Everything® Feng Shui Book
Everything® Feng Shui Decluttering Book, $9.95
Everything® Fix-It Book
Everything® Green Living Book
Everything® Home Decorating Book
Everything® Home Storage Solutions Book
Everything® Homebuilding Book
Everything® Organize Your Home Book, 2nd Ed.

KIDS' BOOKS

All titles are $7.95
Everything® Fairy Tales Book, $14.95
Everything® Kids' Animal Puzzle & Activity Book
Everything® Kids' Astronomy Book
Everything® Kids' Baseball Book, 5th Ed.
Everything® Kids' Bible Trivia Book
Everything® Kids' Bugs Book
Everything® Kids' Cars and Trucks Puzzle and Activity Book
Everything® Kids' Christmas Puzzle & Activity Book
Everything® Kids' Connect the Dots
     Puzzle and Activity Book
Everything® Kids' Cookbook, 2nd Ed.
Everything® Kids' Crazy Puzzles Book
Everything® Kids' Dinosaurs Book
Everything® Kids' Dragons Puzzle and Activity Book
Everything® Kids' Environment Book $7.95
Everything® Kids' Fairies Puzzle and Activity Book
Everything® Kids' First Spanish Puzzle and Activity Book
Everything® Kids' Football Book
Everything® Kids' Geography Book
Everything® Kids' Gross Cookbook
Everything® Kids' Gross Hidden Pictures Book
Everything® Kids' Gross Jokes Book
Everything® Kids' Gross Mazes Book
Everything® Kids' Gross Puzzle & Activity Book
Everything® Kids' Halloween Puzzle & Activity Book
Everything® Kids' Hanukkah Puzzle and Activity Book
Everything® Kids' Hidden Pictures Book
Everything® Kids' Horses Book
Everything® Kids' Joke Book
Everything® Kids' Knock Knock Book
Everything® Kids' Learning French Book
Everything® Kids' Learning Spanish Book
Everything® Kids' Magical Science Experiments Book
Everything® Kids' Math Puzzles Book
Everything® Kids' Mazes Book
Everything® Kids' Money Book, 2nd Ed.
Everything® Kids' Mummies, Pharaoh's, and Pyramids
     Puzzle and Activity Book
Everything® Kids' Nature Book
Everything® Kids' Pirates Puzzle and Activity Book
Everything® Kids' Presidents Book
Everything® Kids' Princess Puzzle and Activity Book
Everything® Kids' Puzzle Book

Everything® Kids' Racecars Puzzle and Activity Book
Everything® Kids' Riddles & Brain Teasers Book
Everything® Kids' Science Experiments Book
Everything® Kids' Sharks Book
Everything® Kids' Soccer Book
Everything® Kids' Spelling Book
Everything® Kids' Spies Puzzle and Activity Book
Everything® Kids' States Book
Everything® Kids' Travel Activity Book
Everything® Kids' Word Search Puzzle and Activity Book

LANGUAGE

Everything® Conversational Japanese Book with CD, $19.95
Everything® French Grammar Book
Everything® French Phrase Book, $9.95
Everything® French Verb Book, $9.95
Everything® German Phrase Book, $9.95
Everything® German Practice Book with CD, $19.95
Everything® Inglés Book
Everything® Intermediate Spanish Book with CD, $19.95
Everything® Italian Phrase Book, $9.95
Everything® Italian Practice Book with CD, $19.95
Everything® Learning Brazilian Portuguese Book with CD, $19.95
Everything® Learning French Book with CD, 2nd Ed., $19.95
Everything® Learning German Book
Everything® Learning Italian Book
Everything® Learning Latin Book
Everything® Learning Russian Book with CD, $19.95
Everything® Learning Spanish Book
Everything® Learning Spanish Book with CD, 2nd Ed., $19.95
Everything® Russian Practice Book with CD, $19.95
Everything® Sign Language Book, $15.95
Everything® Spanish Grammar Book
Everything® Spanish Phrase Book, $9.95
Everything® Spanish Practice Book with CD, $19.95
Everything® Spanish Verb Book, $9.95
Everything® Speaking Mandarin Chinese Book with CD, $19.95

MUSIC

Everything® Bass Guitar Book with CD, $19.95
Everything® Drums Book with CD, $19.95
Everything® Guitar Book with CD, 2nd Ed., $19.95
Everything® Guitar Chords Book with CD, $19.95
Everything® Guitar Scales Book with CD, $19.95
Everything® Harmonica Book with CD, $15.95
Everything® Home Recording Book
Everything® Music Theory Book with CD, $19.95
Everything® Reading Music Book with CD, $19.95
Everything® Rock & Blues Guitar Book with CD, $19.95
Everything® Rock & Blues Piano Book with CD, $19.95
Everything® Rock Drums Book with CD, $19.95
Everything® Singing Book with CD, $19.95
Everything® Songwriting Book

NEW AGE

Everything® Astrology Book, 2nd Ed.
Everything® Birthday Personology Book
Everything® Celtic Wisdom Book, $15.95
Everything® Dreams Book, 2nd Ed.
Everything® Law of Attraction Book, $15.95
Everything® Love Signs Book, $9.95
Everything® Love Spells Book, $9.95
Everything® Palmistry Book
Everything® Psychic Book
Everything® Reiki Book

Everything® Sex Signs Book, $9.95
Everything® Spells & Charms Book, 2nd Ed.
Everything® Tarot Book, 2nd Ed.
Everything® Toltec Wisdom Book
Everything® Wicca & Witchcraft Book, 2nd Ed.

PARENTING

Everything® Baby Names Book, 2nd Ed.
Everything® Baby Shower Book, 2nd Ed.
Everything® Baby Sign Language Book with DVD
Everything® Baby's First Year Book
Everything® Birthing Book
Everything® Breastfeeding Book
Everything® Father-to-Be Book
Everything® Father's First Year Book
Everything® Get Ready for Baby Book, 2nd Ed.
Everything® Get Your Baby to Sleep Book, $9.95
Everything® Getting Pregnant Book
Everything® Guide to Pregnancy Over 35
Everything® Guide to Raising a One-Year-Old
Everything® Guide to Raising a Two-Year-Old
Everything® Guide to Raising Adolescent Boys
Everything® Guide to Raising Adolescent Girls
Everything® Mother's First Year Book
Everything® Parent's Guide to Childhood Illnesses
Everything® Parent's Guide to Children and Divorce
Everything® Parent's Guide to Children with ADD/ADHD
Everything® Parent's Guide to Children with Asperger's
     Syndrome
Everything® Parent's Guide to Children with Anxiety
Everything® Parent's Guide to Children with Asthma
Everything® Parent's Guide to Children with Autism
Everything® Parent's Guide to Children with Bipolar Disorder
Everything® Parent's Guide to Children with Depression
Everything® Parent's Guide to Children with Dyslexia
Everything® Parent's Guide to Children with Juvenile Diabetes
Everything® Parent's Guide to Children with OCD
Everything® Parent's Guide to Positive Discipline
Everything® Parent's Guide to Raising Boys
Everything® Parent's Guide to Raising Girls
Everything® Parent's Guide to Raising Siblings
Everything® Parent's Guide to Raising Your
     Adopted Child
Everything® Parent's Guide to Sensory Integration Disorder
Everything® Parent's Guide to Tantrums
Everything® Parent's Guide to the Strong-Willed Child
Everything® Parenting a Teenager Book
Everything® Potty Training Book, $9.95
Everything® Pregnancy Book, 3rd Ed.
Everything® Pregnancy Fitness Book
Everything® Pregnancy Nutrition Book
Everything® Pregnancy Organizer, 2nd Ed., $16.95
Everything® Toddler Activities Book
Everything® Toddler Book
Everything® Tween Book
Everything® Twins, Triplets, and More Book

PETS

Everything® Aquarium Book
Everything® Boxer Book
Everything® Cat Book, 2nd Ed.
Everything® Chihuahua Book
Everything® Cooking for Dogs Book
Everything® Dachshund Book
Everything® Dog Book, 2nd Ed.
Everything® Dog Grooming Book

Everything® Dog Obedience Book
Everything® Dog Owner's Organizer, $16.95
Everything® Dog Training and Tricks Book
Everything® German Shepherd Book
Everything® Golden Retriever Book
Everything® Horse Book, 2nd Ed., $15.95
Everything® Horse Care Book
Everything® Horseback Riding Book
Everything® Labrador Retriever Book
Everything® Poodle Book
Everything® Pug Book
Everything® Puppy Book
Everything® Small Dogs Book
Everything® Tropical Fish Book
Everything® Yorkshire Terrier Book

REFERENCE

Everything® American Presidents Book
Everything® Blogging Book
Everything® Build Your Vocabulary Book, $9.95
Everything® Car Care Book
Everything® Classical Mythology Book
Everything® Da Vinci Book
Everything® Einstein Book
Everything® Enneagram Book
Everything® Etiquette Book, 2nd Ed.
Everything® Family Christmas Book, $15.95
Everything® Guide to C. S. Lewis & Narnia
Everything® Guide to Divorce, 2nd Ed., $15.95
Everything® Guide to Edgar Allan Poe
Everything® Guide to Understanding Philosophy
Everything® Inventions and Patents Book
Everything® Jacqueline Kennedy Onassis Book
Everything® John F. Kennedy Book
Everything® Mafia Book
Everything® Martin Luther King Jr. Book
Everything® Pirates Book
Everything® Private Investigation Book
Everything® Psychology Book
Everything® Public Speaking Book, $9.95
Everything® Shakespeare Book, 2nd Ed.

RELIGION

Everything® Angels Book
Everything® Bible Book
Everything® Bible Study Book with CD, $19.95
Everything® Buddhism Book
Everything® Catholicism Book
Everything® Christianity Book
Everything® Gnostic Gospels Book
Everything® Hinduism Book, $15.95
Everything® History of the Bible Book
Everything® Jesus Book
Everything® Jewish History & Heritage Book
Everything® Judaism Book
Everything® Kabbalah Book
Everything® Koran Book
Everything® Mary Book
Everything® Mary Magdalene Book
Everything® Prayer Book

Everything® Saints Book, 2nd Ed.
Everything® Torah Book
Everything® Understanding Islam Book
Everything® Women of the Bible Book
Everything® World's Religions Book

SCHOOL & CAREERS

Everything® Career Tests Book
Everything® College Major Test Book
Everything® College Survival Book, 2nd Ed.
Everything® Cover Letter Book, 2nd Ed.
Everything® Filmmaking Book
Everything® Get-a-Job Book, 2nd Ed.
Everything® Guide to Being a Paralegal
Everything® Guide to Being a Personal Trainer
Everything® Guide to Being a Real Estate Agent
Everything® Guide to Being a Sales Rep
Everything® Guide to Being an Event Planner
Everything® Guide to Careers in Health Care
Everything® Guide to Careers in Law Enforcement
Everything® Guide to Government Jobs
Everything® Guide to Starting and Running a Catering
  Business
Everything® Guide to Starting and Running a Restaurant
**Everything® Guide to Starting and Running
  a Retail Store**
Everything® Job Interview Book, 2nd Ed.
Everything® New Nurse Book
Everything® New Teacher Book
Everything® Paying for College Book
Everything® Practice Interview Book
Everything® Resume Book, 3rd Ed.
Everything® Study Book

SELF-HELP

Everything® Body Language Book
Everything® Dating Book, 2nd Ed.
Everything® Great Sex Book
**Everything® Guide to Caring for Aging Parents,
  $15.95**
Everything® Self-Esteem Book
Everything® Self-Hypnosis Book, $9.95
Everything® Tantric Sex Book

SPORTS & FITNESS

Everything® Easy Fitness Book
Everything® Fishing Book
Everything® Guide to Weight Training, $15.95
Everything® Krav Maga for Fitness Book
Everything® Running Book, 2nd Ed.
Everything® Triathlon Training Book, $15.95

TRAVEL

Everything® Family Guide to Coastal Florida
Everything® Family Guide to Cruise Vacations
Everything® Family Guide to Hawaii
Everything® Family Guide to Las Vegas, 2nd Ed.
Everything® Family Guide to Mexico
Everything® Family Guide to New England, 2nd Ed.

Everything® Family Guide to New York City, 3rd Ed.
**Everything® Family Guide to Northern California
  and Lake Tahoe**
Everything® Family Guide to RV Travel & Campgrounds
Everything® Family Guide to the Caribbean
Everything® Family Guide to the Disneyland® Resort, California
  Adventure®, Universal Studios®, and the Anaheim
  Area, 2nd Ed.
Everything® Family Guide to the Walt Disney World Resort®,
  Universal Studios®, and Greater Orlando, 5th Ed.
Everything® Family Guide to Timeshares
Everything® Family Guide to Washington D.C., 2nd Ed.

WEDDINGS

Everything® Bachelorette Party Book, $9.95
Everything® Bridesmaid Book, $9.95
Everything® Destination Wedding Book
Everything® Father of the Bride Book, $9.95
Everything® Green Wedding Book, $15.95
Everything® Groom Book, $9.95
Everything® Jewish Wedding Book, 2nd Ed., $15.95
Everything® Mother of the Bride Book, $9.95
Everything® Outdoor Wedding Book
Everything® Wedding Book, 3rd Ed.
Everything® Wedding Checklist, $9.95
Everything® Wedding Etiquette Book, $9.95
Everything® Wedding Organizer, 2nd Ed., $16.95
Everything® Wedding Shower Book, $9.95
Everything® Wedding Vows Book, 3rd Ed., $9.95
Everything® Wedding Workout Book
Everything® Weddings on a Budget Book, 2nd Ed., $9.95

WRITING

Everything® Creative Writing Book
Everything® Get Published Book, 2nd Ed.
Everything® Grammar and Style Book, 2nd Ed.
Everything® Guide to Magazine Writing
Everything® Guide to Writing a Book Proposal
Everything® Guide to Writing a Novel
Everything® Guide to Writing Children's Books
Everything® Guide to Writing Copy
Everything® Guide to Writing Graphic Novels
Everything® Guide to Writing Research Papers
Everything® Guide to Writing a Romance Novel, $15.95
Everything® Improve Your Writing Book, 2nd Ed.
Everything® Writing Poetry Book